YOUTH ON THE MOVE

T0322959

/ AFRICAN
/ ARGUMENTS

African Arguments is a series of short books about contemporary Africa and the critical issues and debates surrounding the continent. The books are scholarly and engaged, substantive and topical. They focus on questions of justice, rights and citizenship; politics, protests and revolutions; the environment, land, oil and other resources; health and disease; economy: growth, aid, taxation, debt and capital flight; and both Africa's international relations and country case studies. Additional longer monographs and edited volumes are published in association with the series, under the auspices of the IAI.

Managing Editor, Stephanie Kitchen

Series editors

Adam Branch
Alex de Waal
Alcinda Honwana
Ebenezer Obadare
Carlos Oya
Nicholas Westcott

Associate editors

Eyob Gebremariam
Elliott D. Green
Jon Schubert

ASNAKE KEFALE
FANA GEBRESENBET
(*Editors*)

Youth on the Move

*Views from Below on
Ethiopian International Migration*

HURST & COMPANY, LONDON

IAI   International African Institute

Published in collaboration with the International African Institute.
First published in the United Kingdom in 2021 by
C. Hurst & Co. (Publishers) Ltd.,
83 Torbay Road, London, NW6 7DT
Copyright © Asnake Kefale, Fana Gebresenbet and the Contributors, 2021
All rights reserved.
Printed in the United Kingdom by Bell and Bain Ltd, Glasgow

The right of Asnake Kefale, Fana Gebresenbet and the
Contributors to be identified as the authors of this
publication is asserted by them in accordance with the
Copyright, Designs and Patents Act, 1988.

A Cataloguing-in-Publication data record for this book
is available from the British Library.

ISBN: 9781787385702

This book is printed using paper from registered sustainable
and managed sources.

www.hurstpublishers.com

CONTENTS

CONTENTS

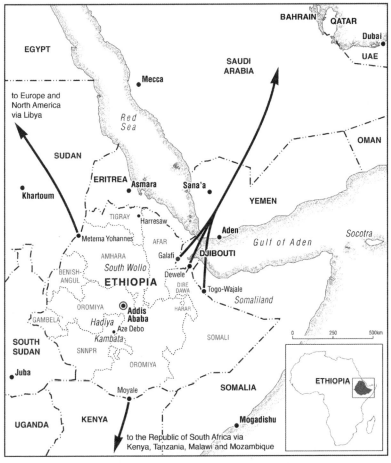

Major sending and transit areas of irregular migration covered in this book

LIST OF FIGURES AND TABLES

List of Figures

List of Tables

ABOUT THE EDITORS AND CONTRIBUTORS

Note: Contributors are listed alphabetically following the book editors first. As is customary, the first names of Ethiopian authors appear first when they occur in the list as well as in citations and references and are alphabetised accordingly—unlike the Western practice where people are alphabetised by surname.

Asnake Kefale is Associate Professor of Political Science and International Relations, Addis Ababa University. Formerly he was Director of Research and Publication at the Forum for Social Studies (FSS), a policy think tank in Addis Ababa, Ethiopia. Asnake's research interests include the politics of development, governance, federalism and migration. He is the author of *Federalism and Ethnic Conflict in Ethiopia: A Comparative Regional Study* (Routledge, 2013).

Fana Gebresenbet is Assistant Professor at the Institute for Peace and Security Studies (IPSS), Addis Ababa University. His research focuses on the politics of development, state developmentalism, pastoralism and migration. He co-edited *Lands of the Future: Anthropological Perspectives on Pastoralism, Land Deals and Tropes of Modernity in Eastern Africa* (Berghahn, 2021). He was previously engaged in various research projects with a focus on irregular migration from Tigray, northern Ethiopia, and is currently a researcher for a multi-country research project, Migration for Development and Equality (MIDEQ) with a focus on the Ethiopia-South Africa corridor.

Alemu Asfaw Nigusie is Assistant Professor in the Department of Political Science and International Studies at Bahir Dar University,

ABOUT THE EDITORS AND CONTRIBUTORS

Ethiopia. His areas of research include migration and refugee studies, internal displacement, political economy, and identity politics. He has previously published articles in *Bandung: Journal of the Global South*. Currently, he is doing his PhD on refugee flows, state responses, and North–South cooperation in Africa, with particular reference to the Ethiopian state.

Priya Deshingkar is Professor of Migration and Development at the University of Sussex. She is best known for her research on internal and South–South migration, which has challenged conventional under-standings of the relationship between migration and poverty. Her research is multidisciplinary, drawing on the fields of labour geogra-phy, anthropology and sociology, and focuses on precarity and agency in labour migration, migration brokerage and the migration industry as well as trafficking and modern slavery. Priya has a strong publica-tions record and regularly advises governments on migration policy.

Catherine Dom is an independent researcher, a member of a team conducting longitudinal qualitative research on change and continuity in twenty rural villages of Ethiopia since 1994 (www.ethiopiawide. net). Her work focuses on youth, migration, and education. She has authored several publications based on this research, including a chap-ter on 'Migration for work in rural communities (2010–13)' in *Changing Rural Ethiopia: Community Transformations*, edited by Pankhurst, Bevan, Dom, Tiumelissan and Vaughan (Tsehai, 2018).

Fekadu Adugna Tufa is Associate Professor of Social Anthropology at Addis Ababa University, where he served as chairman for over three years. He has been conducting research on a variety of issues including inter-ethnic relations, identity, border studies, land use systems, forced displacement and migration. He has published widely on migra-tion facilitation, smuggling and the migration industry. Currently, Fekadu is engaging in multiple research assignments on forced displace-ment and refugees in the Horn of Africa.

Firehiwot Sintayehu is Assistant Professor in the Department of Political Science and International Relations at Addis Ababa University. Her main research interests are migration in Ethiopia, gender issues and hydro-politics in North-East Africa. Her recent co-publication is

xii

an article titled 'Managing irregular migration in Ethiopia: A case for policies centering the right to development', *Ethiopian Journal of Human Rights* (2019).

Kiros Birhanu is currently a freelance research consultant. She used to work as a research assistant and communications coordinator for Young Lives in Ethiopia. She holds a BA in Sociology and Social Administration and a Master's in Public Health. She has participated in many qualitative research projects. Her research interests are in migration, reproductive health, nutrition and education.

Kiya Gezahegne is a lecturer in Social Anthropology at Addis Ababa University. Her work mainly focuses on the intersection between migration, borderlands, gender and identity. Her interests extend to religious identity and conflict. She has published research articles on migration from Ethiopia to the Middle East, Sudan and Europe.

Mulugeta Gashaw Debalke works as a National Research Coordinator for Water Witness International in Ethiopia for the multi-country Accountability for Water Action and Research Programme. He obtained his PhD in Sociocultural Anthropology at the University of Alberta in 2012. His main research interests are resource stewardship, smallholder agriculture, climate change, and traditional knowledge's contribution to global challenges such as ecological degradation. Previously, Mulugeta worked as a research fellow, social adviser, and consultant for different organisations, including the World Bank, FHI/USAID, PDRC and the Miz-Hasab Research Centre.

Teferi Abate Adem is a Research Anthropologist associated with Human Relations Area Files at Yale University and an affiliate faculty of the Yale Council on African Studies. Academic positions he held prior to this include Visiting Assistant Professor of International Development and Social Change at Clark University, postdoctoral fellow at the Program in Agrarian Studies, Yale University, and Assistant Professor and Chair of the Department of Sociology and Anthropology, Addis Ababa University. Teferi's research interests encompass a variety of historical and comparative themes related to the household and community-level effects of expanding state powers, global market forces, and climate change-related agrarian shocks.

ABOUT THE EDITORS AND CONTRIBUTORS

Tekalign Ayalew Mengiste is an Assistant Professor of Social Anthropology at Addis Ababa University and affiliated researcher at Stockholm University, Sweden. Currently he is Chair of the Department of Social Anthropology at Addis Ababa University. He has widely researched and published on issues such as forced mobility, human smuggling, migration governance, and children on the move, focusing on Ethiopia and East Africa. His recent article, 'Intensifications of border governance and defiant migration trajectories in Ethiopia', was published in *Geopolitics* (2021).

Yordanos S. Estifanos graduated with an MA from the European Masters in Migration and Intercultural Relations (EMMIR) programme at the University of Oldenburg, Germany. He also earned a Master of Science (MSc) in Population Studies from Addis Ababa University. He was a research fellow at the Bielefeld Graduate School of History and Sociology (BGHS) in Germany. He has previously worked for national and international organisations and has published migration-related monographs, research articles and commentaries. Yordanos is currently a researcher for the Ethiopia–South Africa Migration Corridor research project.

Zerihun Mohammed is Executive Director of Good Governance Africa (Eastern Africa) and formerly was a senior researcher at the Forum for Social Studies (FSS), Ethiopia. He holds a PhD from the University of Cambridge in Human Geography. Zerihun has extensive research experience in various subjects including migration, social relations, livelihoods and resource management.

ACKNOWLEDGEMENTS

This book is the result of a collaborative effort and has benefited from the support of many people. First and foremost, we would like to express our gratitude to our contributors. This volume would not have been possible without their hard work and dedication.

Second, we would like to thank the organisers of the 20th International Conference of Ethiopian Studies (ICES), which was held in Mekelle, Ethiopia in October 2018, for accepting our panel on migration. The majority of the chapters included in this volume were originally presented at that conference.

Third, we wish to express our gratitude to the Carnegie Corporation of New York, which supported this book through a Book Manuscript Completion Grant from the African Peacebuilding Network (APN) at the Social Science Research Council (SSRC). The support of the APN enabled us to organise a book workshop in which all the chapters were critically discussed and feedback was given to each author. We also want to thank the MIDEQ research project for the intellectual input and allowing one of the editors (Fana Gebresenbet) to dedicate sufficient time during the editorial work. The APN's support also enabled us to copy-edit the manuscript before submitting it to the publisher. Here, we would like to acknowledge Melissa Mahama, who undertook this important copy-editing work.

Fourth, we thank the two anonymous reviewers found by the publisher for their critical remarks. Their comments helped us to improve the manuscript.

ACKNOWLEDGEMENTS

Last but not least, we would like to express our deep appreciation to Stephanie Kitchen, the Managing Editor of African Arguments, for her unfailing support and enthusiasm throughout the publication process.

Asnake Kefale and Fana Gebresenbet
Addis Ababa, June 2021

FOREWORD

In a rapidly globalising world, where human mobilities and interactions are continuously reconstituted and are giving rise to complex relationships and impacts across space and time, *Youth on the Move* is a critical intervention into debates on the nature and ramifications of migration out of Ethiopia.

Drawing on 'voices from below', this book speaks eloquently to the dominant discourses on international migration out of Ethiopia, interrogating structuralist and securitised readings of human mobilities across international borders. It makes a strong case for a nuanced approach prioritising the 'voices and agencies of individuals and sending communities.' Bringing together the reflections of numerous young scholars, Asnake Kefale and Fana Gebresenbet, two former fellows of the Social Science Research Council's African Peacebuilding Network's (APN) grants program, have successfully put together a compelling collection of essays which provide a distinct African perspective on international migration involving Ethiopian youth.

The efforts of the editors are a testament to their intellectual capacity to engage with and transform the conversation on African migration. Of note is the important role of the APN in providing funding with the support of the Carnegie Corporation of New York, in the form of a book completion grant in line with one of the programme's principal goals of promoting innovative African thinking and scholarship. The contributions to *Youth on the Move* challenge received wisdom on the pull-and-push factors driving youth migration out of Africa's second most populous country, by giving agency to migrants, their households, and their communities.

Beyond this, the chapters provide explanations as to why migration has been predominantly irregular, unpack the nexuses between socio-economic, political and migration transitions, as well as examining how assemblage has shaped migration—in terms of the aspirations of migrants and their capacity to migrate. By giving voice to Ethiopian migrants and communities at home and abroad, the contributors point to the limitations of approaches that seek to criminalise or securitise youth migration. Not only this, but they also explain how migration is seen as a means for resolving contradictions and pressures emerging from demographic transitions, rapid economic growth, urbanisation, and a significant expansion in the educational sector. Equally important is how various contributors reflect on the ways global–local connectedness and transformations shape the nature and direction of international migration—with direct implications for Ethiopia.

This collection of essays and the powerful introduction authored by the co-editors represent a highly informative addition to both Ethiopian and migration studies. It draws on multidisciplinary perspectives that clearly mark a shift in migration studies in Africa and beyond. By giving voice both to the youth and the hitherto invisible families and communities in sending countries, the book provides unique insights into the drivers of migration and captures developments at the grassroots— particularly in relation to the impact of migration, including remittances from migrants, on community and socio-economic wellbeing. This book underscores the significant impact of the APN network of scholars and their capacity to lead conversations that increasingly shape new thinking and knowledge production about Africa, particularly in ways that reflect and contribute innovative perspectives to global scholarly discourses and practices in the field of post-conflict peace and development.

Cyril Obi

Program Director, African Peacebuilding Network
and Next Generation Social Science in Africa,
Social Science Research Council, New York

INTRODUCTION

MULTIPLE TRANSITIONS AND IRREGULAR MIGRATION IN ETHIOPIA

AGENCY AND ASSEMBLAGE FROM BELOW

Asnake Kefale and *Fana Gebresenbet*

Ethiopian youth are on the move in large numbers to places that are far from home. The motivation for the majority of the migrants is changing their and their families' lives for the better. It is our contention in this book that a more nuanced understanding of migration from Ethiopia can be made by going beyond the pull and push factors that are frequently used to explain migration decisions, and the tendency to view migrants as victims. This book breaks from the dominant trend in migration studies, which gives too much emphasis to structural factors,[1] and, instead, gives more attention to the voices and agency of migrants and sending communities. In doing so, it considers migrants, their households and communities not as hapless victims of illegal traffickers and brokers but as active agents who consciously take part in the migration process. While this volume gives agency to migrants, their households and communities, we do not dismiss the implications of macro-level socio-economic and political factors, which in migration studies are explained in terms of push and pull factors. Following Anthony Giddens's[2] and Rob Stones's[3] conceptualisation, we take the 'duality of structure' seriously. As Stones states: 'structure enters into the constitution of the agent, and from here into the practices that this agent produces. Structure is thus a significant *medium* of the practices of agents' (italics in original).[4]

Ethiopia's international migration rate of 0.7% is much lower than the sub-Saharan Africa average of 2.5%.[5] There has, however, been a significant spike in outward migration from Ethiopia in recent years.[6] Much migration from Ethiopia is undocumented (irregular), and hence official statistics on the number of migrants are not accurate. Some indicative reports, however, show the magnitude of migration from the country. In this respect, the Horn of Africa and Yemen Regional Mixed Migration Secretariat reported that between 2008 and 2016, more than 365,000 migrants and asylum-seekers arrived in Yemen, of whom more than 80% were Ethiopians.[7] In addition, the South African Department of Home Affairs reported that Ethiopians constituted the second-largest number of asylum applicants (9,322), after Zimbabweans, in 2015 (17,785).[8]

Every year, tens of thousands of young Ethiopians try to reach the oil-rich Gulf countries (primarily Saudi Arabia), South Africa and Europe, braving dangerous and tortuous routes, facilitated by networks of brokers and smugglers. The majority of Ethiopian migrants are irregular,[9] meaning they enter or reside in the destination countries without possessing the requisite permits.[10] The structural causes for irregular migration are to do with Ethiopia's social, economic and political conditions, which have shown some dynamism over recent decades. In the 1970s and 1980s, the primary push factor for migration was political—persecution by the military government that ruled the country from 1974 to 1991. This changed from the early 1990s to socio-economic drivers, though political factors continued to play a significant role in the decision of some potential migrants.

Irregular migration from Ethiopia takes place via three major routes (see the Map). First, the eastern route to the Gulf countries, predominantly Saudi Arabia (see chapters 2, 3, 4, 5, 6, 10 and 11). This route is taken by a large proportion of Ethiopian migrants originating from various parts of the country. Female migrants are more likely to be contracted and fly directly to the Gulf, only to become irregular later on. The banning of legal labour migration in late 2013 pushed many women into making the risky journeys across the deserts and the Red Sea. Second, the southern route to South Africa, taken mainly by migrants originating from the densely populated highlands of Hadiya and Kambata areas, passes through Moyale town on the border with Kenya (see chapters 2, 5, 7 and 8). Third, the western route to Western Europe passes through Sudan and Libya. This is a more expensive route, and migrants originate from major towns with no particular core sending area.

More often than not, irregular migration from Ethiopia is seen from the perspective of the proverbial push and pull factors. Consequently, the Ethiopian government and Western donors promote the idea that irregular migration from Ethiopia could be stemmed by a combination of economic development, i.e., the creation of job opportunities, and law enforcement interventions.[11] This perspective, however, fails to consider the nuances of the youth's decision to migrate (or not), shaped in close coordination and consultation with sending households, and with consideration for the expected personal, family and community-level changes.

Structural explanations fail to explain why migrants tend to concentrate in some geographic areas and communities where norms and social networks that support migration have emerged. We contend that a view from below illustrates how information, knowledge and capabilities become concentrated in some communities in the form of migration networks. Moreover, while aspirations to migrate may be pervasive in such communities (compared with others), not all aspiring migrants will be able to realise their plans owing to limited capabilities—be they social capital or finance. A perspective from below also enables us to examine the agency of the youth, the migrant families and communities. This is clearly visible in risk assessment and risk-taking as part of the decision to migrate; despite the position of policy-makers and NGOs, the youth decide to undertake dangerous journeys to migrate through the intermediary of brokers and traffickers, by and large after calculating the risks involved (see chapter 2). In some cases, the agency of the youth extends to deciding to migrate without the knowledge of their parents and 'getting stranded or being taken for ransom by traffickers and smugglers' in transit points in faraway places (such as Yemen) and forcing their parents (and the wider family network) to financially support their migration.

Therefore, this volume goes beyond macro-level discussions and offers insights about individual and community-level perspectives. It also examines the roles that are played by individuals and social networks in facilitating the movement of youth across international boundaries. The majority of the chapters are based on 'voices from below', be they potential migrants, returnees, failed migrants, sending households and communities, or brokers and traffickers. Our focus on agency from below is not divorced from macro-level structural considerations. Chapter 1 addresses these by paying attention to policy processes, while other chapters integrate the interaction between agency and structures. To recap, we adopt Giddens's and Stones's notions of structuration. We consider the processes and dynamics that accompany migration from Ethiopia from two interrelated analytical frameworks—transition and assemblage (see below)—which contribute to processes of structuration.

Socio-economic and political transitions as precursors to migration transitions

In political science literature, the concept of transition is largely used to explain the factors leading to, and the problems associated with, the transition of formerly authoritarian countries to democracy.[12] In this book, we use the term 'transition' to broadly encompass social, political, economic, global and technological changes in order to understand the wider context in which irregular migration happens. In the second decade of the twenty-first century, an astute observer would not miss the fact that Ethiopia is a country undergoing and engrossed by multiple transitions. We contend that these transitions, outlined briefly below, create the structural conditions that impact heavily on the migration decision-making of the youth.

Migration from Ethiopia is heavily affected by the country's demographic transition, the first dimension of transition that we consider as impacting on migration dynamics. Demographic transition refers to 'a series of declines in fertility, morbidity, and mortality which accompany modernization'.[13] In an influential work published in

INTRODUCTION

1929, Warren Thomson described four stages in the demographic transitions of countries in relation to economic progress. In the first, pre-modern phase, 'both mortality and fertility are high and overall population growth is low'.[14] In the second, industrialising phase, 'there is a decline in mortality rates while fertility continues at its historically high level, leading to a rapid increase in population growth'.[15] In the third, industrial phase, 'under conditions associated with urbanization and economic demands for a more educated workforce, the birth rate falls'.[16] In the fourth, post-industrial phase, both 'fertility and mortality decline'.[17]

The second phase, where there is a decline in mortality and high fertility, captures the contemporary Ethiopian situation. At present, Ethiopia has an estimated population of over 100 million and is Africa's second-most populous nation, after Nigeria. The country also has a high population growth rate. Although slightly lower than the annual growth rate of 1984–94 (2.8%), the current annual population growth rate of Ethiopia (2.6%) is considered high.[18] At this rate of growth, the population is projected to reach around 105 million by 2022, although many consider this an underestimate.[19]

The high fertility rate translates into a very broad base in Ethiopia's population pyramid, making the population very youthful. In 2012, the proportion of the population aged 14 or younger was 41.5%.[20] This means a constant influx of young people annually into the labour market, keeping youth unemployment high, estimated at 23.7% in 2010.[21] The Government of Ethiopia (GoE) estimates that about 2 million young Ethiopians join the labour market each year.[22] What the economy offers in terms of employment is limited and it is no wonder that international migration is seen as an option by the unemployed and underemployed Ethiopian youth. This is in accord with scholars like Wilbur Zelinsky who contend that migration tends to coincide with the second phase of demographic transition.[23]

It is, however, important to note that in spite of the growing importance of the concept of 'youth' in both popular discourses and academic writing, 'what is meant by "youth" is still open to question'.[24] There are different notions of who should be included in the category of youth. The United Nations (UN) definition of youth is of people between the ages of 15 and 24, while the African Union (AU) has a wider understanding of youthhood and includes those between 15 and 35 in its definition.[25] The Government of Ethiopia's Youth Policy defines youth as those aged 15 to 29.[26] The variation that exists among various countries and societies in defining youth shows how the youth category is differently conceptualised.

In spite of the differences that exist about the age categories across cultures, the youth concept refers to a transition between childhood and adulthood.[27] While transition to adulthood is important to the concept of youth, 'the meaning of adulthood and how it is achieved, marked, acknowledged and maintained is ambiguous'.[28] Moreover, youth transition more often than not is neither smooth nor linear (see chapter 4). There are several obstacles that cause delays in the transitioning of youth to adulthood. One of the major factors is unemployment, which forces young people to stay in youthhood status for an extended period of time.[29] Because of the problematic nature of youth transitions, scholars have increasingly avoided the use of age categories in defining youth and have shown a preference for social status.[30] In this respect, Alcinda Honwana considers youth as a social construction 'based on social expectations and responsibilities'.[31] Her definition of youth includes 'all those who have not yet been able to attain social adulthood, despite their age as youth'.[32] In this volume as well, we do not limit ourselves to distinct biological age categories. We also consider how the individual agency of the youth, and family and societal expectations of the youth and young adults (including married women), facilitate the migration of youth.

The second dimension of transition that continues to impact on migration has been political. Indeed, the first wave of forced migrants (refugees) left Ethiopia immediately after the 1974 revolution which toppled Haile Selassie's government. Because of the persecution of the opponents of the military regime, known in Amharic as Derg, a large number of Ethiopians left the country during the period 1974–91. Like other socialist or communist authoritarian regimes, the Derg restricted the movement of people. Under the Derg, one needed to carry permit papers to travel within the country, and overseas travel was even more restricted.[33] As a result, it was difficult for Ethiopian citizens to get passports and exit visas. This changed when the military regime was toppled in May 1991 by a coalition of rebel movements, the Ethiopian People's Revolutionary Democratic Front (EPRDF).

The EPRDF government introduced a radically different approach to freedom of movement. Accordingly, the government recognised the right of citizens to obtain travel documents, such as passports, without preconditions. Within the country, the requirement for citizens to carry permit papers was lifted. The EPRDF further enhanced citizen's rights to movement when, in July 2004, it lifted the exit visa requirement for Ethiopians to travel abroad. All these changes greatly facilitated both legal and irregular migration out of the country. Those able to secure an entry visa to a foreign country could travel without restriction, while those using neighbouring countries as transit points could easily travel to border towns such as Moyale and Metema.

The EPRDF government, which could be considered pro-migration, not only encouraged the growing Ethiopian diaspora communities to invest in the country (especially after 2005) but also recognised the overseas labour migration of Ethiopians early on. As Asnake and Zerihun note, labour migration started to the Gulf, particularly to Saudi Arabia, before the 1990s.[34] Mostly young females migrated to carry out domestic work in Saudi Arabia during this period under the guise of making religious pilgrimages. Later on, Ethiopian migrants began to travel to Lebanon and other Gulf countries to perform domestic work in large numbers.[35] The Ethiopian government, intending to formalise and regularise labour migration to the Gulf countries, enacted a series of laws in 1998, 2009 and 2016 (see chapter 1). During the period 2008–13, according to the Ministry of Labour and Social Affairs, close to 380,000 migrants travelled along formal channels to the Gulf countries, largely for domestic work.[36] Following the Saudi Arabian crackdown on undocumented Ethiopian migrant workers in late 2013 and early 2014, the Ethiopian government ceased documented labour migration to the Gulf countries. However, the ban did not stop migrants, who left the country using irregular channels (see chapters 1, 2, 3 and 4).

The other political reform introduced by the EPRDF that continues to have an impact on migration was the restructuring of the country's internal administration based on ethnolinguistic identity.[37] By emphasising the congruence of ethnic identity and territory,[38] the ethnofederal system directly and indirectly engendered tensions and conflicts over a range of issues, including land and residency.[39] As a result, tens of thousands of Ethiopians were displaced from their homes.[40]

Since April 2018, Ethiopia has been in yet another political transition. This transition came about with the change of political leadership at the top of the EPRDF following massive popular protests from 2015 in the two larger and populous ethnic regions, Oromia and Amhara. The EPRDF agreed to political reforms and introduced a new leadership. The appointment of Prime Minister Abiy Ahmed, in retrospect, can be seen as one of the watershed moments in the country's contemporary politics. Detailing the causes of the protests and the trajectories of Ethiopian politics since 2018 is beyond the purpose of this introductory chapter. Nonetheless, it is important to point out that the protests were, by and large, responses to the political and economic hegemony constructed by the EPRDF. The political reforms since 2018 include recognition of freedom of association and speech and the relaxation of restrictive laws. As a result of these changes, thousands of political prisoners have been released and political parties, previously banned, are now allowed to operate within the country. The political opening-up has, however, been accompanied by inter-ethnic strife, breakdowns in law and order, and conflicts. As a result, millions of people have been displaced from their homes. Furthermore, in November 2020 armed conflict commenced between the federal government and the TPLF regional government of Tigray. This has the potential to become protracted. At the time of writing, the conflict has displaced hundreds of thousands (if not millions) of people internally, while some 60,000 crossed the border into Sudan. If the current trend continues, the new political transition could lead to the forced or irregular migration of vulnerable communities outside the country.

The third dimension of transition in recent years in Ethiopia has been brought about by sustained and rapid economic growth, and the expansion of social services and infrastructure. For about ten years, from 2003/04 to 2013/14, the Ethiopian economy, on average, grew at the high rate of 10%.[41] In 2012, Ethiopia had the fastest-growing economy on the continent. The economy appeared to be on the verge of a structural change, from agriculture towards manufacturing. In this respect, the significance of the agricultural sector, in terms of its contribution to GDP, has been declining. Since 2012, the service sector has grown in terms of contribution to GDP but what it provides by way of employment is limited.[42]

INTRODUCTION

In addition to the expansion of the economy, Ethiopia witnessed a massive expansion of social services and infrastructure. One notable feature was the expansion of the education sector. Even if much more is needed in raising the quality of education, Ethiopia showed commendable progress in expanding educational services at all levels. Citing the UNESCO Institute of Statistics, Stefan Trines reported remarkable growth in the net enrolment rate (NER) in elementary schools from 29% in 1989 to 86% in 2015, with a huge surge of enrolments from 3 million in 1996 to 18 million in 2014.[43] A massive expansion of tertiary education was also observed. With just three universities in 1991, the country now boasts more than 40 public universities. In 2018, more than 800,000 students were receiving college and university education in governmental, private and non-governmental institutions.[44] As a result, tens of thousands of young people complete their university and college education and join the labour market every year. In 2019, government universities alone graduated more than 150,000 students. A comparable number of students also completed their studies at private and non-governmental institutions in the same year.[45]

However, what the labour market offers is limited. Hence, graduate unemployment is a serious problem that the country needs to grapple with. Graduate unemployment diminishes education's longstanding and cherished role in Ethiopia in enabling social mobility, thereby undermining the value of education in youth aspirations. As chapters 3, 4 and 7 explain, given the limited expectations of young people of finding rewarding employment after finishing college or university, migration is increasingly regarded as an important way of changing one's life. Educated unemployed youth also seek to transform their lives through migration. Those who pursue education from the countryside, where subsistence agriculture is the mainstay of the local economy, rarely return to their villages, be it after high school or university education. Combined with other socio-economic impacts, education—including primary education—increases migration aspirations in Ethiopia.[46]

The other aspect of the socio-economic transition with a direct and indirect impact on migration is a higher rate of urbanisation. Citing UN estimates about the growth in the urban population from 16% in the

2007 census to 20.31% in 2017 and the projected increase of the urban population to 25.8% in 2028, Pankhurst and colleagues noted the importance for policy-makers of paying attention to the rapid urbanisation taking place in the country.[47] Urbanisation in Ethiopia is the result of two processes: a high level of rural–urban migration and the urbanisation of rural areas.

Processes of urbanisation have implications for international migration from Ethiopia. On the one hand, rural–urban migration serves as a first step towards international migration. This is particularly true of the migration of young women for domestic work in major urban centres of the country. As chapter 3 notes, a significant number of young women first migrate from the countryside to the urban areas, particularly to Addis Ababa, and work as housemaids before their further migration to the Gulf countries. Moreover, remittances from migrants have been important sources of income which have resulted in the expansion of urban settlements in the countryside (see, for example, chapters 4 and 7). As chapter 11 indicates, one major way of asset-building by migrant households has been the construction of rental houses in peri-urban areas, contributing to the expansion of rural urbanisation. The other impact of urbanisation on migration is the widening of the worldview of its residents in comparison with those in the countryside, particularly as urbanites have better access to information technology.

The fourth dimension of transition that has implications for migration is the challenges that the youth face in their transition to adulthood. A large number of youth in traditional agrarian societies are unable, because of economic difficulties, to mark important social milestones that signal this transition. As chapter 4 notes, in the highland Tigray culture, marriage and the formation of one's own household are important milestones in the transition of a young person to adulthood. This culture is widely shared by many agrarian communities in Ethiopia. The delay in the youth transition is a result of a combination of factors, including a prolonged time in the schooling system, shortage of arable land, and joblessness. As Juárez and colleagues show, migration is increasingly used as a way for the youth to transit from youthhood to adulthood.[48] This does not mean that migration is impossible after the conclusion of a marriage. Married couples also decide that one or both of them will migrate to contribute to their early asset-building attempts. Moreover, the institution of marriage is also being utilised to subvert strict norms around controlling girls' sexuality. It is now becoming common for parents to have a daughter marry only to make sure that she loses her virginity in a dignified manner, and then let her migrate irregularly to countries where the risk of being raped is high (see chapter 6).

Finally, globalisation, or glocalisation (see chapter 5), is an aspect of global transition that has an important bearing on youth migration. The expansion and increased access to smart phones, internet and social media have changed how young people across the world, including Ethiopia, communicate among themselves and receive information about their communities, their countries and the world (see also chapters 2, 8 and 9). Globalisation, even defined in the narrow sense of the rapid flow and circulation of information and ideas, increases youth migration in two interrelated ways. First, information technologies facilitate irregular migration; both the migrants and the brokers (called facilitators in chapter 2) use social media extensively. Second, globalisation allows the easy flow of information and thereby increases knowledge among young people about the way people live and the standards of living abroad. This, in addition to the success stories of earlier migrants and returnees, has helped to change youth aspirations. It is no wonder that the youth increasingly see migration abroad as a crucial move to realise their aspirations. As Dom argues in chapter 5, the 'global idea' does not simply replace the local; rather, it is hybridised and becomes 'glocalised.' In more general terms, the 'fleeting images' and 'unfulfilled promises' of globalisation are enough to maintain a high rate of (irregular) migration.[49]

These plural transitions occur simultaneously while following different logics, and create the structural conditions within which the decision to migrate (or not) is made. It should be emphasised that the youth are not only influenced by these transitions, but they also contribute to structural instantiations in their communities, for example through remittances (see chapter 9), and the use of social media to form opinions and make sense of the transitions themselves. Government officials also respond to these transitions, such as by working towards job creation and banning irregular migration (see chapter 1). These multiple transitions coalesce to influence migration patterns—internal and international, formal and informal—from Ethiopia. These amount to migration transitions.[50]

Structure alone does not determine the fate of the youth. As active agents, potential migrants consider various global, national and local factors before making their decisions. Their decision is also influenced by dominant narratives and norms held by the local community, social networks, and brokers or facilitators. Accordingly, (irregular) migration is a complex social phenomenon. The following section contends that assemblage thinking provides a useful analytical tool to help us simplify and capture this complexity, and unpack how agency and structure interact and become enmeshed.

Bringing assemblage thinking to migration research

The concept of assemblage is gaining currency as a useful analytical tool to explain complex social and political realities.[51] It is, by and large, used to create a better understanding of complex social realities, especially in the face of rapid socio-political and technological change and societal reconfiguration.[52] It focuses on the fluidity of social, economic and political relations within periods of stability, rather than reifying existing socio-political ontologies and relations.[53] Put another way, assemblage anchors on the thinking that 'relations are not fixed and stable, nor are they always and everywhere the same'.[54] Moreover, the concept discourages the use of strict dichotomies but recognises differences and pluralisms and considers how disparate elements can be made to cohere harmoniously or competitively.

We contend in this book that migration from Ethiopia could be productively seen from the assemblage analytical perspective. In this respect, we define assemblage in respect of migration as the process within which various players, including prospective migrants, brokers and traffickers, state officials, and formal and informal institutions, link in a harmonious as well as competitive fashion to shape outward migration from Ethiopia.

We justify the use of assemblage as an analytical tool in migration research because of the range of qualities it affords for understanding migration more comprehensively and with more sensitivity to voices from below. First, migration is a complex phenomenon, especially in situations of irregularity, involving numerous actors, often with contending and contradictory interests and objectives, and located at various levels. Part of the complexity emerges from the plural transitions detailed above and the nature of the actors involved in the process (see chapter 2). The actors include the migrant, the family and community at local levels, state actors in Ethiopia, transit countries and destination countries, and the facilitators and brokers. As chapters 2 and 3 document, irregular migration involves the active agency of migrants and brokers as well as the informalisation of actors in formal spheres, often through bribes.

The complexity of migration is expressed in the range of its heterogeneous material and non-material dimensions. The discursive enunciations about migration cover the aspirations and driving interests of migrants and the range of policy directions that the government designs and attempts to implement (see chapter 1). There are material aspects related to remittances and their contribution to the national and local economy as well as local livelihoods (see chapters 9, 10 and 11). The remittances and material instantiations of the economic benefits of migrating are represented, for example, in the housing and urban development sectors (see chapters 4, 7 and 11), which inform and contribute to maintaining, sustaining and reifying migration dynamics.

The key role of smart phone technology in information exchange and flow is a major part of this complexity. Assemblage thinking, in such very complex social realities, offers useful ways of negotiating differences and complexities, and produces a contingent whole.[55] This analytical tool helps us trace the connections, relations and linkages between the various actors, discourses, technologies and normative positions. The existing conceptions of 'migration infrastructure' will not fully capture these dynamics, as they tend to give a strongly economic understanding of migration.[56]

Second, migration dynamics respond to changes in the socio-economic, political and security situation of the sending locality or country, the transit country and the destination country. As stated above, (irregular) migration happens in the context of coterminous multiple transitions. Moreover, policies designed by the Ethiopian government to control and regulate irregular migration and those

designed by Saudi Arabia to control illegal workers have direct consequences for how migration happens from Ethiopia. The actors respond
to constraints (physical, economic and legal barriers) as well as opportunities, and reconfigure their migration. New routes are created and
time of travel is adjusted to match periods of lesser control (see chapter
2). Moreover, the nature of migration itself changes across decades,
responding to conditions in sending communities as well as in migrant
communities in destination countries. For example, as chapter 8
shows, there have been different phases of Ethiopian irregular migration to South Africa, with more recent phases being responses to the
demand for labour and wives. Chapter 10 also shows us that what
started as a coping mechanism to repay government loans metamor-
phosed into a livelihood strategy.

The third benefit of the assemblage analytic to migration research is
its capacity to capture multi-scalar processes with equitable attention
to actors located at all levels. This helps us avoid the existing destination country bias in migration research and policy.[57] Greater attention
is paid to actors with greater power to make migration happen, rather
than state actors in the sending or receiving country.[58] We believe that
avoiding dichotomies (local/global; formal/informal) helps to provide
thick descriptions of the social world as it unfolds. This essentially
means that there will not be a strict dichotomisation in approach;
rather, we take the boundary between categories as fuzzy and see processes as playing out on a long continuum. Moreover, we view each
extreme form in the other, such as the local in globalisation in the
service of glocalisation.

The fourth factor which makes assemblage a useful analytical tool is
its focus on agency. According to Li, assemblage automatically implies
practice, 'to assemble', which 'flags agency'.[59] The dominant trend in
migration research and policy views migrants as simply responding to
opportunities or challenges presented by structures, with little agency
to influence or subvert such structures. This dichotomous view of
agency and structure has been critiqued by Giddens's notion of structuration and also in the more recent migration literature.[60] Assemblage
thinking goes beyond the aspiration to focus on both agency and structure, by concentrating on processes, dynamics and interactions of (re)
assembling.[61] De Haas advances the 'aspiration-capability model',

which pays due attention to the agency of migrants and sending communities.[62] This is further strengthened by the adoption of the assemblage analytic, as it recognises the agency of the heterogeneous actors involved. It is particularly helpful as it brings the agency of non-state actors, brokers and facilitators, and migrants themselves to the fore (see chapter 2).

We should concede here that an assemblage framework will not resolve the difficulties of creating a comprehensive theory of migration. The focus is more on thick description than explanation and theorisation.[63] This challenge could be addressed by taking the assemblage analytic as complementary to the aspiration capability theory.[64] By considering macro-, meso- and micro-factors influencing migration (see chapter 3), this theory takes migration as a function of the aspiration of the potential migrant and the capability to migrate. This is broad enough and could explain migration dynamics in a broad range of situations. In this way, the assemblage concept could be used as a methodological and analytical tool or approach complementing the aspiration capability model.[65]

As indicated above, the assemblage process brings disparate elements—both material and non-material—to construct the phenomenon. The analytic ignores dichotomies (formal/informal, legal/illegal, state/non-state, regular/irregular), and considers how the enunciations and representations of different interests, logics and ideas are interwoven with the material dimensions in making migration a significant part of life. The different components will not fall into their slotted constraints by themselves: rather they will be actively 'assembled' by the agency of situated actors. It is the agency of these situated agents which shapes and moulds the very structures which enable or disable migration in the first place, thereby reifying or eroding it.

The genesis of the book and its organisation

The majority of the chapters included in this volume were presented to a migration panel organised by the editors at the 20th International Conference of Ethiopian Studies (ICES) held in Mekelle, Ethiopia, in October 2018. Consequently, in August 2019, a writing workshop was set up to help revise the first drafts of the chapters in the light of comments from reviewers of the book proposal. The chapters by Catherine Dom, Kiros Berhanu and Mulugeta Gashaw (5, 7 and 10) came from the WIDE longitudinal research programme, started in 1994 with a study of 15 rural communities, later expanded to 20.[66] The WIDE team has been collecting longitudinal data on a number of interrelated development issues and tracking change in these communities for about a quarter of a century now. Although not representative in a statistical sense, the study sites represent diverse ecological settings, livelihoods and social mixes contributing to diversity in the communities' trajectories of change over time. The aforementioned authors predominantly used the 2018 data collected by WIDE, when migration-related themes were included in the study, to write their chapters.

All of the chapters in this volume deal directly with the overall theme of the book, i.e., giving voice to the agency of migrants, their households and communities in the migration discourse. The volume is divided into four parts.

Part I deals with the governance of irregular migration in Ethiopia. In Chapter 1, 'Interrogating the Inter-linkage between Ethiopian Migration Policies and Irregular Migration', Alemu Asfaw Nigusie examines how Ethiopia's migration policies, as a sending country, contribute to the perpetuation of irregular migration, even if the policies and laws are intended to limit the very same phenomenon. Alemu contends that migration-related policies and laws have serious shortcomings. He also shows how brokers and human traffickers and private employment agencies circumvent and bypass the laws by devising creative methods to facilitate irregular migration from Ethiopia.

Chapter 2 is a joint contribution by Fekadu Adugna Tufa, Priya Deshingkar and Tekalign Ayalew Mengiste, vividly entitled '"Say What the Government Wants and Do What Is Good for Your Family": Facilitation of Irregular Migration in Ethiopia'. These authors examine the multiple actors and complex processes involved in the facilitation of irregular migration in Ethiopia. Based on fieldwork in Hadya and South Wollo, two important places of origin, as well as the transit towns of Desheto and Moyale, they examine the role of kinship and other social relationships in the facilitation of irregular migration in the context of the Ethiopian government's intensification of migration control. This chapter gives agency to prospective migrants, their households and communities, and contends that the Government of Ethiopia, by restricting mobility, plays a significant role in the decisions of prospective migrants to take the irregular migration route. Using empirical data, the authors also make a fascinating argument that explicates the limitations of criminalising migration facilitation (brokerage). They stress that the organisation of migrants' departure at places of origin is initiated and reinforced by kinship and religious relations. The chapter also shows the social embeddedness of migration facilitation and how this challenges the government's criminalisation of brokerage or facilitation at the community and local levels.

Part II is made up of three chapters that deal with the decision-making dynamics of irregular migrants and investigate the complex ideas, practices and discourses which drive irregular migration. All three highlight ideas and concerns of great importance at the local level with a dominant bearing on migration decision-making. In Chapter 3, 'The Drivers of Youth Migration in Addis Ababa', Firehiwot Sintayehu focuses on Addis Ababa, Ethiopia's capital, as a sending area of irregular migrants to the Gulf countries, Europe and South Africa. Firehiwot examines the interactions between what she calls macro-(structural) problems (such as unemployment and underemployment and other manifestations of poverty), meso-factors (such as social networks and a culture of migration), and micro-factors (the agency of potential migrants). She contends that individuals decide to migrate by considering the experiences of their predecessors, their prospects, and their practical evaluation of viable available choices. Dense social networks and a well-developed culture of migration reduce costs and risks and increase information flows, thereby favouring the decision to migrate and perpetuating further migration.

In Chapter 4, 'Hopelessness and Future-Making through Migration in Tigray', Fana Gebresenbet, using empirical data collected in the core sending areas of Tigray National Regional State, persuasively contends that the difficulty or, in some cases, the impossibility of transitioning into adulthood informs the decision of many youth to migrate. Another unconventional argument contained in the chapter is that the decision to migrate is not solely determined by economic hardships in the place of origin and better opportunities at the destination. Fana contends that what matters most is not the economic plight of the potential migrant, but what Firehiwot describes as meso-factors: strong networks with previous migrants from the same area, a rich repertoire of adventures and opportunities, and real-time information flows. In such contexts, irregular migration becomes a viable pathway to a decent future compared to available alternatives locally. The chapter furthermore contends that, in the eyes of potential migrants, the risks associated with irregular migration are accepted as something one has to bear to build a successful future. Fana sums up his chapter by underscoring how the long history of migration to the Gulf countries has led to the practice becoming a socially acceptable norm and has contributed to the building and reification of the culture of migration.

In Chapter 5, 'Migration Aspirations and "Glocal Ideas of the Good Life" in Two Rural Communities in Southern and North-eastern Ethiopia: A Comparative Perspective', Catherine Dom uses longitudinal qualitative data to explore how globalisation influenced international migration in two rural communities, Aze Debo in the south and Harresaw in the north of Ethiopia. In both sites in early 2018, the number of people migrating abroad was large and rising. Most were young, and increasingly female, and used irregular routes. In Aze Debo migration money helped local economic growth; by contrast, in Harresaw, after a few promising years, it had become a highly risky coping strategy. The chapter looks at how 'ideas of the good life' interacted and coevolved with aspirations to, and experiences and effects of, migration abroad in each site. Dom shows that in the two sites, both global and local factors shape migration abroad, as an intrinsic component of youth transition to adulthood, while ideas of the good life are 'glocalised' through a context-specific assemblage of what is conventionally called the global and the local.

Part III, made up of three chapters, brings micro-views of migration further to the fore. In Chapter 6, Kiya Gezahegn shows that labour migration to the Middle East and Sudan is a popular option for Amhara youth. Her focus is on rituals performed before migration, en route and in the destination country, captured in the title 'Rituals of Migration: Socially Entrenched Practices among Female Migrants from Amhara National Regional State'. Following her anthropological study, Kiya expertly examines the ideologies and rituals performed by migrants. She takes ritual as an analytical framework to understand migrants and the migration experience in general, and sheds light on how performing rituals has become part of the migration process.

In Chapter 7, 'Irregular Migration among a Kambata Community in Ethiopia: Views from Below and their Implications', Mulugeta Gashaw highlights the deficient, but dominant, perspective in the migration literature which overlooks the views of migrants, returnees, their families and communities. Based on insights from Aze Debo, Kambata, from where irregular migrants largely travel to the Republic of South Africa and Sudan, the chapter presents views from below. This approach, Mulugeta argues, helps to highlight nuances and complexities, which are important for correcting the views from above.

In Chapter 8, 'Gender Relations in a Transnational Space: Ethiopian Irregular Migrants in South Africa', Yordanos S. Estifanos uses ethnographic data collected both in South Africa and Hadiya, Ethiopia, to make several interesting insights. These include the position of smugglers, which he stresses should be seen as an element in a complex web of transnational social networks. Moreover, Yordanos illustrates the recently increasing trend of nuptial migration financed by prior male migrants to South Africa. He further explains the exploitative nature of relations that prevail between Ethiopian husbands and wives in the transnational space. He also notes the exploitation of female labour for the success of businesses owned by more established Ethiopian male migrants.

Part IV, made up of three chapters, focuses on the impacts of irregular migration, primarily from the perspective of sending communities and the national economy. In Chapter 9, 'Remittances and Households Socio-economic Well-being: The Case of Ethiopian Labour Migrants in the Gulf Countries and South Africa', Asnake Kefale and Zerihun Mohammed examine the socio-economic impacts of remittances in Ethiopia at national and local levels. The chapter shows the growing importance of remittances to the national economy in generating much-needed foreign currency and for households at the local level. In addition, the chapter shows that informal channels are mainly used by migrants in the Gulf countries and South Africa to send remittances. Moreover, it examines how remittances are used by migrant families.

In Chapter 10, 'Heterogeneity in Outcomes of Migration: The Case of Irregular Migration to Saudi Arabia in Harresaw, Eastern Tigray',

Kiros Birhanu stresses the need to unpack the impacts of migration through micro-level analyses so as to develop policies which are aligned with the situation on the ground. Using data collected from Harresaw, she contends that migration has changed from a way to improve economic status, to a strategy merely to cope with shocks and disasters. The importance of migration and the income that is generated for the local community is such that young people are dropping out of school to migrate. She notes that the known adversities and negative experiences of irregular migration do not seem to deter prospective migrants. She also maps the changing nature of the impacts of migration between men and women, and across time (mid-1980s, 1990s, mid-2000s, 2012 and 2018), and the durability of the gains.

In Chapter 11, 'The Moral Economy of Irregular Migration and Remittance Distribution in South Wollo', Teferi Abate Adem focuses on culturally expected developmental cycles of households, and related kin- and neighbourhood-based moral-economic entitlements, which are relevant for understanding the local drivers of informal labour migration. Using ethnographic data and stories collected from villages in South Wollo, Teferi contends that migration decisions need to be considered as part of a range of pragmatic and flexible strategies by which smallholder household heads and their adult members in South Wollo cope with changing demographic, economic and environmental conditions. The chapter examines this link between the decision-making agency of individual migrants and sending households, by discussing the kind of culturally expected entitlements and related moral-economic resources both of these actors seek to access at three analytically separable decision nodes in the migration process: the initial decision to depart; financing informal migration; and the micro-politics of remittance distribution.

Read together (as summed up in the conclusion section), these eleven chapters make a nuanced and more accurate representation of the decision-making process of migrants from the local level. Contrary to the dominant view of potential migrants as irrational and unaware of the high risks involved, this book depicts migrants as rational, strategising actors making the decision to migrate in the light of other options for the future. These arguments are made with a central focus on empirical insights at local level, but also drawing on national and global processes and factors.

PART I

GOVERNING IRREGULAR MIGRATION FROM ETHIOPIA

POLICY-MAKING AND (UN)DESIRED OUTCOME

1

INTERROGATING THE INTER-LINKAGE BETWEEN ETHIOPIAN MIGRATION POLICIES AND IRREGULAR MIGRATION

Alemu Asfaw Nigusie

Introduction

This chapter examines how the migration policies of Ethiopia, as a sending country, contribute to the perpetuation of irregular migration, even if the policies and laws were intended to limit the very same phenomenon. The chapter also examines the evolution of Ethiopia's migration-related legal instruments, and their contexts and assumptions, that serve as the basis of Ethiopian migration laws and policies. As shown in this chapter, migration-related policies and laws suffer from serious shortcomings. Besides, human traffickers, employment agencies and other actors circumvent and bypass the laws by devising creative methods.

International migration has increased significantly in the decades following the end of the Second World War, with a pronounced rise in the rate of migration in the 2000s.[1] As the International Organization for Migration's report shows, between 1970 and 2015 the number of international migrants rose from 84 million to around 244 million, constituting 3.3% of the world's population.[2] As a result, the twentieth century has been called 'the age of migration', a reference to the fact that there are more migrants in the world today than ever before.[3]

In recent decades, migration has become one of the most controversial political and policy issues in the West. Indeed, policies relating to integration and border management tend to be divisive.[4] In many Western countries, as Bourbeau notes, 'abrasive rhetoric about migration is gaining popularity' and governments become engaged in migration issues for security and populist reasons.[5]

The campaign against migration has been supported by a range of policy measures by both sending and receiving countries. In their study on boat migration from West Africa to Spain's Canary Islands, Carling and Hernández-Carretero identified eight policy measures: (1) detection and apprehension of migrants, (2) post-arrival processing, (3) repatriation, (4) pre-border surveillance and control, (5) awareness campaigns in countries of origin, (6) prevention of illegal employment in Europe, (7) employment creation in countries of origin, and (8) programmes for legal migration.[6] These policy measures could be categorised under three labels: 'control', 'externalisation', and 'alternative approaches'.[7]

Yet, the evidence for whether such policies are effective in decreasing unauthorised migration is mixed. Scholars such as Mallett and his colleagues suggest that, while migration policies are unable to control the absolute volume of migrant flows, they tend to change the underlying dynamics of the phenomenon.[8] Similarly, a number of other scholars contend that the preventive approach has not been effective in slowing down irregular migration to Europe.[9] Browne argues that 'there is extremely little evidence on the impact and effectiveness' of campaigns launched against irregular migration, as 'conditions of poverty, inequality, conflict and lack of economic opportunities at home' fuel irregular migration,[10] not to mention the impact of the persistently high demand for migrant workers from the destination countries. There is, however, little discussion of the unintended consequences of migration policies on prospective migrants' decision-making and their experience. Moreover, although the majority of African migration takes place within the continent, much of the existing literature focuses on the policies of the destination countries, not the sending countries.[11] As a result, contemporary migration debates, by and large, ignore the perspectives of the Global South. In other words, little attention has been given to inter-linkages between the migration policies of the destination and the source countries.

This chapter investigates the contexts of and the interplay between migration policy measures and migration phenomenon in the sending countries by taking the case of Ethiopia. It problematises Ethiopia's migration policy responses by looking at the contexts in which the policies were introduced and the interrelationships between migration policy measures and migration trajectories. As a sending country, Ethiopia has mainly tried to apply control and alternative approaches of migration management, including detection and apprehension of migrants before they cross international borders; awareness campaigns that focus on the dangers of irregular migration; employment creation within the country; and promotion of legal migration. Also, facilitating the release and safe deportation of Ethiopians imprisoned in countries along the three main migration routes has emerged very recently, particularly since Abiy Ahmed became Prime Minister in 2018.[12] Moreover, the concept of migration has been understood and used negatively by policy-makers and the public, who view migration as 'sidet',[13] not 'felset',[14] which, in the Amharic language, has a negative meaning and connotation, reflected in the migration discourse. This, in turn, reveals a 'restricted perspective of migration from Ethiopia', which is limited to work, not broader aspirations and self-improvement, like study.[15] Such misunderstandings have an impact on the formulation of migration policies. Thus, in this chapter, I contend that even if migration policies are, by and large, intended to reduce irregular migration, they actually perpetuate it.

In writing this chapter, I used both primary and secondary information, including books, journal articles, newspapers, government policy documents, reports, and online sources. The chapter is divided into four sections. Section one provides insights into the background contexts that gave rise to international migration from Ethiopia. Section two presents the evolution of Ethiopia's international migration policies and laws. Section three examines how migration policies contributed to the perpetuation and transformation of irregular migration. The final section provides a few concluding remarks.

Contextualising international migration from Ethiopia

International migration is a recent phenomenon in Ethiopia. Before the 1974 revolution, which overthrew the monarchy, the main reasons for Ethiopians to travel overseas were education, religious pilgrimages, and trade.[16] Religious, trade and other forms of regional migration to neighbouring countries (such as Djibouti, Sudan, Kenya, Yemen and Saudi Arabia) are said to have accelerated during the military regime (the Derg).[17] International (forced) migration became an important trend after the revolution. During the 1970s and 1980s, the military regime unleashed the Red Terror to clamp down on opposition to its rule. As a result, tens of thousands of Ethiopian youth left the country and migrated to North America and Western Europe.[18]

Since the beginning of the 1990s, there has been a steady increase in international migration from Ethiopia compared to the past, but the net emigration rate has still been below 1%.[19] The number of Ethiopian international migrants was 445,926 in 2005 before it declined to 355,930 in 2015.[20] Of this figure, more than two-thirds of Ethiopian migrants are said to have used illegal routes.[21] Thus, the perception that there is a high rate of emigration from Ethiopia is an exaggeration of the current migration rate, as it is still below 1% of the total population of the country, and this view may be linked both to the centrality and 'externalisation' of the migration agenda among destination countries and to the Ethiopian state's acceptance and amplification of this narrative as well as its own experience compared to the past.

There are several factors that facilitated the rise in international migration from Ethiopia. First, there was the overthrow of the military regime in 1991, whose policies could be described as anti-migration, as they restricted the right of mobility within and outside the country. Since the 1990s, the Government of Ethiopia (GoE) has taken various measures that eased restrictions on international mobility such as lifting the requirement of Ethiopian nationals to secure an exit visa to travel abroad. Second, demands for migrant labour in the oil-rich Gulf countries, and the immigrant-friendly policies pursued by the post-apartheid government of the Republic of South Africa at least during the 1990s, fuelled migration from Ethiopia to the Gulf and South Africa.[22]

Ethiopians reach destination countries by regular, irregular or a combination of both mechanisms. Irregular migration is undertaken via three major routes: the northern route to Europe (through Sudan, Libya and the Mediterranean); the eastern route to Yemen, the Kingdom of Saudi Arabia and other Gulf countries (through Djibouti and Northern Somalia); and the southern route to South Africa (through Kenya, Tanzania, Malawi and Zimbabwe). Data from the Regional Mixed Migration Secretariat shows that between 2006 and 2016, more than 512,000 Ethiopian migrants travelled along the eastern route and reached Saudi Arabia.[23] In 2015, the total number of Ethiopian regular international migrants was estimated to be 355,930, which is below 0.5% of the total national population. The most popular seven destinations at this time had the following shares of this small percentage: Europe (48%), the United States of America and Canada (15%), the Gulf States (9%), Israel (8%), Sudan (6%), South Africa (5%) and other African countries (7%).[24] Today, a large number of Ethiopian migrants are concentrated in the Middle East, the US, Canada, Europe and African countries (such as Sudan, Kenya, South Africa and Botswana).[25] International migration from Ethiopia is also characterised by mixed migration, as it includes migrant workers (both regular and irregular), refugees, and other groups of individuals with various vulnerabilities.[26]

In Ethiopia, contemporary international youth migration is unfolding against a backdrop of several interrelated macro-level structural factors. First, there is a high level of population growth, with youth and children constituting about two-thirds of the population; the bulge in this age group essentially determines the extent of migration.[27] Second, there is a high level of youth unemployment (about 22% among those aged 15–24).[28] Third, there is a high level of rural–urban migration, which then transforms into international migration in what is called the mixed migration phenomenon.[29] The GoE policy responses to the problem of youth unemployment include job and employment creation through micro and small enterprises (MSEs);[30] the establishment of the Youth Revolving Fund (YRF); and the expansion of technical and vocational education and training (TVET). Formulated by the Ministry of Urban Development and Housing, the Micro and Small Enterprise Development Policy and Strategy paid huge attention to MSE development and considered these enterprises as 'the key instruments of job creation in urban centers'. The intended end goal of such schemes is to increase income, reduce poverty, and enhance the equitable distribution of income.[31]

However, the MSE Development Policy and Strategy failed to properly recognise the critical problems that circumvent the ecology of MSE development implementation, namely, the attitude, skill and knowledge of the government officers who implement the policy and strategy; the human and material resources and capacity of TVET schools; the commitment of the leadership; the skill, attitude, financial capacity and character of the beneficiaries; local politics and favouritism involved in the allocation of support to beneficiaries; the gap between supply and demand; and the like. Moreover, the promotion of MSEs, entrepreneurial skills and self-employment has been hampered by a lack of finance as well as access to markets.[32] Employment schemes in MSEs not only neglect rural areas but also, by and large, fail to provide sustainable economic opportunities.[33] Moreover, job creation efforts through MSEs schemes suffer from corrupt and bureaucratic administration procedures, and the training offered by TVET centres fails to provide skills that are in high demand by the market.[34]

As noted above, the focus of MSEs was the urban unemployed youth. Indeed, rural unemployment was ignored by policy-makers until the introduction of the National Youth Policy (NYP) in 2004.[35] The NYP identified access to land and expansion of off-farm activities as major solutions to address the rural unemployment problem.[36] After realising the limitations of its policies towards rural unemployment, the GoE introduced two measures: the Youth Development Package (which aims to offer jobs through environmental protection activities) and the Rural Youth Opportunities Creation Package (which allows rural youth to access microfinance institutions to start micro- and small businesses).[37] Both interventions have been found to lack breadth, consistency and focus.[38] As a result, migration serves as a way out of this problem and an alternative means of livelihood for rural youth.

The Youth Revolving Fund was announced to provide the youth with financial and technical support so that they could become self-employed. Ten billion Ethiopian birr (about US$370 million) has been earmarked for this.[39] However, the fund has been riddled with problems relating to budget allocation, limited availability of workshops, requirement for collateral, selection of beneficiaries, and attitudes of the youth.[40]

Accordingly, the root causes of contemporary international youth migration from Ethiopia go beyond economic poverty and youth unemployment in Ethiopia alone; rather, it is a complex phenomenon that has been triggered by a host of factors, including high levels of youth unemployment, demand for migrant labour in the destination countries, the presence of dense networks that facilitate youth migration, the 'culture' of migration (where migration is seen as a socially legitimate phenomenon) among the people, and the agency of migrants (self-improvement, personal development and the like).

Evolution of Ethiopia's migration policies

The GoE has tried to regulate international migration to maximise the benefits that migration brings to the country and to safeguard the well-being of migrant workers. The major policy decisions of the government are briefly discussed below.

The 1998 Private Employment Agency (PEA) Proclamation

Despite the 1994 Directive Issued to Determine the Manner of Employment of Ethiopian Nationals Abroad by the Ministry of Labour and Social Affairs (MoLSA), people were already migrating to the Middle East using the *hajj* and *umrah* religious pilgrimages as pretexts.[41] The need for an institution that would facilitate employment abroad and better protect the rights, safety and dignity of Ethiopians working abroad was clear to the GoE. This led to the introduction of the Private Employment Agency Proclamation in 1998.

This proclamation made overseas employment permissible only through private employment agencies (PEAs) unless the MoLSA permitted the direct recruitment of an Ethiopian national by an employer. Moreover, it compelled agencies to have a branch office or representative in the receiving country; to submit a procedure for the recruitment and registration of job-seekers for approval by the relevant authority; to submit contracts of employment to the relevant authority for approval; to provide potential workers with the necessary orientation with regard to the work and the country of employment before signing a contract; and to deposit a monetary guarantee for the workers in financial institutions, the amount depending on the number of workers an agency sent. Most importantly, the proclamation made the PEAs responsible for ensuring the rights, safety and dignity of the workers.

The Ethiopian PEA proclamation was introduced after the adoption of the International Labour Organization's Convention on Private Employment Agencies (no. 181/1997) and it reflected many of the convention's universal norms and values. For instance, Article 2(1) of Ethiopia's proclamation on the definition and character of an 'agency' is a reflection of ILO's Articles 1(1) and 7(1). But Ethiopia's PEA proclamation failed to include provision for the bilateral agreements highlighted in the 1994 directive and minimum wages mentioned in the ILO convention.

In contravention of the PEA proclamation, PEAs failed to establish legal representatives in the receiving countries. In Yemen, for example, some agencies did not want to become registered and work unofficially because of registration requirements and the government control that would follow registration.[42] Recruitment agencies in Yemen and elsewhere also received payments and benefits from migrants. The rights of domestic workers were often violated by withholding passports, restricting mobility, delaying payment of salaries, and rape.[43] It was not usual for domestic workers to sign a contract, either before departure or upon arrival in the receiving country. When they did sign, it was a document written in a language they did not understand and one that did not represent their interests. For instance, some contract agreements stated that the domestic worker could not leave the house of employment for the duration of the contract, and if they returned to Ethiopia before the end of the contract, they would be fined $3,000.[44]

The 2009 Employment Exchange Services Proclamation

The 2009 Employment Exchange Services Proclamation (no. 632/2009) was introduced because of the limitations of the 1998 proclamation and its implementation. More specifically, it was designed to achieve three major objectives: to differentiate between the role of public and private employment agencies in employment exchange, something that did not exist before; to strengthen the protection of the rights, safety and dignity of Ethiopians going abroad for employment; and to strengthen the mechanism for monitoring and regulating domestic and overseas employment exchange services.

In comparison with the previous proclamation, the 2009 proclamation can be seen as an improvement, particularly because of its emphasis on the protection of migrant workers' rights before departure, during employment, and upon return. For instance, the proclamation made payment of costs (visa, flight ticket, insurance, and residence and work permit), deployment and contractual issues (age, consent of the worker, and registration in embassies) the responsibility of PEAs. The proclamation, moreover, allowed Ethiopians and non-Ethiopians with a permanent residence permit to establish an agency.[45] An applicant wishing to operate a PEA was required to have a branch or representative in the receiving country and provide evidence thereof to Ethiopian diplomatic missions in the receiving country. They were also required to provide food and temporary shelter to Ethiopian migrant workers in distress.[46] When renewing their licences, PEAs were required to submit their foreign representative's renewed licence (Article 10(2c)). Unlike the 1998 proclamation, the 2009 proclamation indicated the amount of money that PEAs were required to deposit in cash (50%) and surety bonds (50%) to comply with the law to ensure satisfaction of liabilities to workers. However, like the 1998 PEA Proclamation, the amount still depended on the number of workers an agency sent.[47] If an employment agency sent workers to more than three countries, it was required to deposit an additional guarantee, equivalent to the number of workers deployed (Article 23(2)). The proclamation also included new clauses laying down a minimum wage for overseas workers (although the amount was not stipulated), depending on the situation in each receiving country; defining unlawful acts (for example, deploying a person under the age of 18 or withholding a worker's travel or other pertinent documents); stipulating the deployment of a labour attaché with strong and well-defined powers and duties; and creating a national committee to ensure that the rights, safety and dignity of workers abroad were protected as required by the proclamation.

However, just like its predecessor, the 2009 proclamation had serious shortcomings. PEAs were found to be carrying out activities in clear violation of the proclamation, namely, not fulfilling their obligation to cover all expenses by themselves; not providing protection to migrant workers; and collaborating with agencies and individuals in the destination country known for human trafficking or working closely with traffickers.[48] Furthermore, PEAs did not provide assistance to migrants who were facing difficulties in the course of employment; rather, they became part of the problem, forcing migrants to continue working by threatening to impose a financial penalty on them on their return to Ethiopia.[49]

The October 2013 ban on overseas employment

In 2013 a ban was introduced on overseas employment in response to the massive deportation of undocumented migrant workers from Saudi Arabia in 2013 and their inhuman treatment.[50] Saudi Arabia, which depicted irregular migrants as the source of all its economic, political and social ills, adopted a new labour law (*Nitaqat*) in April 2013.[51] In four months starting from November 2013, Ethiopia witnessed the deportation of more than 160,000 migrants from Saudi Arabia.[52] Again, following the renewed attack on undocumented migrants, around 260,000 were deported to Ethiopia from Saudi Arabia between March 2017 and March 2019.[53] The mass deportations were accompanied by severe human rights abuses, like beatings and detentions.[54]

Ethiopia, which labelled the magnitude of the irregular migration to the Gulf countries including Saudi Arabia as an 'exodus', blamed traffickers and smugglers for the suffering of its nationals. As the Foreign Affairs spokesman Dina Mufti stated, 'this exodus, being pushed by illegal human traffickers, has created immense problems for the people of the nation [and] for the image of the country'.

The Ethiopian government imposed the ban to address the lack of safety of its nationals en route and in Saudi Arabia, and also the negative image it was casting on the country at large. It also vowed that the ban would not be lifted until a 'lasting solution' was found for the suffering of Ethiopian migrant workers. The 2013 ban was not the first of its kind. In 2008, the government banned the employment of Ethiopian domestic workers in Lebanon. The ban was in response to widely reported human rights violations, abuse and a large number of deaths of Ethiopian domestic workers in Lebanon. From 1996 to 1999, around 67 Ethiopian domestic workers were reported to have died from various causes (for example, hanging, drowning, and falling). Thus, the suspension of work travel to Beirut was 'the only solution to minimizing the human rights abuses and dangers facing' Ethiopian migrants in Lebanon.[55] The 2013 ban was lifted in February 2018, following the introduction of the revised overseas employment law in 2016. The extended ban shut down the legal operations of the private employment agencies.[56]

The 2015 Anti-trafficking and Anti-smuggling Proclamation

To address irregular migration, Ethiopia introduced the 2015 proclamation for the Prevention and Suppression of Trafficking in Persons and Smuggling of Migrants. This proclamation was made three years after Ethiopia ratified two protocols relevant to international migration that supplemented the United Nations Convention Against Transnational Organized Crime: the 2000 Protocol to Prevent, Suppress and Punish Trafficking in Persons, Especially Women and Children; and the 2000 Protocol Against the Smuggling of Migrants by Land, Sea and Air. The most important element of this proclamation was the much stronger powers it gave the police and other security officers to use special investigation techniques like infiltration and surveillance in the prevention and investigation of crimes. The campaign against trafficking and smuggling was to be led by a National Committee that consisted of different stakeholders from federal and regional level governments, religious institutions, charities, and other bodies.

This National Committee was presided over by the Deputy Prime Minister. An Anti-Human Trafficking and Smuggling of Migrants Task Force, accountable to the national committee and led by the Federal Attorney General, was established to carry out the campaign against human trafficking and smuggling. Before the enactment of this anti-trafficking proclamation, illegal migration was addressed by the interministerial task force, which was first established in June 2007 and revived and expanded to the *woreda*[57] and *kebele* levels in 2012. As part of this expanded task force structure, the Deputy Prime Minister assumed the chairmanship of the national task force, while presidents of regional states became chairs of their respective regional task forces.[58] The anti-trafficking proclamation was understood to be 'comprehensive, integrative' as it contained the key strategies—partnership, prevention, protection and prosecution—that are imperative in the fight against human trafficking and smuggling.[59]

That being said, this Anti-trafficking and Smuggling Proclamation was introduced within two important contexts. The first was internal. The Ethiopian government sought to stop the increasing irregular migration out of the country that was happening despite the overseas work travel ban that it imposed in 2013.[60] The second was external. The proclamation was supported by the Western powers, particularly European countries, as it aligned with their interest in stemming the flow of irregular migrants to their shores. Since the 1980s, European countries have introduced migration policies that discourage the arrival of immigrants and asylum-seekers.[61] Fear of being 'flooded' with migrant populations, and the resulting socio-cultural and security threats, have alarmed the European Union to the extent of provoking intolerant practices, spearheaded by far right-wing political forces.[62]

The EU developed an external migration policy called the Global Approach to Migration and Mobility (GAMM) in 2005.[63] Within this external policy framework, the EU focused on establishing a partnership with Africa at bilateral, regional and continental levels with the overall objective of 'addressing the root causes of irregular migration and forced displacement'.[64] Accordingly, joint summits were held, producing plans such as the Khartoum Process (2014), the Valletta Action Plan (2015), and the EU–Horn of Africa Regional Action Plan (2015).[65] Bilaterally, the EU and Ethiopia signed a Common Agenda on Migration and Mobility (CAMM) on the sidelines of the Valletta Migration Summit.[66] As part of these dialogues on migration, the EU pledged to invest in and provide development aid to source and transit African countries, including Ethiopia.

Thus, it is probably no coincidence that the Ethiopian proclamation came out in the same year as the 2015 'summer of migration',[67] backed by the European Union and its member states. Part 5 of the proclamation covers issues relating to the establishment of a fund to 'prevent, control, and rehabilitate victims' of human trafficking and smuggling. According to Article 33, the fund would rely on 'grants from different international organizations and donors and other financial sources'. It is from this perspective that we should view such multi-million-dollar initiatives as the EU's Better Migration Management (BMM), Regional Development Protection Programme (RDPP), and Stemming Irregular Migration in Northern and Central Ethiopia (SINCE), and the World Bank's Development Response to Displacement Impacts Project (DRDIP) and Jobs Compact, which aims to create employment opportunities for Ethiopians (70%) and refugees (30%). Because the participants of irregular migration from Ethiopia are both Ethiopians and refugees (particularly Eritreans), some of these programmes have targeted both of these groups.[68]

The 2016 Overseas Employment Proclamation

The Overseas Employment Proclamation was passed at a time when the legal overseas employment channel was shut down and when the country was being destabilised by widespread protests which saw the imprisonment and flight of young people in their thousands.[69] Thus, there was an imperative for a new and improved proclamation to address the gaps in the earlier legislation. This proclamation was premised on the need to safeguard the rights, safety and dignity of Ethiopian workers abroad; the need for bilateral agreements to help solve some of the problems in overseas employment, irregular migration and human trafficking; and the need to enhance the government's follow-up and regulation of overseas employment.

Thus the 2016 proclamation introduced significant improvements to the 2009 proclamation. For instance, there needed to be a bilateral agreement with the recipient country if one was to consider taking up employment in that country; direct employment was generally discouraged; minimum age (18), education (completion of Grade 8), and skill level (certificate of competence) were all stipulated; licensing requirements were imposed on private agencies (only Ethiopian, and with capital of not less than one million birr) as well as financial guarantees (a deposit of $100,000 or its equivalent in birr in a blocked bank account); a Foreign Employers' Guarantee Fund was established; and incentive schemes for agencies were set up to encourage good performance. Operation in more than one country is discouraged, and agencies are required to acquire separate licences for different destinations.

The irregular migration and human trafficking and smuggling problems linked to the 2013 overseas ban are also reflected in this proclamation. A task force, accountable to the National Coordinating Committee, which was, in turn, established by the 2015 Anti-trafficking and Anti-smuggling Proclamation, was given the authority to 'ensure the proper implementation of the proclamation' (Article 15(2a)). This task force was mandated to establish a conducive environment for bilateral agreements with receiving countries on issues relating to employment, to cooperate with appropriate organs, and to carry out other relevant activities. The Deputy Prime Minister was entrusted with the leadership of the national task force.

Following the adoption of the new proclamation, and the lifting of the ban on overseas employment in February 2018, Ethiopians were allowed to take up domestic work and leave for the Gulf countries of Kuwait, Jordan, Saudi Arabia and Qatar, with which Ethiopia had signed and ratified bilateral agreements.[70] Ethiopia and Saudi Arabia are reported to have agreed to a monthly minimum wage of 1,000 Saudi riyal (about $266) for Ethiopian domestic workers.[71] In addition, TVET schools, medical centres and sending PEAs, which have become the vital features of the new legislation, started to provide training to equip prospective migrants with the necessary skills.

Loopholes in Ethiopia's migration policies and the perpetuation of irregular migration

Despite Ethiopia's various policies and proclamations to regulate international migration by both legalising overseas employment and tackling irregular migration and human trafficking and smuggling, individuals have continued to leave the country irregularly in large numbers. According to data from the RMMS, between 2011 and 2016 the estimated number of Ethiopian arrivals in Yemen was 92,838 in 2011, and

96,778 in 2012, before it dropped to 54,850 in 2013. After 2013 (when Ethiopia introduced the ban on overseas employment in the Middle East and the Anti-trafficking and Anti-smuggling Proclamation in 2015), irregular migration increased dramatically to 71,950 in 2014, 82,000 in 2015 and 97,198 in 2016, a return to the pre-2013 number of irregular migrants.

Therefore, it is the contention of this chapter that the increase in irregular migration is linked to what Castles calls the 'regulatory failure' of the state (such as poor formulation and implementation of policies) as well as to the agency of actors involved in the migration phenomenon—individual migrants, employers, and intermediaries, such as registered PEAs, unregistered brokers, and social networks.[72] These actors exploit the existing regulations (or lack of them) to their advantage. Some of these regulatory failures and ways of circumventing the regulations are discussed below.

Despite the Private Employment Agency Proclamation, designed to provide migrant workers with rights, safety and dignity en route and in duty through a legally established employment agency, some problems arose that caused this not to happen. Few agencies operated in the business owing to the huge deposits they were required to make as a guarantee of workers' rights. In the early stages of the proclamation of 1998, only one agency operated.[73] Later this increased to 122.[74] The deposit requirement forced many agencies to operate underground; and migrants, with the help of traffickers and smugglers, would travel to Kenya and Tanzania as an alternative route so as to reach Lebanon and other countries in the Middle East.[75]

The financial and administrative requirements became the source of grievance and illegal conduct by private agencies.[76] PEAs were required to open a branch or have a legal representative in the receiving country (as part of the 2009 and 2016 Employment Exchange proclamations), but administrative and legal obstacles in receiving states made fulfilling this requirement problematic.[77] PEAs also faced competition from traffickers who provided services at a minimum cost that were attractive to migrants. Formal and regular migration through a PEA was slow because of cumbersome bureaucratic rules and procedures. Documents had to pass through various processes according to the laws and regulations in both Ethiopia and the receiving countries. This put agencies at a disadvantage compared with human traffickers, as 'a trafficker will send a migrant worker within two weeks, while it takes, on average, one to three months for a PEA to do so'.[78] Irregular migration is perceived to be a cheaper, more rewarding, less bureaucratic and less time-consuming option than legal migration.[79] Added to this is the three-month competence training required to take up work abroad, as required by the 2016 proclamation. This proclamation demands a higher investment of money and time from potential migrants.

As noted above, the October 2013 ban was imposed as a response to severe human rights violations. It did not, however, deter Ethiopians from trying to enter Saudi Arabia and other Gulf countries via alternative mechanisms. Ethiopia's imposition of this ban without addressing the underlying causes that trigger people to migrate abroad was doomed to fail from the very beginning. The fact that the highest number of Ethiopian arrivals in the now conflict-ridden Yemen was recorded after this ban was imposed confirms this policy gap. In the end, the recognition by the GoE that the ban was being circumvented by operators led to its lifting in 2018. According to Assefa Yirgalem, communications director at the Ministry of Labour and Social Affairs, 'The number of illegal migrants has reached as much as 1,300 people a day. Therefore, we immediately started preparations to lift the ban.'[80]

The 2015 Anti-trafficking and Anti-smuggling Proclamation, which aimed to curb irregular migration, also has weaknesses. The proclamation was premised on the argument that human trafficking and smuggling is a crime and should be addressed as a law enforcement problem; and, therefore, it paid due attention to the prosecution of human traffickers, the protection of victims, and partnership and cooperation with relevant stakeholders. It failed to see human trafficking as part of the larger migration phenomenon. Traffickers and smugglers operate in networks and are embedded within communities from local to international levels. Sometimes, people involved in smuggling activities may not be part of a larger criminal network and may carry out smuggling for personal, moral reasons, helping their relatives and kin.[81] The preventive dimension of the proclamation does not discuss the root causes of migration and why individuals engage in it and seek the help of traffickers and smugglers in the first place, rather than proceed through the formal migration channel. Admittedly, this problem has been recognised by the government. During a meeting on 17 January 2020, Demeke Mekonnen (the Deputy Prime Minister) and the National Committee he leads urged that any preventive action should be community-centred (starting from the family) and should help resolve unemployment.[82]

Moreover, one major challenge regarding the implementation of the proclamation has been the collusion of government officials in Ethiopia with criminal networks for personal benefit from the smuggling business.[83] This collusion and misuse of power 'ranges from turning a blind eye to smugglers' actions to actively participating in trafficking operations or directly enforcing abuse on migrants'.[84] As a result, bribery and the payment of ransoms have become the most common approach among smugglers, traffickers and migrants themselves.[85]

Apart from a few reports of the capture and imprisonment of a small number of individuals suspected of participating in illegal migration, the National Task Force has failed to deliver meaningful outcomes to date.[86] Of the 186 cases handed to the public prosecutor's office by the police, only 10 cases ended in conviction between 1995 and 2008; and only 13 individuals were convicted out of 309.[87] The data collected from a focus group discussion[88] conducted in February 2017 with participants who monitor the northern route highlighted a lack of coordination, finance, human power, and clear enforcement mechanisms within the government itself as reasons for the task force's failure, making the impact of migration management policies limited and less effective. They also highlighted the methods that smugglers use to overcome government restrictions. These include using public transport (to cross the Ethiopian–Sudanese border) instead of goods vehicles as previously; bribing government officials so that security checkpoints could be 'opened'; changing drivers and vehicles as they enter various Ethiopian regions and checkpoints to avoid capture by the police; and placing migrants in established 'guest houses' before departure.

In spite of the improvements meant to address both legal and irregular migration, Ethiopia's 2016 Overseas Employment Proclamation not only lacks clear guidelines on implementation but also suffers from inherent limitations. First, it does not stipulate how the rights of citizens will be practically guaranteed and protected in receiving countries. In the past, Ethiopian diplomatic missions abroad failed to ensure fair treatment of Ethiopian nationals in the receiving countries, giving the impression that the GoE is powerless to defend its nationals and hold perpetrators to account. Whether Ethiopia can allocate the necessary attention and resources to collaborate with the destination countries and make them comply with agreed rules this time round is open to question. Second, issues around return migrants and their reintegration have not been properly addressed;[89] and, third, looking at the profile of current irregular migrants, it is likely that for a significant proportion, the minimum requirements are unattainable, leaving most with no other option than to migrate irregularly.

The long time the government took to lift the ban, even after new legislation was adopted, has apparently been the source of complaint and irregular migration too. Although the revised overseas employment proclamation was issued in 2016, it took two more years to allow legal (regular) migration through the intermediary of private employment agencies. PEAs complain that the time taken for the conclusion of the bilateral agreements and other related preconditions have caused havoc to their operations and cost them money.[90] Because of the long delay, the first cohort of overseas workers left for Saudi Arabia in August 2019,[91] more than a year after the ban was lifted. The prolonged delay in allowing legal migration left the operation open to illegal operators.[92]

Moreover, the various proclamations issued by the government to regulate legal migration needed to be backed up by the necessary financial, human and institutional arrangements and capacity. The management of migration in Ethiopia involves different government ministries and agencies, but it is MoLSA that is mandated to look after legal labour migration. But this ministry has not gained the government's attention or been equipped with the necessary infrastructure to carry out its stated tasks.[93] Ethiopia does not have the capacity or the will to carry out its mission of protecting its citizens.[94] The government has not been able to monitor the treatment of its nationals or offer support when needed in the receiving countries.

Finally, the management of migration in Ethiopia has not been treated as an integral part of the country's development endeavours. The Growth and Transformation Plans (GTPs)[95] do not explicitly recognise the importance of labour migration as an employment opportunity and part of the economic development of the country.[96] The 2012 National Social Protection Policy document does not mention the role of migration for employment opportunities at all. National awareness-raising activities and the dissemination of information about international migration and overseas employment have not been continuous, correct or up to date, and have focused on the downsides of migration rather than its benefits.

Conclusion

This chapter provided insights into the nexus between Ethiopia's migration management policies and laws and irregular migration by examining the national economic, social and political contexts of international migration, the history of the migration management laws and perspectives so far developed, and the major loopholes of the policies, both in theory and in practice, that promote irregular migration. The laws and policies passed, from the 1998 PEAs proclamation down to the recent 2016 Overseas Employment Proclamation to manage migration, appear to be progressive, as they have paid due attention to the protection of the rights, dignity and safety of workers abroad by focusing on the export of a skilled labour force, increasing the accountability of PEAs, establishing labour attachés, and making bilateral agreements mandatory.

But they also reveal the important interplay between structure and agency. Promulgating new laws to promote legal migration does not automatically mean that legal routes will be utilised; and at the same time, banning legal channels does not mean irregular migration will be halted, as closing legal channels diverts migration flows to irregular channels. As the discussion above showed, the formulation of laws and policies at a structural level (with all their inherent limitations) has triggered the agency of non-state actors like migrants, PEAs, and human traffickers and smugglers, and encouraged them to devise ways of circumventing the policies and laws put in place. The net effect of the interplay between the migration management approaches of the state and the response from non-state actors has been nothing but the perpetuation of irregular migration, rather than a decline in its importance. The Ethiopian government thus needs to analyse its migration policies and systems critically and entirely, including assumptions, implications, benefits and costs, and its will and capacity to bring benefits to the country and to those actors involved.

2

'SAY WHAT THE GOVERNMENT WANTS AND DO WHAT IS GOOD FOR YOUR FAMILY'

FACILITATION OF IRREGULAR MIGRATION IN ETHIOPIA

Fekadu Adugna Tufa, *Priya Deshingkar* and *Tekalign Ayalew Mengiste*

Introduction

Earlier scholarship on migration facilitation has emphasised the entrepreneurship and business dimensions of migration brokerage.[1] The actors involved were characterised as an 'ensemble of entrepreneurs who, motivated by the pursuit of financial gains, provide a variety of services facilitating human mobility across international borders'.[2] This approach paid less attention to non-economic factors, such as kinship and other social obligations that aid the organisation of migratory trajectories and encourage the diverse and dynamic relationships that emerge between migrants, their families, brokers and the officials working in the domain of control.[3] Recent works on migration echo sensationalist media coverage that portrays migrants as silent victims of various kinds of abuse including sexual abuse, forced labour and physical abuse by trafficking rings and smuggling operations.[4] However, an emerging strand of the literature argues that such approaches ignore the agency of migrants and their families in mobilising migration resources. In this way, the dominant literature downplays the dynamism and social complexity of the organisation of migration facilitation, which includes family and religious relations at the places of origin and transit.

Similarly, the media rhetoric that links youth migration to the 'greedy and immoral' behaviour of brokers and smugglers has the effect of portraying potential migrants and their families as irrational and desperate victims of the smugglers.[5] However, as Andersson and Achilli correctly analyse, while such an approach is effective in activating public opinion and some policy interventions, these representations have consistently failed to address the problems of irregular migration and the complex social and cultural dynamics behind migration facilitation, including smuggling.[6]

This chapter departs from the widespread emphasis on the business aspects of migration facilitation and the victimisation of migrants by individual criminal brokers and smugglers. We highlight the role of aspiring migrants, their families, and other social relations such as religious networks. In other words, we try to understand migration facilitation from the perspective of both the migrants and their families, and emphasise the active roles that kinship, friendship and religion play in the facilitation of migration. This represents a departure from seeing the process as a hegemonic statist legal paradigm.[7] We draw on Deleuze and Guattari's concept of assemblage to understand the multiple actors in Ethiopian migration facilitation, and the multifaceted interweaving between them in an extremely dynamic and complex environment (see also the Introduction).[8] The ways different actors assemble and relate to each other and respond to constraints and opportunities created by policy, resource availability and networks are crucial in the success of the migrants' journey. We also emphasise how this assemblage facilitates the agency of the migrants and their families in planning, finding brokers and playing an active part in initialising the smuggling process and its financing to realise the young migrants' desired future and the well-being of their families.

This approach opens up a scholarly opportunity to revisit migration brokerage, the organisation of departure, and the smuggling of migrants across borders.[9] It provides a more nuanced and comprehensive understanding of migration facilitation and the actors involved.[10] Such an analysis also helps us understand why aspiring migrants trust migration brokers or smugglers regardless of government criminalisation campaigns and gloomy media reports about the situation for irregular migrants, including horror stories supported by graphic images from the Mediterranean and Red Sea.[11] We argue that deeper insights into the local social relations underpinning migration facilitation are critical to understanding the clandestine organisation of migration. This localised aspect of migration facilitation also lies behind the resilience of irregular migrations in the face of the government's organised campaigns.

Setting the migration context

This chapter is based on the data gathered from the Migrating Out of Poverty (MOOP) research consortium funded by the UK's Department for International Development (DFID) on the migration industry in Ethiopia, which ran between February 2018 and September 2019. The empirical data for this chapter was drawn from fieldwork in two major origin locations (Hadya and South Wollo) and two routes to transit towns: the eastern route (up to the Ethiopia–Djibouti border town of Desheto, which is a transit point in migration towards Yemen and Saudi Arabia) and the southern route (up to the Ethiopia–Kenya border town of Moyale, towards South Africa).

The data was collected over three months of fieldwork conducted between March and December 2018 in Hadya, South Wollo, Moyale and Desheto. We conducted semi-structured interviews and focus group discussions (FGDs) with aspiring migrants, deportees, returnees, families of migrants, informal brokers, law enforcement officials, border guards, immigration officials, officials of international organisations and local NGOs. These included eight brokers, five border guards and twenty officials and personnel working in migration-related government offices, and three personnel working for non-government and international organisations engaged in migration management activities. In addition, we interviewed fifty aspiring and deported migrants, thirty families or households of migrants, and fifty returnees as well as five migrants en route.

The two origin locations differ significantly in terms of the dominant religion and provide an interesting comparison as to how religion is operationalised within those networks and belief systems. South Wollo is a predominantly Muslim majority area situated in north-central Ethiopia, and most of the migrants are young women who aspire to work as domestic workers in the Gulf countries. Hadya is a Protestant Christian majority area situated in south-central Ethiopia where most of the migrants are young men who aspire to work in South Africa.

The two routes are also situated in very different territories and landscapes. The migrants cross the vast arid lowland area to the east of Wollo that continues to and includes Djibouti, a territory inhabited by Afar pastoralists. There is no regular public transportation on the route and most travel is made by minibus with several checkpoints along the route. Migrants on this route take either minibuses or trucks, which are used by *khat* (a mild stimulant crop) and vegetable traders until they arrive at the border towns, of which Desheto is one. The plain lowland allows the migrants to navigate the everyday cross-border economies of the pastoral system, which is important in the organisation of departures and journeys from South Wollo. Brokers in South Wollo arrange departures and transportation with *khat* and vegetable traders. When migrants reach the border area, they make use of the knowledge of the pastoralists to circumvent border control. The smuggling infrastructure from Hadya to the border town of Moyale is completely different. Hadya is connected to Moyale by an asphalt road with regular transportation lines. Thus, migrants' departure and journeys from Hadya to the border town of Moyale are relatively straightforward as migrants can travel by public transport. However, crossing the Ethiopian–Kenyan border is facilitated by the wide range of brokers and smugglers based in Moyale town. When control is very tight in the town, smugglers may use pastoralists to facilitate border crossings.

Restrictions on mobility and its consequences

In 1998, the Ethiopian government issued a proclamation that allowed the establishment of overseas employment agencies. As a result, some 400 licensed Private Employment Agencies (PEAs) served as the main mediators of labour migration from the country until 2013. For instance, according to the Ministry of Labour and Social Affairs (MoLSA), the ministry responsible for labour migration, PEAs assisted the regular migration of over 480,000 labour migrants between 2008 and 2013, mainly to Saudi Arabia, Kuwait and United Arab Emirates.[12] Most of these (94%) were less-educated females who engaged in domestic labour.[13]

In late 2013, the Government of Ethiopia banned all PEAs, accusing them of anomalies such as working with informal brokers, and failing to follow up and support the migrants in the countries of destination. Reports of Ethiopian domestic workers suffering abuse in Gulf countries and mass deportations from Saudi Arabia triggered the ban. In late 2013 and early 2014 Saudi Arabia deported more than 163,000 undocumented Ethiopian migrants, mainly female domestic workers.[14] On the southern route, as well, deaths of Ethiopian migrants en route to the Republic of South Africa were reported several times, the worst being in 2012 when several dozen migrants suffocated to death in a container in Tanzania.[15]

With increased media coverage of the deaths of Ethiopian migrants en route and of abuses they endure at destinations mainly in the Gulf countries, the Ethiopian government responded by banning all PEAs and criminalising informal brokers.[16] With more tragic incidents, such as the murder of 30 Ethiopians (with two Eritreans) in Libya by Islamic extremists broadcast in the international media, the Ethiopian government's response was to extend the criminalisation of brokers and to portray migrants as victims of human trafficking practices. To that end, it intensified migration control by using regulatory infrastructure. Anti-human trafficking and smuggling legislation was adopted swiftly and anti-human trafficking task forces were established at all administrative levels with the aim of targeting migration brokers. In order to broaden migration control activities, the government formed a joint anti-human trafficking committee with representatives of law enforcement agencies and religious and traditional leaders. More importantly, the Deputy Prime Minister at national level and regional presidents chaired these committees. Checkpoints were set up on the main migration routes. Thus, the government criminalised brokerage and subjected brokers to an organised campaign. As a result, hundreds of brokers were convicted, and are currently serving long-term prison sentences.[17] According to a report by SAHAN, the Ethiopian Federal Police investigated 400 cases of smuggling and trafficking and made more than 200 arrests.[18] In 2017 and 2018, 84 brokers (77 males and 7 females) were detained in the Kombolcha district of Wollo, which is an important place of origin for Gulf migrants. At the same time, 54 smugglers (43 males and 11 females) were detained en route in Afar on suspicion of smuggling and guiding migrants to Djibouti.[19] In Hadya, between 2014 and 2016, 145 people were detained, and accused of human trafficking and smuggling in persons,[20] and the courts sentenced 50 to long prison sentences.[21]

Despite the criminalisation and incarceration campaigns, there has been a further rise in the migration of Ethiopian youth using informal brokers.[22] In 2018, a record number of 160,000 migrants are estimated to have arrived in Yemen irregularly by land and sea, and in the first half of 2019, 84,378 migrants arrived in Yemen. Of these arrivals 90% were from Ethiopia. If these trends continue, the number of migrants arriving in Yemen will substantially increase in later years.[23]

In June 2018, the Ethiopia Immigration Office reported that an average of 1,100 women were leaving the country every day for the Gulf countries, mainly to Saudi Arabia and UAE, using tourist visas.[24] The employment agencies in the Gulf countries have continued to work with their banned Ethiopian counterparts, who because of the ban became informal brokers. The Ethiopian government's ban on licensed agencies for more than five years (2013–19), in the absence of any alternative routes to legal migration, paradoxically not only encouraged informality but also created a market for informal brokers. Accordingly, hundreds of former licensed labour brokers turned into informal brokers engaged in clandestine recruitment, organising and sending documents, organising job interviews, and finally arranging passage with a tourist visa. Data from Moyale Immigration Office shows that in 2018 an average of 60 migrants applied for an exit stamp to cross to Kenya every day, and close to two-thirds were from Hadya and its neighbour, Kambata Zone in southern Ethiopia. Smugglers in Moyale estimate that around the same number, if not more, cross the border with their assistance every day, an increase from a decade ago.[25]

After these statistics from the Immigration Office were broadcast on national television, the Ethiopian government ordered the Federal

Police, Attorney General's Office, Immigration and Nationality Affairs, Civil Aviation and Ethiopian Airlines to coordinate efforts to curtail illegal travel out of the country through airports. Officials targeted Ethiopian girls who were travelling on tourist visas. Security officials standing near immigration clearance at Bole International Airport would stop women whom they identified by their appearance, clothing and luggage. These women were forced to give interviews regarding their travel and were turned back if suspected of having been recruited for overseas employment.[26]

We focus on two issues here. One is that, regardless of how they are recruited and where they are heading to, any individual has the constitutional right to travel as long as they have a valid visa. Two, in Ethiopia, what we are witnessing is the determination of the youth to migrate at any cost (see chapter 4), including using highly risky land and sea routes. In this situation, obtaining a visa for overseas employment could have been tolerated until better arrangements were made. Belaynesh is a deportee from Saudi Arabia. Originally, she is from Wollo, though we interviewed her in Addis Ababa.

> I got a tourist visa through a broker who is a family member. When I was about to leave, my friends who left before me were forced to return from the airport and some of them had their passports taken away. When I heard about that I consulted with the broker and travelled by land instead to Kenya through Moyale. He put me in contact with brokers in Moyale who arranged for me to get an entry stamp from the Kenyan immigration officials to travel by bus to Nairobi. I flew from Kenya to Saudi Arabia.

Belaynesh's case shows the unintended consequence of restriction on mobility that leaves informal brokers as the only agents of mobility at the moment when an aspiring migrant is ready to migrate at any cost. Though Belaynesh had already paid for the different stages of the process—recruitment, visa and flight—the new restriction regime at the airport forced her to make another unexpected payment to travel to Kenya. The new restriction did not stop migrants but forced them to take an additional irregular route, with additional risks. Indeed, our research confirms the positive correlation between the intensification of control on migrants' mobility and the rise in the price for the service of migration facilitation. For instance, from

2013 (when the campaign against brokers started) and 2018 (when we did our fieldwork), the price of brokerage from Wollo to Saudi Arabia by the land and sea route increased from around US$300 to $700 per person. At the same time, the price for the southern route from Hadya to South Africa, for a similar service, increased from around $2,500 to $5,000. Many women migrating to the Gulf countries typically enter into a debt arrangement, finally paying more than 50% on top of the original price.

Belaynesh's account, besides showing her determination to migrate, demonstrates the strong relationship between customers and brokers, and also the resourcefulness of these brokers, evidenced by the speed by which they can effectively mobilise their connections to switch the migrants' route when necessary. Although these new routes are potentially more dangerous than the old ones, they may help to fulfil the migrants' aspirations to migrate and thus show that the brokers are a part of migrants' agential strategies. These are the moments when the brokers or smugglers show their positive contributions 'as service providers who satisfy a need that people cannot satisfy through legal channels', and, of course, earn a positive reputation from the migrant communities.[27] An illustration of this can be found among the Hadya, where brokers are nicknamed '*berri kefach*', meaning 'door openers'.[28]

In October 2018, the Ethiopian government stopped issuing passports to citizens who had no 'proper' reason to travel. According to our discussion with an immigration official, to get a passport, citizens now had to present an invitation or official letter from an employer, mentioning the reason for travel to the immigration authorities. When travelling for commercial purposes, they needed to present trade licences.[29] With these restrictions on passports, the government was aiming to stop people seeking overseas employment through 'illegal' means. To the aspiring young migrants, it confirmed that their only option was to try the land and sea routes using brokers or smugglers, which do not require official documents, not even a passport. In this way, the state created a situation where migrants consider brokers or smugglers as their only alternative.

Government officials required aspiring migrants to wait while preparations were made to restart official or formal labour migration through newly licensed agencies. However, migration management actors should have understood that, given past experience and the criteria set in the new legislation, even when formal labour migration restarted, it would not be the only or even the main means of labour migration. Even when the services of legal overseas private employment agencies were operational, finding employers, arranging travel documents or employment contracts, and organising skills and language training before departure required time, and so the informal brokers have become alternatives in organising direct flights or overland journeys.[30] On top of that, according to the new Overseas Employment Proclamation (923/2016, Article 7), any worker taking up overseas employment must have completed a Grade 8 education, and possess a certificate of occupational competence, a document issued by an authorised government organ evidencing that the worker is capable of performing a particular task. Indeed, according to our data, both from Wollo and Hadya, many aspiring migrants who were registered to undergo training as part of the new Overseas Employment Proclamation requirements left by overland routes using migration brokers, owing to the time the formal preparations had taken. In addition, even if the provisions of the proclamation were implemented, it would only help women or, broadly, those going to the Gulf countries. In other words, it is not applicable, for instance, to those going to South Africa.

With intensified pressure from the domain of control, including checkpoint and border control regimes, smugglers explored new routes. Every time a new route is taken, smugglers along transit points are more likely to be inexperienced, the local transporters new to the business and less knowledgeable, and transport infrastructure, including boats, flimsy. These factors contribute to the risks of smuggling and account for some of the tragic news we hear about irregular migration. Our data from the southern route shows that migrants and their smugglers who were pursued by the police have been forced to use poor-quality boats and over-loaded containers, resulting in tragic deaths.[31] Several deaths on the eastern route, on the Red Sea crossing to Yemen, happened for similar reasons. Such incidents were reported in December 2018 and April 2019, with the deaths of many migrants, most of them from Wollo and Tigray (north of Wollo). Similarly, in our recent fieldwork on the Ethiopia–Sudan border, we were told that migrants died from dehydration when using a newly discovered desert route.[32] These routes are remote and there is little likelihood of obtaining help in an emergency. What we are trying to assert is that because of the absence of a legal migration route, intensification of migration control structures stood no chance of stopping migration. Instead, that control contributed to an increase in the participation of more migration facilitators, some with less experience, resulting in more tragic incidents.[33] Next, we discuss the modus operandi of migration facilitation from below, to help explain how irregular migration, in general, and facilitation of irregular migration, in particular, are sustained regardless of the government's efforts to control it.

The role of family in migration facilitation

Migration facilitation mostly involves family members, whether at home or abroad. In this regard, Belloni has analysed the role of transnational family networks in facilitating irregular migration by taking the case of Eritrean refugees' migration to Europe.[34] Families participate in the facilitation of their children's migration, starting from initiating the process and planning, to looking for brokers and financing. Many of our informants in Hadya and Wollo had even sold their farmland or only house to realise their young child's aspirations to migrate. From the parents' perspective, this is just part of caring for the future well-being of their children or close kin member. As a result, covering migration expenses is viewed as a parent's responsibility. The reasons for deciding to facilitate a son or daughter's migration vary. For some families, sending a family member abroad goes beyond the well-being of the migrant and is considered an investment in the family's future. According to one of our interlocutors, 'in Hadya, if you do not have a brother or a son in South Africa, you do not have a life'. Similarly, in Wollo, having a daughter in the Gulf countries increases the family's status. When discussing their future, a couple might decide to finance the migration of the wife or husband temporarily, to build the financial stability of the family. Whether it is the husband or wife who migrates often depends on the destination, with the Gulf labour market mainly demanding females for domestic work, and the South African informal petty economy 'fitting' males.[35]

In this desperate situation, brokers enable the aspiring migrants and their families to realise their desires. Brokers are accessed through migrants who have used their services to manage their migration. Moreover, family members are usually involved in organising their aspiring children's or spouse's migration, including the selection of and negotiation with brokers. Family involvement reinforces the social relationship between the migrant and broker. At times, the deal between the migrant and the broker evokes the relationship between their two families. This social relationship is the principal guarantee the migrants and their families have to get their money back in case the migration fails. In other words, the relationship serves as a form of social pressure on the brokers to fulfil their obligations. On the other hand, brokers also count on the same social relations as a source of protection from the domain of migration control. That is why migrants and their families often refuse to expose the identity of brokers and smugglers to law enforcement agents, even when the journey has failed and the migrants are deported.

Brokers also facilitate the migration of their own family members. Hamud (pseudonym) was a leading broker in the small town of Mersa in Wollo with many years' experience in facilitating migrants' departure from Wollo, smuggling them from Djibouti to Yemen, and working with smugglers in Yemen. When we asked him about the extent to which families participate in the facilitation of migration and the relationship between families of migrants and brokers, Hamud related his experience:

> My mom and her sister asked me saying, 'You have changed the lives of many people in Mersa, why don't you change your family's life?' They wanted me to send my cousin and my sister. In the beginning I was hesitant to accept the request because they were kids. But as they kept nagging me to send them, I finally decided to do so.

It is common for a family to approach a broker to facilitate the migration of younger family members. However, there has been a widespread development in the migrant–family relationship, discussed by Milena Belloni, since the political crisis in Libya.[36] Family members in the diaspora are pressured into providing finance to migrants when they reach transit points in Libya, although they refused to do so before the migrant's departure. In other words, migrants deliberately cause themselves to be stranded, for example, in Libya, and call their family or kin members in the diaspora or at home to intervene. This is also becoming common in Wollo, following the crisis in Yemen. Many young people, whose families do not support their desire to migrate, leave after consulting with brokers who are willing to facilitate their journey to Yemen without charge. The crisis in Yemen has created the space for smugglers to mistreat such people, detaining, beating and abusing them until a relative pays for their smuggling service. Having a family member in the diaspora, especially in the Gulf countries, is preferable as they can be contacted, they tend to respond sooner, and the money transfer is much easier than from villages in Ethiopia. If the migrant has no one in the diaspora willing to pay for him or her, the brokers have a local arrangement whereby family members in Ethiopia can settle the payment.

Interestingly, aspiring migrants intentionally make themselves the hostages of smugglers to coerce their families into funding their migration. Horrendous media images of the situation in Yemen and stories from deportees don't stop them. For instance, the IOM assisted the return of 2,100 Ethiopians stranded in Yemen in June 2019 alone, many of whom, according to our informants, were from Wollo.[37] Moreover, according to our informants, aspiring migrants not only know that migration through Yemen involves abuses, especially when they have insufficient funds for the smuggling service, but they also are familiar with some of those carrying out the abuse. Like Hamud, the broker we quoted above, there are several Ethiopians working with the Yemenis in smuggling migrants first to Yemen and then to Saudi Arabia. These brokers are involved in detaining, beating and abusing the migrants in Yemen. As the overwhelming majority of migrants crossing Yemen come from rural Ethiopia, it is no surprise that Yemeni smugglers work with their Ethiopian counterparts or assistants in basic tasks such as language interpretation and the arrangement of money transfers.[38]

The agency that migrants exert by putting pressure on their families is not limited to being stranded in transit. As outlined in the introductory section, and discussed in detail in chapter 4, unemployed youth feel they are not progressing in their lives in general nor in their transition to manhood, such as being unable to get a job or get married. They live in a situation of being 'stuck' at home, suffering from a lack of opportunities. Given the profound desperation in their lives, they put pressure on their families to support their migration. We interviewed Dengamo, a father of four children, in a small town in Hadya. He lives on a small income as a village tailor. His daughter and son migrated to South Africa several years back, the daughter through marriage and the son taking the overland irregular route. But to the disappointment of the family, neither has remitted any money. The third son completed high school in 2017 but did not pass the national exam required for admission to university. This son also wanted to migrate to South Africa; however, because his two siblings had failed to send remittances, it was not easy to ask his father to finance his migration. The father stated: 'After he completed high school my son started to behave strangely. I knew he was afraid of asking me to send him to South Africa. His behaviour changed. He stopped talking to anyone at home. I feared that he might commit suicide.'

Worried about his son's behaviour, Dengamo sold his only house to finance his son's aspiration to migrate to South Africa. He initiated the facilitation of his son's departure through a 'very reliable broker', his best friend's son. However, the worries of the family were not limited to the financial pressure. Dengamo told us that he could not sleep for the next few days, worrying about the risky long journey to South Africa. Everyone in the villages in Hadya seemed familiar with the risks along the route from the stories of many deportees in the villages and of people returning to the zone. One coping mechanism that came to Dengamo's mind after days of prayer was to cast a lottery on the future destiny of his son, which, of course, showed South Africa. 'I cast lottery three times ... I confirmed that the destiny of my son is in South Africa.' This was an attempt to find an excuse or something to blame should anything happen to his son.

The case of Dengamo and his son shows how the youth in areas known for their 'culture of migration' can persuade their families. The sacrifice that families make—such as selling their only house—shows how migration is considered a better alternative and a solution to their current situation. Other causes of worry for families when they support their son's or daughter's irregular migration are the risks and dangers involved. Recently, as a result of the intensified effort by countries in East Africa to control irregular migration, the frequency of detention, deportation and death of Hadya migrants en route to South Africa has increased. For instance, between June and November 2018, IOM assisted the return of close to 400 Ethiopian migrants stranded in Tanzania, most of them from Hadya.[39] The Hadya Zone Labour and Social Affairs Office recorded the deaths of 4,265 Hadya migrants between 2013 and 2019 en route and at places of destination in South Africa. These reports have not convinced aspiring migrants or their families to subscribe to the Ethiopian government's policy, including the criminalisation of brokers. In places such as Hadya and Wollo, where brokers are found almost everywhere—in the rural villages and in small and big towns—people rarely report them to law enforcement agencies. Rather, the intensification of migration control and the rise in migrant detention rates, deportations and deaths have increased the demand for brokers among aspiring migrants and their families.

Migration control actors and kinship relations

In other recent publications of ours, we analysed the fluid relationship between the domain of migration facilitation and migration control, when border officials, motivated by financial returns, help migrants and smugglers to circumvent state control.[40] In this regard, we used ethnographic data from the Ethiopia–Sudan borderlands to show the involvement of border guards and the militia in facilitating irregular migration.[41] Similarly, in the Ethiopia–Kenya borderlands, the immigration office staff, border guards and the security apparatus became actors in the facilitation of migration, contrary to their official roles of curbing illegal migration. In that situation brokers managed to turn those in the domain of control into facilitators by using their financial power. Our argument was that the smugglers fare better than the control regime in sharing the resources available to all the actors facilitating migration at different levels.[42]

In this chapter, we go a step beyond the economic return argument and examine the actors in the domain of migration control from the perspective of their social and kinship relations with the aspiring migrants and their families as well as with the brokers. At the places of origin, many officials and law enforcement agents are involved in the facilitation of migration not just for financial gains, but also because of their family, kinship or other social responsibilities. As with the relationship between migrants and brokers, the attempt to dissociate migration control agents (such as members of the task force established to curtail illegal migration) from their social context is reductionist and simplistic. Like migrants, families and brokers, members of law enforcement agencies also participate in the everyday life of the community. To substantiate this, we discuss the cases of a higher official and a local socially respected elder, both members of the task force to curtail irregular migration in Hadya. In these cases, in spite of their roles and responsibilities as members of the task force, the two individuals not only allowed but also financed the irregular migration of family members.

In the first case, a top official in Hadya Zone administration, who was also head of the zone's task force, financed his brother's irregular migration to South Africa in 2016.[43] Like any other family member in Hadya, he identified a broker and paid to facilitate his brother's migration. Seen from his political position and from the legal context, this act could be described as hypocritical or even criminal. However, for local people, who view the action from that of his familial responsibility, it would not be seen as criminal. As an older brother with more resources, and when so many youths were migrating from his neighbourhood, the official did what was expected of him—to fulfil a family social responsibility. By viewing the situation from the top down only, we fail to understand the relationship between the migrant and the individuals in the domain of control who have family responsibilities. Attempting to control irregular migration by establishing a task force that sees everything from a law enforcement perspective will not succeed. Ethiopia's migration governance strategy needs to be broader and human-centred and account for the social context.

In areas such as Hadya and Wollo, the Ethiopian government established Anti-illegal Migration Committees at the grass-roots level. In each *kebele*[44] there is a committee of 25 individuals including elders, religious leaders, women and youth. The object of the committees is to discourage irregular migration at the village level by raising community awareness about illegal migration. In addition to sharing information about the negative aspects of illegal migration, the committee members are also told to identify families whose children migrate and report such cases to the government authorities.

In the second case, Adane (a pseudonym) is a respected elder in Soro district and a member of the local Anti-illegal Migration Committee. We interviewed him in the summer of 2018.[45] Adane is economically better off than many in his village. Ten years ago, he financed the migration of his eldest son to South Africa. Adane himself migrated at a young age to Wonji sugar plantation and worked for many years as a labourer. Adane's son, part of the diaspora in South Africa, improved the life of the family by sending remittances. Adane was able to purchase a plot of land and construct a house in the locally admired design called 'Chento mode', a 'standard house' that families who have a migrant in South Africa build—one of the status symbols in Hadya to show that you have 'somebody' in South Africa. The house symbolises the Hadya migration to South Africa in the rural villages.[46]

While he was part of the Anti-illegal Migration Committee, Adane's second son asked him to finance his migration to South Africa. Adane, supported by his first son in South Africa, financed his aspiring second son's migration to South Africa. He contacted brokers, arranged the payment and facilitated his son's migration. In public, Adane speaks in favour of the government position that criminalises illegal migration and downplays the contributions of migration to South Africa to local development. At home, he does what he thinks is good for the future of his son and the family's well-being. Such incongruities between the public domain and private activities have become common when it comes to irregular migration. Government officials, religious leaders and elders all condemn illegal migration in public, but when it comes to their family members, they hardly hesitate to facilitate it. After a local stakeholder meeting in Hosaena, the capital of Hadya Zone, a zonal official murmured to the first author of this chapter that the new modus operandi of migration facilitation in the villages in Hadya, following the government's intensification of control on migration, was: 'Say what the government wants and do what is good for your family'.

The role of religious institutions

Inhabitants of South Wollo and Hadya are predominantly Muslims and Protestant Christians respectively. In both areas, religion plays a major factor in facilitating the aspiring youth's migration. In both Muslim

South Wollo and Christian Hadya, religion supports the realisation of the youth's aspiration to migrate. This starts from neighbourhood prayer groups to institutional backups. In Wollo families invite neighbours and religious leaders to their homes and undertake *du'a*, an Islamic religious ritual of blessing. In *du'a* sessions, people gather and pray for aspiring migrants who will leave soon. During the journey, migrants perform similar rituals in groups guided by the most religiously senior among them. Similarly, in Hadya, fellow Christians in the neighbourhood gather and pray for the success of the departing aspiring migrants. In both cases, the religious performances support potential migrants by giving them hope and courage to face risks during the dangerous journey (see also chapter 6).

Islam shapes and informs the timing of overland migration from Wollo to Saudi Arabia. During the Ramadan fasting season, migration from Wollo reaches its peak because the Yemeni–Saudi border is more or less open, and, according to migrant narratives, it is *haram* (a sin) to imprison migrants at the border during the fasting season. At the same time, employers in Saudi Arabia need more migrant labour to fill roles as cooks, shepherds or cleaners and for other laborious tasks that natives cannot undertake when fasting. While en route, after they leave Ethiopia, particularly in Djibouti, migrants visit mosques and are hosted by fellow Muslims. Labour migration from Wollo to Djibouti has a long history, resulting in the establishment of several mosques that are now dominated by migrants.

Institutionally, Islam provides an opportunity for aspiring migrants to use the *hajj* and *umrah* religious pilgrimage visa to enter Saudi Arabia, and then stay on. Migrants use social and smuggling networks at their destinations to get accommodation and jobs. Mohammed, our returnee informant in Wollo, took this route when he first migrated to Saudi Arabia. He accompanied three women as their *mahram* (a male relative who accompanies women travelling for *hajj* and *umrah*, as women under 45 cannot travel alone according to Sharia law). Neither Mohammed nor the three he accompanied went to Mecca, where *umrah* pilgrimage is performed. On his arrival, Mohammed travelled to Jeddah, where his sister was living, and worked there until he was caught and deported one year later. Similarly, the three women went to their respective relatives and friends and overstayed their visa.

Likewise, churches in Hadya play important roles in the facilitation of irregular migration. Members pray for the success of potential migrants in their aspiration to migrate to South Africa. Moreover, priests and pastors prophesise about the destiny of individual aspiring migrants. In facilitating migration, the church officials have multiple interests: they, like other members of the community, have kin members who want to migrate; they sympathise with members of their congregation; they have interests in expanding their religious congregation; and they also have financial interests.

The institutional linkages that exist between Protestant churches in Hadya and southern Africa indirectly strengthen the role of churches in facilitating migration. Accordingly, churches in Hadya Zone send pastors and members of gospel choirs on exchange programmes to churches in South Africa. The receiving churches support the scheme and issue official invitation letters that ease the issuance of visas. Once in South Africa, many of the clergy from Ethiopian churches permanently overstay the time stamped in their visas. Indeed, Hadya migrants have recently established several churches at several nodes of migration in different countries en route to the Republic of South Africa. Starting from the border town of Moyale, there are churches dominated by Hadya migrants in Malawi, Mozambique, Zimbabwe and South Africa. These churches may not have been built deliberately to facilitate migration. They are rather the result of piecemeal social interaction, starting with prayer groups organised by failed migrants, smugglers and other acquaintances at the important nodes of migration, and gradually developing into churches. Of course, the migration experience itself greatly contributed to the creation of a Hadya community in these major transit towns. After a while, the churches serve as a place where migrants meet each other, and where smugglers meet up with migrants, and as sources of information. In Moyale, for instance, there is a growing Hadya population and a church with most of its members from Hadya. In 2017, a pastor in Moyale, originally from Hadya, was fired by officials of the church, as Ethiopian government intelligence officials accused him of smuggling migrants. More specifically, he was accused of receiving Hadya migrants, hosting them, sometimes using the church buildings for accommodation, and smuggling them to Kenya. A broker called Towfiq (a pseudonym) confirmed the pastor's story:

You see that big church. The pastor first contacted me and asked me to do him a favour. His family members came from Hadya to go to South Africa. He asked me how much they should pay, and if I can help him. He paid me, and I processed his relatives' migration. I did this several times for him. After a while, he asked me for a commission. I paid him 1,000 birr per person for those who came through him. He gradually started brokerage, and we were working together. Last year his congregation learnt that he is a broker and they expelled him from the church. Now, I don't know where he is.

Other research also analyses the role of the church in migration. Hagan and Ebaugh's study of Mayas from Guatemala in Texas found that religion and the church play an important role in decision-making, preparing for the journey and after arrival.[47] The involvement of different categories of the population makes migration facilitation a community enterprise rather than a business run by independent criminal networks alone.

In our interview, officials of the Ministry of Labour and Social Affairs in Addis Ababa and the Hadya Zone Police Department told us that they had warned the churches not to pray for migrants and prophesy in relation to migration as it encourages potential migrants to take risks.[48] Here, we see a variant of the same top-down legalistic and administrative measures against migration facilitation, which we criticised above.

Conclusion

In a context of 'forced immobility' owing to increasing migration and border controls, having a broker in a family with knowledge about how to facilitate migration to Yemen is a resource to be exploited.[49] The multi-layered relationships and strong social bonds between the migrants, their families and the brokers do not feature in the hegemonic discourse that oversimplifies migration brokerage and views it from a 'binary predator–victim perspective'.[50]

In this chapter, our study of brokerage operations, motivations and roles elucidates three points. First, it shows how government restrictions on mobility make brokers and smugglers very important to aspiring migrants and their families. Despite the state's criminalisation campaigns, aspiring migrants and their families are eager to use broker expertise to fulfil the desires of the aspiring migrants who are desperate to migrate at any cost. Second, migration facilitation is 'a complex and layered social process', rather than a simple dichotomous story of smugglers versus migrants or criminals versus innocent victims, as the migration control agencies would like to argue.[51] In this regard, seen from below, migration facilitation is a social practice where family, kinship and religious institutions and relationships are crucial. Third, the chapter explicates that the migrant–broker relationship is much more than a 'business' enterprise, thereby challenging earlier studies of the migration industry. For brokers living in the migrant communities at the places of origin, besides monetary return, migration facilitation is about fulfilling family or kinship responsibilities that force them to deal simultaneously with family and moral responsibilities. When smugglers operate further away from origin areas and there is an increased 'social distance', we recognise that smugglers and traffickers are not held to account by those social bonds and can use their power to perpetrate violence and abuse against migrants.

PART II

BEYOND PUSH AND PULL

DRIVERS OF INTERNATIONAL IRREGULAR MIGRATION

3

THE DRIVERS OF YOUTH MIGRATION
IN ADDIS ABABA

Firehiwot Sintayehu

Introduction

This chapter argues that individuals make the decision to migrate based
on their experiences of the interactive effect of macro-level structural
(i.e., mainly economic and political) factors and meso-level ones (i.e.,
social networks). These macro- and meso-level factors influence the
agency of potential migrants but are not sufficient by themselves to
understand the decision to migrate. Although agency could transform
structures too, what this chapter elucidates is the reification of the
social and economic structures and further entrenchment of the culture
of migration. Despite this, potential migrants make the decision to
migrate for various reasons.

Ethiopia is an origin, transit and destination country for migrants.[1]
Ethiopian migrants leave the country through various regular and
irregular mechanisms. The majority are 'economic migrants' as their
decision to migrate is based on factors relating to employment and

earnings. For some, the reason to leave is political repression or human rights violation by the incumbent political party. In parts of the country where there is an established tradition of migration, migration is a cultural norm.[2] Addis Ababa, an important origin and transit area, is a major hotspot for migration. A migration profile study conducted for IOM by Mehari shows that although residents of Addis Ababa only make up 3.2% of the country's population, it is the source of 16.3% of migrants from Ethiopia.[3]

The existing literature has given significant attention to the risks facing Ethiopian irregular migrants in transit and in the destination countries. Migrants are transported in unsafe vehicles and boats.[4] Traffickers demand additional payment in transit countries. When the migrants are unable to pay, the traffickers demand ransom from family members at home and expose the migrant to different forms of abuse. Abuse from traffickers includes abduction, robbery and sexual assault.[5] Physical attacks accompanied by psychological pressure cause mental health difficulties for numerous migrants. Female migrants, particularly, experience mental health problems, rape and physical injury, as a result of which many commit suicide.[6]

This chapter investigates the drivers of migration from Addis Ababa, looking into structural and non-structural issues. It examines the context within which migrants, predominantly young men and women, decide to migrate. Various studies have been produced about the push and pull factors of migration in structural terms, with migrants moving from less affluent parts of the globe to the richer ones.[7] This study acknowledges that structural factors such as unemployment and underemployment are important in explaining the outflux of young people to various destinations internationally while being further facilitated by meso-level factors such as a culture of migration and social networks as well as micro-level considerations of human agency.

Unemployment and underemployment, as structural factors, are substantial drivers of migration since potential migrants are unable to mobilise income to pay for their economic and status needs. These factors are often considered push factors for international migration. However, high levels of unemployment alone would not suffice to propel people to migrate, were it not for the existence of strong social networks with those who have migrated earlier. In the study area, there are strong webs of social networks which enable potential migrants and their families to communicate with each other and with those who have migrated beforehand. Local brokers, smugglers and facilitators are also available to inform potential migrants about the different mechanisms and paths they may take by establishing links with other brokers in transition and destination countries. This study acknowledges that migration is an individual decision. An individual's decision to migrate is informed by his or her own situation, whether he or she lacks the income to satisfy his or her needs. The decision is also based on individuals' expectation of returns from migration. The discussion of the agency of migrants is framed by Emirbayer and Mische's conceptualisation in which human agency is explained in term of iteration, projectivity and practical evaluation.[8]

This research used a purposive sampling technique. The three target areas were *woredas*[9] in Arada sub-city, Addis Ketema sub-city and Kirkos sub-city in 2017, with a second round of data collection in Addis Ketema in 2018. The field sites were chosen in consultation with the Bureau of Labour and Social Affairs of the Addis Ababa City Administration and their offices at the sub-city level, because of the high level of irregular migration in these *woredas*. Ten key informant interviews (KIIs), seven in 2017 and three in 2018, were conducted with representatives from *woreda* Bureaus of Labour and Social Affairs as well as Micro and Small Enterprise sector offices. These bureaus were selected, as they are responsible for the creation of employ-ment opportunities for the youth in Addis Ababa, which is a major strategy used by the Government of Ethiopia to curb irregular migra-tion and support the reintegration of returnees. Six FGDs, two in each *woreda*, and twelve in-depth interviews in *woredas* from Addis Ketema sub-city were conducted with potential migrants, returnees and families of migrants.

Understanding the drivers of migration in Addis Ababa: The role of structure

Macro-level explanations of migration have dominated migration studies for a long time, and are expressed in various forms.[10] The argument is mainly economic, stressing that increased employment opportunities and expectations of higher income in destination cities and countries attract a flow of people from less developed areas where there are high levels of unemployment and poverty.[11] Accordingly, prospective migrants from less developed countries or areas base their decisions to migrate on their perceptions of employment opportunities and better pay.

According to De Haas, some of the macro-theories of migration, such as neo-classical and other equilibrium theories of migration, manifest themselves in a form of functionalist social theory, which 'tends to see society as a system—or an aggregate of interdependent parts, with a tendency towards equilibrium'.[12] Here, migration is supposed to happen from low-income to high-income areas as a function of spatial disequilibria.[13]

Another set of theories, which come as a critique of functionalist theories, are found within the category of conflict theory, and focus on understanding the sources of socio-economic inequalities.[14] For instance, world systems theory contends that social and economic systems tend to reproduce and reinforce structural inequalities.[15]

Macro-level explanations of migration focus on why migrants move from particular world regions (less-developed countries) to others (developed or prosperous countries) by looking at social, economic and political contexts that are shared by all community members, both migrants and those staying behind.[16] Thus, the main deduction of this theory is that communities facing various manifestations of poverty and violence in the least developed parts of the world are more likely to migrate.

Structural factors of migration are important in explaining migration from Addis Ababa, considering the increasing percentage of unemployment in the city. According to the Central Statistical Agency, one in five of the city's population was unemployed in 2016.[17] The figure is much higher for women, at 30%, and probably higher for younger age groups.

Massive unemployment in Addis Ababa is likely to worsen as a result of growing population. This is specifically significant for Addis Ketema, Arada and Kirkos sub-cities, which are identified as hotspots of migration for the present study. The three sub-cities are among the most densely populated parts of Addis Ababa, with 43,192, 26,755 and 18,970 people per square kilometre respectively. These areas are also known for pervasive poverty. According to a 2015 study conducted by the city's Bureau of Finance and Economic Development, poverty levels in Addis Ketema and Arada sub-cities were 46.9% and 34.5% respectively. The same study argues that the high inflow of migrants from all over the country to Addis Ketema, the location of the largest bus station of the country, Autobus Tera, explains the severe poverty in the area. The poverty level in Kirkos sub-city is lower compared to the other two, at 14.8%, perhaps as a result of the city's urban renewal programme, which relocated many households from the sub-city to the suburbs.[18]

When thinking about their future, informants residing in these areas stressed that the increasing cost of living in the city made the prospect of a good future in Addis unlikely. Employment opportunities offering decent incomes are rare. Large families are forced to live in single-room houses as renting anything larger is unaffordable. Moreover, informants accused the government of making false promises about employment creation opportunities and potential training and related business support initiatives, which never materialised.

Addis Ketema, Arada and Kirkos sub-cities are located in the centre of the city, the location of major parts of Addis Ababa's urban slums. The congestion levels and population density are further manifested in the residence patterns and housing conditions in the sub-cities. More than three-quarters of the residents in Addis Ketema (83.2%), Arada (78.7%), and Kirkos (77.3%) live in rented houses, with the majority of the households living in single-room houses.[19] The houses in the study area consisted of small single rooms with low-quality facilities.

The majority of the people residing in the study *woredas* have either low-income jobs or are unemployed. The informal sector accounts for the greater part of the areas' economy and is a key means of income. Women rely on work in retail trade and services and men on menial jobs, both in the informal sector.[20]

The majority of the youth informants identified as potential migrants or returnees were unemployed or underemployed women. Most had responsibility for looking after, raising and educating children or siblings, and reflected that this had led them to seek various ways to earn an income. Some were engaged in the informal sector selling coffee and tea on the streets or *injera* (flatbread, a staple food in Ethiopia).

The unemployed men were, at times, forced to take up menial labour for lower pay, but, for the most part, the responsibility to assist family members was left to the women.

Many informants consulted for the study felt hopeless about the prospect of living a 'good life' in Ethiopia. This feeling stemmed from a lack of educational attainment, which was felt to be precluding them from higher-paying jobs that would potentially cover the high costs of living in the city. They had also lost hope with the government employment opportunities such as self-employment in Micro and Small Enterprises (MSEs) and in the manufacturing sector. The MSE option does not work for them, as the urban agriculture sector promoted by the government is not of interest to the unemployed youth. Moreover, in instances where the youth establish MSEs, they do not find work premises with viable market links. Employment in the manufacturing sector is also unattractive because of the very low wages. Hence, the men felt powerless to earn an income in Ethiopia and often spent time with friends, building up networks with the goal of making a migration trip.

For potential migrants in the target sub-cities, the main destination countries were Kuwait, Beirut, Saudi Arabia, Qatar and Dubai in the Middle East. After the 2013 large-scale deportations from Saudi, Kuwait and Beirut became the preferred destinations for female migrants, mainly to work as housemaids. Meanwhile, Qatar and Dubai have recently emerged as preferred destinations for male migrants, both skilled and unskilled, to work on construction sites or as drivers. Engineering graduates have taken contractual jobs in Dubai for some years without involving brokers in the process. A comparatively lower number of men also went to South Africa and South Sudan.

Choice of destination is mainly dependent on cost. For most, the preferred destination is the United States. However, it is prohibitively difficult to reach both physically and financially, with the opportunity to move there mainly limited to the diversity lottery or through marriage arrangements. The geographical proximity of Europe makes it a slightly more feasible option, despite the high expense and hardship that young people face on the journey. Mehari classified the routes taken by Ethiopian international migrants according to three levels of cost; expensive routes (mainly Europe and North America), medium-cost routes (Africa and Asia) and budget routes (Middle East countries).[21] For a migrant to reach the borders of Europe, paying each broker in the network, the cost ranges from 150,000 to 300,000 birr (US$4,500 to $9,000). To reach the Middle East, if a migrant takes up regular labour migration channels, in which she or he is only required to pay for a medical examination and the issue of a passport, these costs could go up to 5,000 birr (about $150). Metema and Moyale serve as transit border areas for migrants headed to Europe and South Africa respectively. In the interviews, the eastern route through Somalia and Djibouti was rarely mentioned as a route by migrants starting off from Addis Ababa. Many travel by air, using either a tourist visa or mechanisms established by brokers with their contacts in the Middle East countries.

Social networks as catalysts for irregular migration from Addis Ababa

An individual's decision to migrate is facilitated by common practices in the society. Links between the origin and destination countries are made by pioneer migrants from areas which might eventually become hotspots of emigration. Such initial connections become the basis for a continuous outflow of migrants, forming popular routes. These patterns are referred to as 'chains of migration'. Networks serve as social capital which lowers the costs and risks that accompany migration.[22] Over time, established networks may serve as migrants' sole reason to move after other structural reasons fade.[23] A major assumption of the network approach is that the flow of information from different directions is instrumental in forming and sustaining the social capital necessary for perpetuating migration.

Social networks in migration hotspot neighbourhoods encourage parents to push their children to go abroad. Family members discuss the migration experience of their children when they meet at different social events such as weddings and funerals as well as more frequently while having coffee together. Family members whose siblings have migrated and are sending money back home are very proud of them. Having a family member abroad also grants better privileges. As a result, many parents with children who have decided to stay try to persuade them to join the migration journey that was taken up by their peers. One informant puts it like this: 'My parents do not want to see us sit idle in the house. They prefer that we go to one of the Arab countries and send money back home. They know of the risks in going there, but it is the success stories their ears are hinged upon.'[24] It is, however, not always families that want their children to migrate. In other instances, the migrants themselves make their own decision and contact migration brokers secretly to arrange their journey.[25]

It is very common for the youth to plan and execute migration journeys by themselves as there are many who have undertaken different migration adventures until they became successful and settled in one of their migration destinations. Friends use socialisation platforms to discuss their next migration journey. Social media platforms, particularly Facebook, further enable the youth back home to maintain contact and communicate with migrants in different parts of the world. This allowed irregular migrants to move to the Middle East even during the ban on labour migration between 2013 and 2018.

After successful stories of pioneer migrants emerge from a certain area, migration turns into a life path option and eventually becomes normative. This leads to migration becoming a culturally sanctioned part of life, in which an individual will be expected to take part when he or she comes of age. Kandel and Massey, who conducted a study of the culture of migration in Mexico, argue:

> Young people who grow up and come of age [in particular localities] increasingly expect to migrate internationally in the course of their lives. For young men, especially, migration becomes a rite of passage, and those who do not attempt it are seen as lazy, unenterprising, and undesirable as potential mates. In communities where international labor becomes fully integrated into local culture, young men seeking to become adults literally do not consider other options: they assume they will migrate in preparation for marriage and that they will go abroad frequently in the course of their lives as family needs and personal circumstances change.[26]

In consequence, the dynamic interplay of the constraints and opportunities provided by structural factors as well as social networks results in rising number of migrants, potentially making migration a culturally appropriate norm. Many youth members of society in the research area have migrated, and significantly improved their and their family's material well-being. As a result of such experiences, moving to a second country for employment becomes recognised as a feasible alternative life path. That is why migration which takes place in response to unemployment and underemployment in Addis Ababa is considered normal. But this culture of migration is not built on economic success, as in other areas. 'Successful' migrants from the target sub-cities define success as educating siblings and acquiring new household goods. This point is made in strong terms by the following two informants:

> I know that I will not change my life. I am well aware that I will not go beyond buying a sofa and TV or painting the house. But at least I will not be dependent on my family anymore. They will have one less person to feed and shelter. Even if I am not able to send money, I will at least be able to take away their expenses [on me].[27]

> I have been in Saudi Arabia for the past eight years but when returning home, I still do not have any assets. My family used the money I sent to pay for my children's school fees and house rental. If I am not going to get a better job here, I will definitely return to Saudi Arabia.[28]

When contemplating their future life choices, including the possibility of migration, young people consider the experiences of their predecessors. Informants mentioned that seeing friends migrate and start to earn a 'good income' had been instrumental in making their decision to migrate to one of the Middle Eastern countries. They observed neighbours receiving remittances which resulted in a relatively improved quality of life. This view of the past is an essentially selective process, in which bad experiences and risks are downplayed and success stories are trumpeted.

Agency in migration decision-making

The structural macro-level and meso-level explanations influence the decisions individuals make, without reducing the agency of the individual. Micro-level theories of migration focus on how migrants, as individuals, make conscious decisions to migrate. The value expectancy model of migration contends that the decision to migrate is not based exclusively on economic considerations.[29] Motives to migrate depend on multiple values that are related to the anticipated migration outcomes and expectations. Values, here, are defined as the objectives behind migration. These values depend on the characteristics of individuals and on societal norms. The values are not always economic; they may also be social—for example, to gain the respect of the community. For the value expectancy model, the decision to migrate is influenced by the objectives held by prospective migrants and the direct and indirect expectations of individuals and society.[30]

In the study areas, the informal sector is a major source of employment and income. Informal sector jobs are mainly menial, dominated by men, low-paying and temporary.[31] Many employed in such jobs are from outside Addis Ababa. For example, unskilled youth are employed as bus ticket officers, janitors, guards or daily labourers. In the FGDs and individual interviews, the potential migrants expressed the conviction that they would not be willing to engage in such menial labour or domestic work in Addis Ababa. These kinds of jobs are considered 'denigrating and depreciatory'. Nonetheless, potential migrants are well aware that when they move to a second country, the jobs left for migrants and those that they take up will be menial. Informants said that this is acceptable to them and their families, since working abroad is perceived as a privilege, and they also think that the pay for such unskilled labour in Europe or the Middle East will be higher.

Without skills and educational qualifications, the youth do not expect good employment opportunities. However, even those who do have qualifications and skilled jobs decide to migrate because of insufficient pay. Education has thus failed to guarantee better livelihoods, as it had done in previous times. This is confirmed by research conducted for the Addis Ababa Bureau of Finance and Economic Development. One of the informants of the study says, 'In our country, many people do not accept the idea that education is a tool that helps to lead a good life. You spend 15 years on education but you find out that 15 years have been a waste. This has made many youth despair. Some say, "God forgive those who are at school/college."'[32]

Migration involves a complex decision-making process which includes choosing from information coming from various sources; migrants' destinations, timing and the routes they may take are based on such information. Potential migrants make a judgement about whether migration is a better option than their existing situation or not, taking monetary and non-monetary considerations into account.

While it is easier to point out monetary issues as drivers of migration, looking into the non-monetary ones is always a challenge.[33]

The contribution made by such micro-level theories of migration is immense as migration is, in the end, an individual decision, even if it is influenced by structural macro- and meso-level factors. Any macro-level assumption should have a link to micro-behavioural foundations, as the agency of individuals is important in the decision-making of migrants, and vice versa. De Haas argues that people do not migrate because of abstract concepts such as demographic transitions, declining fertility, ageing, population density, environmental degradation or factor productivity.[34] Individuals will migrate if they aspire to benefit from better opportunities elsewhere and possess the capability to move there. Accordingly, individual agency plays a crucial role in understanding large-scale migration from particular places.[35] Emirbayer and Mische define human agency as 'the temporally constructed engagement by actors of different structural environments—the temporal relational contexts of action—which, through the interplay of habit, imagination, and judgement, both reproduces and transforms those structures in interactive response to the problems posed by changing historical situations'.[36]

Human agency has three constitutive elements: iteration, projectivity, and practical evaluation. Iteration is the selective reactivation of past actions. Projectivity is the way actors think of future possible outcomes of their actions, which are reconfigured by hopes, fears and desires for the future. Practical evaluation refers to the capacity of actors to make normative and practical judgements from a list of alternatives.[37] While discussing the agency of migrants, Bakewell, De Haas and Kubal put judgement at the centre—informed by iteration and projectivity, linking the present to the past and the future, and allowing migrants to consciously create space for manoeuvre.[38]

Each informant had their own considerations in making the decision to migrate. Their decisions are affected by the structural situation of poverty, which is worsened as a result of unemployment and underemployment. Moreover, the challenges facing community members that make them flee the country are gendered, resulting in a common decision-making process among female potential migrants.

When female potential migrants and returnees think of the future, they are highly influenced by their responsibilities for supporting family members. This has to do with the gendered societal responsibility women hold in communities and is reflected in the following quote from a returnee: 'I have earned a degree in management but decided to migrate to one of the Arab countries when I was unable to get a job here. I had to migrate in order to support my sisters and brothers to complete their education.'[39] The impact of migration on women is also gendered and serves as a driver to remigrate. When women return home, they are usually past the age at which they would be desirable for marriage. Hence, marriage is not an attractive prospect for female returnees in particular. The phrase '*shi-be-shi*', literally 'thousands upon thousands', illustrates the expectation that migrants will bring back money from destination countries. Conversely, unless they have savings, returnee migrant women are seen as less desirable for marriage. As a result, most of the women who have returned from the Middle East intend to go back or have already done so. As illustrated in the following quote, marriage for female migrants reverses the usual transactional terms. In conventional practice, the man is expected to provide income to the household and sometimes pay dowry for marriage.

> I think I need to pay a dowry for a husband. What people here do not know is that we only change our clothes. We do not have anything more than that. Even if I want to settle down and have a family here, it is going to be hard. And I need to have money to support my family.[40]

Family members and the environment may have their own impact on the decisions of potential migrants while the final judgement is made by the migrants themselves. In some instances, potential migrants decide to move to a second country despite being conscious of bad experiences very close to them. A mother who was interviewed in Addis Ketema sub-city talked at length about her daughter's desire to migrate to the Middle East using a migration broker or smuggler, despite her sister suffering from mental illness after her migration to Saudi Arabia. She says:

> Even if my younger daughter sees her sister who is staying at home as a result of her mental illness, she still insists on going because she has lost hope of the situation in Addis Ababa. She has obtained her degree in Management but because of being unable to find a job she is resorting

to the migration option. When I tell her not to do it, she insists on trying her luck.

Most returnees interviewed reported that they migrated when they were in elementary or secondary school. They argued that going abroad for employment and starting to earn an income is better than going to school for another four or five years when employment opportunities after graduation are not guaranteed. This shows the practical evaluation that migrants conduct in order to choose from available alternatives. A returnee who migrated to Kuwait when she was in Grade 9 says:

> I went to Kuwait dropping out of Grade 9. I decided to go, thinking of the long years I would have to stay in school and I was not even sure whether I will make it to college or not. My friend went there before me and she was sending money to her parents. When leaving Ethiopia, I was hoping to achieve a better life for myself and my family.

In the study area, the youth are frustrated and have lost hope for the future in Addis Ababa. As a result, migration to a second country has become a feasible alternative. In these parts of the city, the migration of young women with responsibility for supporting family is a norm, bringing the culture of migration into play. Moreover, individuals' urge to migrate is facilitated through social networks which connect migrants from their origin to destination countries. Migrants consider past experiences, project what kind of future they would like to achieve, and practically evaluate their decision when making up their minds about moving to a second country.

Conclusion

This study attempts to understand the drivers of migration by looking at factors at different levels, ranging from the structural to individual, and applying them to selected hotspot areas in Addis Ababa. The study intends to contribute to the existing debate with regard to the drivers of migration from different parts of the world.

The drivers of migration in Addis Ababa can be explained more comprehensively by looking at structural factors at the macro-level, social networks and migration brokers at the meso-level, and the agency of individual migrants at the micro-level. Structural factors, mainly unemployment and underemployment, are pushing the youth of Addis Ababa to migrate to countries that are believed to offer better employment opportunities—predominantly in the Middle East and Europe. The structural factors of migration are further complemented by meso-level drivers for migration, namely social networks, which eventually lead to a culture of migration, as young people consider migration as a viable option when choosing from alternative life paths.

Addis Ketema and Arada sub-cities, areas which were identified as hotspots of migration in Addis Ababa, are characterised by rampant poverty. Moreover, the types of jobs that are available here are informal or involve manual labour, which are regarded as denigrating in the society. Hence, the youth are not willing to engage in such employment opportunities and they prefer to migrate for employment in menial jobs where their community members are not present. In fact, family members with children who have travelled abroad have higher social status.

The existing perception is that better education will enable the youth to obtain better-paying jobs. However, many graduate from college and endure unemployment for a long time. This has resulted in education acquiring a reduced value. The youth prefer to drop out of school and migrate since the belief that education will not enable them live a better life is widely held.

This chapter acknowledges that human agency is important in migration, as the decision to migrate is an individual decision. Migrants are found to make their own decisions based on the gains they expect from migration, as they project the kind of future they would like to achieve, which is described in terms of improving the quality of their housing, extending support to parents, and opening businesses upon return. Migrants' decisions are also informed by the experiences of peers who migrated and improved their lives in different ways.

4

HOPELESSNESS AND FUTURE-MAKING THROUGH IRREGULAR MIGRATION IN TIGRAY, ETHIOPIA

Fana Gebresenbet

Introduction

Government officials explain the pervasive irregular migration from Atsbi Wenberta and Raya Alamata *woreda* in Tigray region as the result of youth being duped by traffickers and brokers or being irrational and trying to take shortcuts, rather than working hard in their home country. The youth depict a totally different reality. They view potential migrants as active agents doing something to realise the futures they aspire to in the face of pervasive and near-permanent unemployment that constrains the resources at their disposal.

This chapter argues that international irregular migration is a spatial response to a temporal problem faced by Ethiopia's unemployed youth both in the present and in the future. Unemployment brings a temporal problem in the present, in the form of 'passing' or 'killing' 'overabundant' amounts of 'unstructured' time.[1] The result is the youth 'thinking too much' about their futures, and how to actualise the futures they aspire to. Youthhood—a transitory social stage between childhood and adulthood—is a period of working towards economic independence, establishing one's own family, and taking charge of family and community responsibilities. Ideally, this is a linear process, passing through socially sanctioned stages.

The reality in many small towns in Tigray (and Ethiopia at large) is that the expectations and aspirations of the youth have been heightened by ever-increasing access to primary, secondary and post-secondary education.[2] Each level of education attained raises expectations, especially of joining the prestigious public service, which is not attainable for most.[3] The official approach adopted by the Ethiopian government stresses that the EPRDF is building a developmental state, is committed to putting the country in the league of middle-income countries, and is keen to distribute an equitable share of the growing economic pie to the poor and the youth.[4] As a result, state 'narratives of unfolding and imminent development'[5] contribute to increasing youth aspirations and expectations, partly fuelled by developmental narratives of the state surrounding the creation of millionaire model farmers.

The difficulty of reaching this aspired-to future leads to experiences of boredom, often characterised by a lack of change and progress and, with that, hopelessness. Hopelessness is a common and pervasive feeling of the youth in the study areas, and one of the few ways to escape, in their view, is irregular migration. Irregular migration is thus conceptualised as fleeing from excruciating hopelessness and a frustrated future, and working towards a socially acceptable future, which can be summarised as transitioning to adulthood. Migration, however, does not necessarily remedy the situation the youth are in. Only a few returnees succeed in gaining economic independence and, with that, achieving the socially sanctioned transition to adulthood.

Employment does not provide an escape from the quagmire, as the youth earn wages that do not cover the increasing cost of living. Consequently, employment in the formal sector or through self-employment does not give the youth the economic means to transition into economic independence and form a family.[6] The employed are also unable to make good on the future to which they aspire. Most of the employed are thus in a similar state to the unemployed, facing 'temporal problems' and using irregular migration as a fix. Despite this, most of the discussion in this chapter draws on interviews with and experiences of the unemployed.

Methodologically, this research is based on interviews and FGDs conducted in January and October of 2017 in three towns, Atsbi Endasellassie (of Atsbi Wenberta *woreda*), Waja Timuga (of Raya Alamata *woreda*) and Abi Adi of Tigray regional state. As will be indicated below, geographical proximity to the Afar lowlands (and therefore proximity to the Red Sea coastline and the Middle East, particularly Saudi Arabia) and the long tradition of going to Saudi Arabia to make 'quick money' justify the selection of the first two. Abi Adi was included to represent *woredas* linked to the western route and also as a site where migration is a relatively recent phenomenon.

The study is based on interviews at regional and *woreda* levels, on FGDs with representatives of the youth, and on document analysis. Interviewees representing various government offices were purposely selected for the relevance of their work to the issue under investigation. Officials and experts of relevant sectoral offices were interviewed, i.e., Labour and Social Affairs, Planning and Finance; Youth and Sport Affairs; Agriculture and Natural Resources; Urban Development, Trade and Industry; and Micro and Small Enterprises Development Agency, at regional and *woreda* levels. A total of 42 interviews were conducted, 13 with key informants at regional level and 29 with key informants at *woreda* level. FGD participants were selected in collaboration with experts from the Labour and Social Affairs and Youth and Sport Affairs offices of the respective *woreda*. After an initial purposive sampling of the youth, the technique of snowballing was used to get more FGD participants. A total of 72 young informants participated in 14 FGDs across the three *woredas*.

The remainder of this chapter is structured into four parts. The first gives the socio-economic context of Ethiopian, and more specifically Tigrayan, irregular migration to the Middle East, mainly to Saudi Arabia, particularly from the core migration *woredas* of Atsbi Wenberta and Raya Alamata. The second gives an ethnographic account of the context in which many decide to migrate irregularly, with a focus on notions of time and progress as shaped by prolonged and pervasive urban youth unemployment. The third argues that migration provides a spatial solution to the pervasive sense of hopelessness the youth feel, which follows Appadurai's conceptualisation of the future as cultural fact, particularly the centrality of imagination and archives. The fourth section concludes the chapter.

Context of irregular migration from Tigray to the Middle East

Ethiopians dominate the stock of irregular migrants heading to Saudi Arabia through Yemen. Undeterred by the regional war in Yemen and the associated cholera epidemic,[7] according to the UNHCR, Ethiopians made up 171,131 of the total of 207,186 new arrivals, i.e., more than 82%, in Yemen from the Horn of Africa between March 2015 and March 2017.[8] The IOM estimated that between March 2017 and the end of 2018, some 230,000 Ethiopians were returned from Saudi Arabia.[9] Additionally, hundreds of thousands of Ethiopians are thought to still live in Saudi Arabia without legal documents. This huge number of Ethiopian migrants to Saudi Arabia (and the Middle East in general) is a reflection of the inability of concerted government measures to halt irregular migration, including legal measures against traffickers[10] and 'creating awareness'. On top of this, migrants face horrifying risks and inhumane treatment en route and in destination countries. More than 160,000 Ethiopians were deported from Saudi Arabia between November 2013 and April 2014, and 230,000 between April 2017 and January 2019.[11] These deterrents indicate that there is a strong drive pushing the youth to migrate, though they most likely know too well that it might be a tough bargain.

Not all areas of Ethiopia contribute equally to this stock of migrants heading to the Middle East. According to official records, 99% of formal labour migrants destined for the Middle East between the 2008/09 and 2012/13 fiscal years were from Oromia (32.4%), Amhara (31.1%), Addis Ababa (18.1%), SNNP (12.2%) and Tigray (5.03%).[12] Addis Ababa is the exception in contributing a much higher number of migrants proportionally than its share of the national population size. This Asnake and Zerihun attribute to 'the tendency that the city serves as a transit passage for female migrants from rural areas, who spend the interval required to process the procedures of their labour migration by working as housemaids in Addis Ababa'.[13]

Thus, Tigray, the region of interest for this study, is one of the important origin areas for Ethiopian labour migrants. The region's Youth and Sport Affairs Bureau compiles data related to irregular migration and returnees per *woreda*. It is well known in Tigray that some *woredas*, such as Atsbi Wenberta, send more migrants than others. Data for the 2015/16 fiscal year shows that migrants do not come from all administrative zones at an equal or comparable rate. The highest number come from Eastern Zone (4,875; 1,361 female), followed by Southern (1,907; 570 female), Central (1,503; 350 female) and South-Eastern (1,005; 371 female). Official data shows that women make up about one-third of irregular migrants from Tigray, while formal labour migration in the few years prior to its banning in late 2013 was overwhelmingly dominated by women.[14]

When comparing *woredas*, of the 9,331 recorded irregular migrants from the region in the 2015/16 fiscal year, the highest number come from Atsbi Wenberta in Eastern Zone (2,320; about 25%), followed by Ahferom in Central Zone (1,437; 15%), Hintalo Wajirat in South-Eastern Zone (1,428; 15%), and Kelete Awlalo in Eastern Zone (1,216; 13%).[15]

By 2017 the regional government, well aware of these differences, had identified 22 core *woredas* with the highest levels of migration; 13 *woredas* are linked to the Eastern Route (ER) and 9 *woredas*, closer to the border with Sudan, are linked with the Western Route (WR), which leads to Israel–Europe through Sudan. These *woredas* have a relatively smaller number of irregular migrants leaving in a given year and the route itself has been established more recently (see Table 4.1).

Factors such as geography and historical trade and migration routes have led to migrants taking particular routes and migrants from particular *woredas* being present in higher concentrations in certain destination countries. Through stronger networks with family and relatives in the sending *tabia* (parish) in Tigray, migrants further determine the extent and dynamics of migration. Historically, for example, migrants from areas close to the Afar lowlands or the Red Sea coast across from Eritrea sought to reach the Middle East. Currently, this route involves travelling to Afar or Somali region, onwards to the border with Djibouti or Somaliland, and crossing the Red Sea into Yemen. After reaching Yemen, migrants trek into Saudi Arabia using a combination of walking and vehicles. Migration from Tigray to Saudi, according to an expert from the region's BoLSA,[16] has taken place at least since the early 1970s.

Table 4.1: Migration hotspot *woredas* from Tigray

Zone	Woreda
Southern	Raya Alamata (Eastern Route, hereafter ER)
	Raya Azebo (ER)
	Alamata Ketema (ER)
South-Eastern	Hintalo Wajirat (ER)
	Enderta (ER)
Central	Ahferom (ER)
	Abi Adi (Western Route, hereafter WR)
Eastern	Atsbi Wenberta (ER)
	Kelete Awlalo (ER)
	Wukro Ketema (ER)
	Tseade Emba (ER)
	Ganta Afeshum (ER)
	Gulo Mekeda (ER)
	Erob (ER)
Western	Kafta Ketema (WR)
	Kafta Humera (WR)
	Humera (WR)
	Sheraro (WR)
North-Western	Shire (WR)
	Asgede (WR)
	Tselemti (WR)
	Tahtay Adiabo (WR)

Source: Author's compilation based on data from Assefa Tegegn, Senior Expert, Regional BoLSA (interview, 9 January 2017).

Over time, migration from a particular locality to a particular destination builds a 'migration system'.[17] Stronger networks between a sending *woreda* and the destination facilitate the flow of information,

ideas, money and migrants. Accordingly, in *woredas* that have a migration system, irregular migration will be culturally sanctioned and
accepted by the majority as a feasible life alternative. This will be closer
to what is dubbed a 'culture of migration'.[18] Migration in such areas
will be self-perpetuating, involve larger volumes, and is more likely to
remain high despite anti-migration policies and practices.[19]

This is the case in Atsbi Endasellassie and Waja Timuga towns,
where migration is a pervasive part of social and economic life. It is
difficult to find a young man or woman who is not well informed about
migration and what it takes to migrate irregularly from the two towns.
Many, especially in Atsbi Endasellassie, are confident in stating that all
households have someone in Saudi Arabia, be it from immediate or
extended family. Migrants are mostly young men,[20] but they come
from all socio-economic backgrounds. Employment status does not
determine the likelihood of migration. Informants state that teachers
migrate more than other public employees, encouraging their students
to migrate as well. The unemployed find it difficult to raise the
30,000–35,000 birr (roughly US$1,000) needed at the time of the
fieldwork to start their journey if they do not have a relative or friend
already in Saudi Arabia or parents to sponsor them. Priests and deacons
also migrate, despite the fact that they will most likely be unable to
follow strict Orthodox Church rules surrounding meat, specifically the
rule forbidding the consumption of meat slaughtered by a Muslim,
which is considered 'Muslim meat'.

By contrast, migration is not yet an entrenched part of life in Abi
Adi. Migration from western parts of Tigray, including Abi Adi, com-
menced recently, particularly after 2014/15, with the youth acquiring
knowledge from Eritrean refugees hosted in the region's Western and
North-Western Zones.[21] Eritrean refugees leave the refugee camps in
Tigray and move onwards to Europe by crossing the border with
Sudan.[22] The Tigrayan youth are learning from Eritrean refugees, and,
at the time of fieldwork, irregular migration was just picking up steam.
This migration was so new that *woreda* officials and experts were quick
to comment that we were in the 'wrong neighbourhood', as migration
was not an issue in their *woreda*. Some considered it an insult to equate
them with other *woredas*, particularly Atsbi Wenberta, by doing the
fieldwork in the town.[23]

Moreover, it is common for migrants to fail to reach their destination and return to Abi Adi, mainly because their parents could not cover the expenses required to proceed along the journey. Higher costs and risks involved in the Western Route and the lack of information about irregular migration in the town contribute to this. While it was a challenge to find returnees in Abi Adi, finding deportees or returnees in Atsbi Endasellassie and Waja Timuga was easy. In Atsbi Endasellassie, one informant ridiculed our description of his 'migration status' as a returnee (*temelash*), and added that 'there is no *temelash* (returnee) in our *woreda*. We only have *temelalash* (commuters).'[24]

'Being stuck': Youth perception of time and progress in Tigray

One characteristic of Ethiopia's proliferating small towns is the presence of many young men hanging around roadsides, cafes and other public places. This is a reflection of the high level of youth unemployment in urban areas. The unemployment rate for urban youth aged 18–29 years between the mid-1990s and early 2000s was about 50%.[25] This sorry state of youth unemployment improved in the following years, but the figure still remains high.[26] Following its March 2012 survey, Ethiopia's Central Statistical Agency indicated that urban youth unemployment had decreased from 26% (33.9% for women) in May 2009 to 23.3% (29.6% for women) in March 2012.[27] This was further reduced to 17% in April 2015, according to a World Bank 2016 report.[28] In Tigray region, urban unemployment was 19.4%, two percentage points higher than the national urban unemployment rate.[29]

Such statistics tell us a lot about the stock of young men and women actively seeking work, mainly in urban areas, but nothing about their experience. Based on ethnographic fieldwork in Tigray, this chapter highlights the excruciating social and psychological pain that long periods of unemployment impose on the youth. Although unemployment figures are much higher for women than for men, unemployment is not experienced in the same way by both genders.[30] Women have the 'luxury' of keeping themselves busy with household and community-sanctioned chores, relieving themselves of some of the burden borne by their male counterparts.[31] Thus, most of the information for this work is drawn from men.[32]

Youthhood is a liminal and transitory stage between childhood and adulthood. The transition to adulthood is non-linear and complex, and can take various forms, including the school-to-work transition, gaining economic independence, and getting married and starting a family.[33] Youthhood can be extended in situations of economic hardship and high unemployment. However, this 'extended liminality' leaves unemployed youth in long periods of disorientation, ambiguity and anxiety regarding if, how and when they will transition into adulthood. Experiencing 'extended liminality' is particularly problematic.[34]

The youth who participated in this research perfectly fit this description. They stress that they are 'stranded'[35] in a situation where they cannot imagine that they will be economically independent anytime soon. All share the discomfiture and shame, which increases with age and years of schooling, of still living under the same roof as their parents or being dependent on them. One informant in his early thirties emotionally stated that, despite his age, he lives with his parents and lives off the money they give him, adding, 'I live like a teenager, without plans for life or for the day.'[36]

Proper dating and planning for a possible married life are luxuries for most young men. *Woreda* Labour and Social Affairs Bureau (BoLSA) experts perceive that the average age for marriage is increasing, more for men than women.[37] One BoLSA expert in Atsbi Wenberta *woreda* shared the increasing perception that the youth are 'burdens to parents, at an age they should have formed their own house'.[38] This situation is less pronounced in the case of women, as it is the man who is expected to amass the required monetary and material wealth to form a family.[39] Thus, it is more common to see younger women getting married to much older men. The concern for young women, therefore, is related to entering a relationship with a desirable man who is simultaneously reasonably older than her and economically capable of supporting a family. The welfare of children is a constant concern for women, expressed in such statements as 'my child is going hungry'[40] and 'what will I feed my child?'[41]

In this situation of a 'crowded labour market', the youth have few livelihood options.[42] With employment opportunities in the formal sector few and far between, the main alternative for an economically viable life is through government Micro and Small Enterprises (MSE) sectors, which are designed to create sustainable jobs for the youth and also reduce the irregular migration of unemployed young men.[43] The significant support for the youth to self-employ through loans from micro-finance institutions, skills training by technical and vocational training institutions, and the provision of working and selling spaces by local administrations is not proving effective.[44] Especially in Atsbi Endasellassie, it is not uncommon to see public servants, teachers particularly, attempting to reach Saudi Arabia.[45] Employment by itself does not suffice to hold someone back from his or her aspiration to migrate; instead, it may finance such migration. Similarly, some people use loans from the regional micro-finance institution, Dedebit Credit and Saving Institution (DECSI), to cover their migration expenses.[46]

Government officials attribute the low success of the MSE sector to a 'lack of awareness' about the value of hard work and the perceived impatience of the youth to become wealthy overnight.[47] It is common to hear officials and experts at MSE Development Agency, Women, Youth and Sport, and Labour and Social Affairs Bureaus characterise the youth in pejorative and pathological ways. The youth are viewed as having 'attitudinal problems',[48] expressed by others as a preference for 'taking short cuts rather than working hard to earn a living'.[49] The policies shaped by these views are meant to raise awareness among the youth both of the importance of entrepreneurship and self-employment and the risks of irregular migration, and to mobilise them accordingly.[50] Such policy misperception of why the youth do what they do is not unique to Ethiopia.[51]

The experience of longer periods of youth unemployment has a temporal dimension. One example of this is a lack of daily activities for people to be engaged in. The youth are concerned by the daily 'absence of things to do', which leads to 'waking up late, and staying up well into nights'.[52] A returnee in Raya Alamata stressed that she 'simply sits idle on the soil (ground)', as her mother and younger sisters do most of the household chores.[53] The situation is very similar to what Mains describes as the challenge for Jimma's youth, of being burdened with overabundant unstructured time in the present.[54] One young man added that in such conditions, with no sign of the situation changing, 'tomorrow is not different from today. The only difference is that the following days will be burdened with worries and concerns carried over from previous days. Thus, the following days will be more and more stressful.'[55]

This stress and anxiety, according to many young informants, come with the inevitable 'overthinking' that takes place during such elastic experiences of time. This 'overthinking' is often focused on ways of circumventing current challenges and living the desired life. It is not exclusively about the here and now, but about the possibility of transitioning to adulthood. This brings a second temporal dimension to the unemployment experience of the urban youth, related to the transition into adults and also to future-making. The unemployed urban youth experience their status as being 'stuck' (*mechekel*)[56] or 'stagnating' (*balenebet mekom*)[57] in what should have been a transient and temporary period of youthhood. A structural, mainly economic, barrier is holding them back from becoming an adult. The entrenched feeling of not making significant progress was described in one FGD as life being '*edme mekuter*' (counting years of age),[58] and in another as '*selalmoten new yalenew*' (living only because we didn't die yet).[59] In addition to an absence of progress, these framings show that the unemployed youth have lost hope in expecting to build a decent adult life.

Hopelessness and irregular migration as future-making in Tigray

The section above tells a depressing story of youth hopelessness. This pervasive feeling is engendered by long periods of unemployment and the challenges, mainly economic, of transitioning to adulthood. The concerns and anxiety of the youth are captured in the following quote:

> At my age (17), dreaming about the future is the norm. But we have no future here. What will I become if I stay? Will I go back to my parents' village and be a farmer? I do not want to do that. I know that I cannot make a good living in town because there are no good jobs, I do not have (marketable) skills and I do not have family or relatives in good places to help me out. So, how can I expect tomorrow to be better than today? Each day I live is the same as the previous, and with that comes anger and hopelessness.[60]

However, this does not mean that the youth is doing nothing to overcome these overbearing socio-economic obstacles. Their agency in circumventing the structural barriers holding them back from becoming adults comes in the form of irregular migration to Saudi Arabia. This choice is mediated by the strong 'migration system' and 'culture of migration' in the case of Atsbi Endasellassie and Raya Alamata.[61] The decision to migrate to Saudi is comparable to starting life after a period of 'stillness' and waiting. This is eloquently expressed by an informant from Atsbi Endasellassie, who compared his life to an interrupted bus ride:

> My life is like a long-distance bus trip. Some years ago, I was coming from Addis Ababa by bus, and the bus had to stop for two or three hours in the middle of nowhere. Other vehicles were passing us, the driver and the assistant trying to repair the bus and get it going. Our life is like that: something is wrong and we are not moving. Others pass us and lead independent lives. We are still here. The key to start moving is going to Saudi …

This sense of feeling stuck or stranded is similar to Sommers's description of Rwanda's post-genocide youth and their difficulties transitioning into adulthood.[62] However, in the migration literature, 'stuck' and 'stranded' are used to conceptualise the experience of migrants who have already embarked on the journey but are yet to reach their desired destination. They are in an insecure position, often with a precarious legal status, be it in the transit or destination country (awaiting a decision on an asylum application). Moreover, this situation also captures the non-linear nature of migration.[63] In our case, the youth feel 'stuck' on a temporal field, without the means to plan for a stable life and transit into adulthood. One of the preferred options to become 'unstuck' is to migrate with the hope of accumulating the necessary amount of resources for the transition.

Thus, migration is not taken up for its intrinsic value. It is rather taken as a 'spatial fix'[64] to the challenges faced by youth in progressing up the social hierarchy into adulthood. Irregular migration, therefore, serves as a genuine path, enabling migrants to imagine and aspire to a better life by building their capacity. Migration here is capability-building and has developmental outcomes.[65]

Appadurai's framework, which takes the 'future as cultural fact', helps us to understand migration in such circumstances.[66] He conceptualised the future as a product of 'three notable human preoccupations that shape the future as a cultural fact … imagination, anticipation, and aspiration'.[67] The first step in future production is imagination, made possible through the construction of what Appadurai calls archives— which constitute 'critical sites for negotiating paths to dignity, recognition, and politically feasible maps for the future'.[68] These archives are filled with and store 'the past' but also serve to inform and shape the future. In the two study areas, Atsbi Wenberta and Raya Alamata, decades of migration to Saudi Arabia have created a continuous flow and store of information, ideas and materials.

One type of archive occurs in the form of real estate, a physical and material storage of the benefits of migration. For example, in Atsbi Endasellassie there is a recently established neighbourhood with more expensive housing structures. It is called Riyadh neighbourhood, signifying that the largest proportion of the owners are migrants or migrants' families.[69] Similarly, migrants from Raya Alamata benefited when Waja Timuga town had its first 'basic plan' made in 2013/14, in the process incorporating surrounding peri-urban areas. When this farmland was put up for auction, prices were upped from the starting 84 birr per square metre to more than 2,000 birr per square metre. This excluded local people but benefited businessmen from other parts of Tigray and migrants and migrant families with some cash.[70]

Migration-related success stories can also be discerned in the life histories of many successful businessmen in Wukro, a more established town close to Atsbi Endasellassie. Most vehicles providing public transport between Wukro and Atsbi Endasellassie towns are bought with money remitted by migrants or returnees. The large size of remittances could also be guessed at by the presence of branches of three commercial banks in Atsbi Endasellassie town, i.e., Commercial Bank of Ethiopia, Lion International Bank and Wegagen Bank Three bank branches would appear too many for such a small town, but an official from the *woreda*'s Planning and Finance Office confirmed that these branches receive awards from their headquarters for good performance, an indication of the importance of remittances to the *woreda*'s economic activities.

The archives do not only involve material wealth and consumption. There is a near real-time flow of information, thanks to the use of mobile phones. The information can be success stories, updating friends and relatives about the glorified aspects of life in Saudi Arabia as well as the risks, ranging from inhumane treatment in Saudi to hor-rifying experiences en route. The most recent of such sad stories is the drowning of about 43 migrants from Atsbi Wenberta who were irregu-larly migrating to Saudi.[71] There were also several individuals from Atsbi Endasellassie attacked and injured in their transit through war-torn Yemen during the time of our fieldwork. Funerals of those killed or who died on the journey or in the destination form a part of the community archive.

However, when it comes to narratives about migration and the future, the youth focus on the positives of the migration experience. When pushed to go beyond this selective remembering and relate to the risks and negative experiences of irregular migration, the youth are generally dismissive and interpret them using fatalistic explanations. Many state that people die *en route* to their destination country because 'their day has arrived.'[72] From a religious point of view, one will not live beyond that date whether one migrates or not. Thus, death—the ultimate risk one faces—is seen as unrelated to the decision to migrate, but as a supernatural decision destined to happen on a predetermined day. Moreover, there is the tendency to look at one's fate during migration in a dichotomised way: 'either my body will come in a body bag or I will come with a bag full of money'.[73]

In Atsbi Endasellassie and Waja Timuga, the archives that inform the youth's understanding of future possibilities available to them are mainly centred on migration. The long history of migration and the densely knit network of migrants linking the sending and destination areas, coupled with ease of information flow, make migration a top priority for discussion in the long aimless chats which the unemployed youth have on a daily basis. This further reinforces the idea of irregular migration as among the chief solutions to building a future into adult-hood. Because of the recent nature of migration from Abi Adi, the youth do not have a strong archive to draw from as yet. Abi Adi's youth appear to be closer to those of Jimma, as described by Mains, in that they mainly dream about migrating based on secondary information.[74] Thus, migration is not yet seen by Abi Adi's youth as a realistic or concrete option for achieving a desired future.

Whatever is drawn from an archive must be supported by the 'capacity to aspire' for it to be realised. Appadurai conceives of aspiration as a mechanism through which 'cultural systems, as combinations of norms, dispositions, practices, and histories, frame the good life as a landscape of discernible ends and of practical paths to the achievement of these ends'.[75] He adds that 'cultural systems also shape specific images of the good life as a map of the journey from here to there and from now to then'.[76] In our case, the aspiration is not limited to migrating, as life in Saudi Arabia is considered temporary, until enough money has been made to return and start the desired life in Ethiopia. As a result, migration is viewed as a necessary detour to build 'aspirational capacity', not an end in itself. It is a culturally sanctioned pathway to building one's capabilities to transit into adulthood and live an independent life.

Migration dynamics can also be explained by the youth's aspiration and capability to migrate. Both are necessary if a potential migrant is to start his or her journey.[77] The aspiration to migrate enables us to consider social, political and cultural factors that shape people's attitude towards mobility, in addition to economic ones. Moreover, while one needs the capability (in the manner understood by Sen)[78] if one is to migrate, the reverse is also true: migration is capability-enhancing. Therefore, migration is an inherent part of development, not an expression of a failure to develop.[79] Moreover, migrants should not be seen as victims only; rather, migration 'itself can be conceptualized as a form, or expression of, agency ... and not only a "functionalist" response to spatial differentials in economic opportunity'.[80]

In our case, irregular migration is a proactive measure, an expression of agency, by the unemployed youth in response to the excruciating challenge of making the transition into adulthood. Viewed this way, migrating to Saudi Arabia has an instrumental value, contributing to building capabilities by giving the commensurate economic independence and ability to form a separate family. This is the success story of only a few migrants. This, however, does not mean that increasingly more male youth won't take migration as a chance to escape from the permanence of youthhood and to transit into adulthood. Obviously, the socio-economic devastation and destruction of infrastructure and industries which ensued following the war in Tigray (from early November 2020) will further dampen the outlook of the youth about their future. Even if the violence ends soon and reconstruction efforts proceed aggressively, it is unlikely that the socio-economic impacts of the war will fade quickly. This suggests a substantial increase in irregular (or even forced) migration from Tigray. The conflict also affects routes for irregular migration. Tigrayan youth who have the feeling of being under 'siege' by Amhara regional forces would avoid the Western Route. Irregular migration along the Eastern Route, which passes through the Afar region and Djibouti, could be intensified. Over the medium and long term, if the more than 60,000 Tigrayan refugees in Sudan are not voluntarily repatriated, they could repeat the experience of Eritrean refugees, and head to Western Europe and North America.

Conclusion

This chapter adds a further dimension to the debate on 'waiting' and migration, which is often made in spatial terms, in transit centres and while processing asylum seekers. Here the argument is that a feeling of 'waiting' is at the centre of the decision to migrate, rather than a manifestation of uncertainties and feelings of being 'stranded' after the commencement of the migration project. Moreover, 'waiting' could as well be about notions of social age, and not only about the economic and material dimensions of life.

Future-making projects of the youth cannot be dissociated from the idea of becoming adult. The economic requirement for this is increasing beyond the means of the majority of aspiring youth. Extended periods of agonising economic hardship, particularly related to unemployment, have serious implications for the temporal experience of urban youth. In Tigray's small towns it is becoming nearly impossible to meet the economic requirements to make the transition to adulthood. This is making youthhood an over-extended and near-permanent period. It is leaving the urban youth with pervasive feelings of being 'stuck' and 'stranded' in time. It is in such situations that migration emerges as one dominant expression of youth agency to extricate themselves, with the hope of accumulating enough resources to make the transition into adulthood. Viewed in this way, migration is capability-increasing and is part of development.

Irregular migration is not an option available to all urban youth. The findings from Abi Adi show that migration does not feature as strongly in the future-making projects of the youth here. A long history of migration from a particular locality leads to the accumulation of narratives, memories, experiences and material remittances that further reify the importance of migration in the limited list of options that the youth draw from.

5

MIGRATION ASPIRATIONS AND 'GLOCAL IDEAS OF THE GOOD LIFE' IN TWO RURAL COMMUNITIES IN SOUTHERN AND NORTH-EASTERN ETHIOPIA

A COMPARATIVE PERSPECTIVE

Catherine Dom

Introduction

This chapter looks at how 'ideas of the good life' interacted and coevolved in partly mutually reinforcing ways with aspirations to, and experiences and effects of, migration abroad in two rural communities, Harresaw in the north and Aze Debo in the south of Ethiopia. In both, migration abroad was large, mostly youthful, increasingly female, and irregular. I use data from the Ethiopia WIDE research (see the Introduction), mostly from early 2012 and early 2018. I also draw on 1994 and 2002 data for historical perspectives. WIDE, whose holistic approach aims to provide 'thick descriptions' of the communities' situations, is not a study of migration.[1] Rather, migration emerged as a fact that seemed increasingly important for understanding the communities' trajectories, especially since the 2010–13 fieldwork. The data, therefore, does not have the same depth as in migration-focused research. Its strength is to situate migration in the 'thick' local contexts of each community as well as in time, thereby providing robust foundations to study migration aspirations, which are 'always an empirical matter'.[2]

In both 2012 and 2018, migration was addressed through protocols exploring major changes and issues in the community as well as people's livelihoods. These protocols were used to talk to approximately 75 women and men (in roughly equal numbers) of different socio-economic profiles and wealth statuses, in interviews and a few FGDs in the two communities. In addition, six to eight young women and the same number of young men, of different age groups and wealth status, were also interviewed about their own lives and those of young people in the community. In 2018, colleagues from WIDE and Mekelle University and I also carried out a few days of fieldwork specifically to further explore migration in each community. In Harresaw, 27 return-ees, deportees, migrants' families, would-be migrants, people not wanting to migrate and other community members were interviewed and FGDs were held (with older, adult, and younger men, and women of different ages, respectively), with a focus on global influences on migration and some attention to migration effects (see chapter 10). In Aze Debo, 33 individuals were interviewed across a similar range of profiles and two FGDs were held with men and women, respectively, on migration decision-making (see chapter 7).

In this chapter, I draw on the analytical concepts of migration aspira-tions and of 'glocal' ideas of the good life. These emerged inductively as particularly relevant to make sense of the data, as well as being closely interrelated. Moving away from the 'figure of the migrant as a utility-maximising individual',[3] I conceive aspiration as an 'emotionally thick representation of what one's future *might* and *should* look like, given the present circumstances and the experiences of the past re-codified from the "here-and-now"'.[4] A 'matter of individual cognition and emotion',[5] aspirations are 'never simply individual ... always formed in interaction and in the thick of social life'.[6] I show how migra-tion aspirations in both sites, often first expressed in economic terms, go beyond this and relate to ideas of the good life and social norms about self-worth. Moreover, far from the cliché of the homogenisation of local cultures under the assault of globalisation, in both sites 'glocal' ideas of the good life have emerged, drawing on both global and local cultural and normative repertoires, by a process, which Robertson calls 'glocalisation', of continuous reconstitution through 'the simultaneity and the inter-penetration of what are conventionally called the global and the local'.[7] Migration aspirations and experiences of migration are both shaping and being shaped by the 'glocal' ideas of the good life, in a complex coevolution also influenced by urbanisation, education and communications, while also reflecting contextual specificities, and the very different transformative potential of the main migration flows, in each locality.

Following this introduction, I outline the historical evolution of patterns of outmigration in each community. This provides the context for the comparative analysis of contemporary migration aspirations and 'glocal' ideas of the good life in the two communities, which follows in the next two sections. After briefly reflecting on the gap between these ideas and government ideas of rural life, the final section concludes.

Migration in Aze Debo and Harresaw: A long history

In both Aze Debo, a food-insecure rural community in Kambata, southern Ethiopia, and Harresaw, a drought-prone rural community in north-eastern Tigray, migration abroad in early 2018 was important in all aspects of people's lives. In both sites, it rested on a longstanding tradition of outward mobility.

Harresaw in 1994 was a place of frequent drought, famine or severe hunger. In 2012, a government large-scale productive safety net programme,[8] which began around 2005, provided support to food-insecure households somewhat more predictably than in the past, extending to 80% of the community in 'bad years'. The development of irrigated farming in some parts of the community, thanks to a dam and rudimentary irrigation canals built in the early 2000s, was promising, and this was seen as the way towards development by government officials. However, this failed to account for the growing number of people, especially the younger generations, who had no access to land, irrigated or not.[9] A severe drought in 2007/08 had prompted a widespread debt crisis, as most households lost livestock bought on credit under a government programme alongside the safety net (see chapter 10). In early 2018 Harresaw was a community in decline. Recurrent drought and poor rains over most of the previous six years had dried up the impounded water at the dam. Irrigation was no longer possible. The consequent reduction in household income harmed the small non-farm sector, and local daily labour opportunities had shrunk, hitting hard the growing number of landless households. Food aid, seen as a lifeline, had decreased and the safety net was less predictable. About 1,400 young people (or an estimated 80% of their cohort, according to some respondents) were unemployed and landless. Roughly 10% among them had studied up to Grade 10, an investment which did not seem to make much difference in terms of prospects.

Historically, Harresaw was accustomed to mass migration especially in times of severe drought and famine. Migration was common even in normal years as farming could not cover basic needs. In 1994 migrants were going to Eritrea or Afar for daily labour for men and domestic work for women, to Humera to harvest cash crops, and in a few cases to towns, for periods varying from two months to two years. In the data from 1994, six men had reportedly been to Saudi Arabia. In the local narrative, historical trade links existed with Saudi through the Afar, carrying butter, goats, sheep and honey brought from Harresaw. A few people from Harresaw went themselves with the goods and, at some point, some stayed longer to work. The 1984 drought led more people to consider this option. People noted that there was no way of becoming rich in the village whereas sometimes migration made an individual wealthy.[10] In 2002/03, people gave the example of a man who, after returning from Saudi, was living in Addis Ababa and had a car.

In 2012 outmigration continued to be very important, in spite of officials' hope that the safety net and irrigation development would make people 'develop their country at home'. The pattern of migration destinations had evolved too. With irrigated farming demanding local daily labour, there were fewer labour migrants to Humera and Afar. The most notable change, however, was how migration to Saudi had become the 'big thing'. The number of those going there had gradually increased over the years as the positive effect of remittances and savings became visible, whereas the 1998–2000 Ethiopian–Eritrean war and ensuing border closure had made going to Eritrea impossible. However, migration to Saudi really shot up with the debt crisis mentioned earlier. For many, it was the only feasible way to be able to refund their loans. Then migrants started staying longer in order to accumulate capital to invest at home.

Migration became an alternative in particular for the many landless and unemployed youngsters, who saw successful returnees as role models. In Saudi, jobs were easily found, payment rates were high, and the riyal was strong, so payment was good. Most migration was irregular, as the legal government-regulated scheme (mostly for women as housemaids) was seen as complicated, slow and costly. The irregular journey was considered by many to be expensive (3,000 to 5,000 birr, or US$170 to $280 in 2011/12) and risky, but worthwhile. Local people talked about better lives and livelihoods in return. They estimated that some 400 to 500 people were going each year, and many returned with capital for investment. Migration to Saudi, back then, was potentially transformative.

In 2018, in the much more difficult local context described above, outmigration continued to be an important outlet, but with far less certainty that it might lead to a 'better life'. Migrating elsewhere in Ethiopia, such as to Afar for daily labour or to towns for more educated youth, was seen to lead only to a hand-to-mouth existence. At the same time, the cost-benefit balance of migration to Saudi had radically changed: the journey through Yemen, already at war, was more expensive (30,000 to 50,000 birr, or $1,100 to $1,800 in February 2018) and riskier; in Saudi, since late 2013 the authorities had regularly deported irregular migrants, and the economic slowdown experienced in that country meant there were fewer job opportunities and salaries were lower. Some 150–300 people in a year still went, but the returns in the rare cases of success were moderate, especially compared to just a few years back and also to the levels mentioned in Aze Debo.[11]

Aze Debo in the 1990s and early 2000s was food-insecure and already very densely populated with acute land scarcity. One in four or five households were estimated to be landless. There also was a fairly high level of schooling, as Protestant missionaries present in the area since the 1930s had popularised education.[12] Migration was seen as a necessity, and a source of wealth and status for people with children sending remittances.[13] More than half of the men coming of working age in Aze Debo migrated temporarily elsewhere in Ethiopia to trade or search for jobs, for periods ranging from a few months to over a year. Those less educated and lacking money to trade went to work on sugar-cane and other state or commercial farms or to farm others' land. There were educated people with professional jobs working all over the country, and traders and people involved in transport in the country's major cities, primarily Addis Ababa, Dire Dawa and Harar.

In 2012, the productive safety net programme was operating in Aze Debo, though assisting far fewer households than in Harresaw (around 20%). Migration continued to be an important alternative to lack of land, capital and jobs locally, especially for the hundreds of high school and college graduates. Two new gendered flows were important. Young men migrated to South Africa to trade in the streets or in shops once they were better established, while a few attractive young women were going there as wives. Alongside this, a growing number of young women migrated elsewhere in Ethiopia and also to the Gulf countries, some of them legally. In the local narrative on migration to South Africa, the well-known ambassador from the area was mentioned (see chapter 8); also, two young pioneering men from Hadiya went there, became very successful and called others, and the word gradually spread to Kambata. The journey was costly (33,000 birr or around $1,800 by land, 100,000 birr or around $5,700 by air with a broker-arranged visa). Remittances and savings from successful migrants were said to be a major source of wealth and development for their families and the community more widely. Beyond the (smaller) economic returns, the greater mobility of women was a major departure from the Kambata tradition of keeping them strictly at home.[14]

In 2018 Aze Debo's trajectory was somewhat hopeful, with the local economy slowly but steadily growing. The expansion of nearby urban markets, including the zonal capital of Durame four kilometres away on a recently asphalted road, incentivised farmers to engage in commercial dairy production and irrigated horticulture. The local non-farm sector was growing. However, as in Harresaw, one major concern was the ever-rising landlessness and, more broadly, the lack of options for young people. There were reportedly 426 unemployed young women and men with at least ten years of schooling and, for one in four, additional technical and vocational or university education.

Migration, and migration savings or remittances, closely interacted with these trends. Alongside continued migration to historically familiar rural destinations, a steadily rising number of young women and men were going to towns and cities for all sorts of work. Successes were modest but appreciated, and this contributed to reducing the very high pressure on land. The trend had also continued of women migrating to Sudan and in a few cases to the Gulf countries. However, the big story was the steady number of young men migrating to South Africa who, if successful, dramatically improved their and their family's life: 60 to 70 men were reportedly going every year.[15]

Migration aspirations in 2018: Similarities and differences[16]

Turning to migration aspirations in early 2018, this section shows that beyond the 'more immediate wants' often first stated, 'the intermediate and higher order normative contexts' of these wants were key shaping factors in both communities.[17] Work and an income were the immediate wants of young people, their parents, and the community at large—being seen as indispensable markers of young people's transition to adulthood. Migration abroad was seen as a way of satisfying these wants while options for doing so locally were limited or not regarded as worthwhile in comparison. Yet in both sites, these were less aims in themselves than means towards the good life, often expressed as a desire for 'change'. There were also important nuances in how migration aspirations were formulated, reflecting the very different 'transformative potential' of migration in each site, and resulting in very different ways in which 'imagined transformations' through migration were 'institutionally embedded'.[18]

Migration aspirations in Aze Debo

In Aze Debo, as one respondent explained, 'South Africa is [seen as] a land of fortune where one can get good money'.[19] So, a father explained, young people migrated 'not because it is good to go in another country but there is no job here'.[20] They 'go rather than trou-bling their parents for land'.[21] Even rich young people wondered 'what would I do if I am living here'.[22] For the many young people failing national exams, 'going' was better than staying at home, 'brawling and frustrated'.[23] Some of those with college education were getting lowly paid jobs, which motivated them to also migrate. For instance, a father explained how his son with a public health degree was being paid 500 birr a month ($20) in a private pharmacy in the regional capital of Hawassa, and concluded: 'What kind of money is that for a person like him? He left …'[24] In the same vein, there was a sense that while jobs in local factories might stop those migrating elsewhere in Ethiopia, those migrating to South Africa were 'looking for a better life'. 'What would you do if you are paid 40–45 birr a day, and you pay for a single meal of *shiro* [beans stew consumed with *injera* or flatbread—consid-ered a cheap meal] 18 birr?'[25]

Beyond these immediate wants, young people (mostly men, as noted earlier) also expressed 'becoming' aspirations, manifested in a strong desire for economic independence and of 'changing oneself and changing one's family.'[26]

> A young man who doesn't go 'will have to ask his father to buy him a pair of shoes when those he has are worn out'.[27]

> How come it is possible to live if you are not supporting your father, your uncle and the rest of your relatives? … We need to go to South Africa to change ourselves, our families and our relatives. This is the objective of young people.[28]

Young people 'need change', and the kind of options offered in government-sponsored schemes didn't match their aspirations. For instance, one young man, reacting to the fact that in Aze Debo the government only supported 'rural activities', explained:

> loans for things like fattening [bulls] … bring nothing significant, it's just hand-to-mouth. The thinking that youth will change by [fattening] bulls is not good. It has to be something that brings new things, knowl-edge and skills … I forward my question to the government so that the youth can be supported with jobs that can transform them.[29]

More vocal young men asked the local administrators: 'You always say we are the backbone of the community, what did you do for us?'

Frustrated by the lack of an answer, one of them concluded that 'everyone wants us to migrate, even the administrators, because we are a burden to them'.[30]

The transformative dimension of successful migration was highlighted in most interviews, and even those who did not want to go reckoned that 'many people here have worked hard, they have done trading, but I have seen no one who has changed',[31] whereas the migrants' families were 'better-off'. People gave examples they saw as especially striking, such as an orphan who had been able to buy a house in Durame and the bus he was driving, or another orphan who had a house and a minibus and had sent his brother to South Africa to replace him.

In turn, as Carling and Collins note, these 'becoming' aspirations were strongly embedded in local social norms. In Aze Debo, outmigration had been seen as a way to support one's family for decades. In 2018, migration to South Africa, with considerable returns (by local standards) in cases of success, was socially accepted and associated with status. 'They [migrants to South Africa] are respected, they are heard.'[32] 'The talk is high about their success.'[33] People respected migrants' ability to support the community's poor (sending money annually for Meskel [commemorating the finding of the True Cross] for an ox for very poor households, supporting poor people with cash, or paying the schooling costs of orphans), some of which was managed by the local Protestant churches. They held in great esteem migrants who met the costs of family funerals, relieving the *idir* of the burden. As one respondent explained, migrants 'have better social acceptance because they are supporting their parents, poor people and the community at large, and come back with new ideas and practices'.[34] In contrast, joblessness and idleness at home attracted shame. One young man noted that if you go, 'even if you don't change yourself, people will smile at you', whereas 'if you remain unemployed and wander around, people's reaction is like punishment'.[35]

In this way, migration abroad also fitted with the prevailing social norm of younger generations 'getting ahead of their fathers'[36] and supporting older ones. At the same time, and together with other transitions in rural Ethiopia, migration abroad contributed to an evolution in the tangible signs of fulfilment of these norms, with urban houses, cars and so on being the new signs of status.[37] It also prompted a sense that one couldn't do less, so that aspirations reflected 'not only socially sanctioned behaviour but also social mechanisms of diffusion'.[38] People observed the success of others and migration became part of their 'aspirations window'.[39] In Aze Debo this sense of emulation was widespread. Some respondents said that children as young as ten started thinking about migration. Like migration itself, this sense of emulation when seeing returnees 'having changed themselves' was not new; it was why going for work in sugar factories became popular in the 1960s and 1970s.

One of the most important ways a migrant could adhere to social norms and help his family, relatives or friends once he or she was established was to 'take them to South Africa' by financing their trip. A father enumerating his son's successes, such as houses in Hawassa and Durame, was also proud to add that 'he has taken six young people to South Africa',[40] including a younger brother, who in turn had taken another two. The newcomer usually repaid his sponsor by working for him free of charge for some time (see chapter 8). But he could then establish himself and start building his own success, like the man who 'has taken two of [his] nephews to South Africa. It's been three years since they left; now they have their own shops and support their families.'[41] Having a link with someone already established in South Africa was therefore almost a precondition: 'a young person doesn't go there if he doesn't have [an established] relative or a friend'.[42] There were also stories of frustration and jealousy when a friend in South Africa did not honour a promise made earlier or when a migrant took some relatives and not others.

In this predominantly Protestant community, religion played a major role in socially embedding the value of migration to South Africa as an object of aspiration. Faith and fatalism were often called upon to vindicate migration aspirations. There were young men saying: 'If God is willing to take my life because I am going, I will never be spared for staying at home',[43] and that they 'will win if God is with [them]'.[44] A migrant's father, for whom 'no one dies without the will of God', explained that he prayed for his son to live well in South Africa and for God to deliver him from the bad things that happen in this 'country with trouble'.[45] Prayers were said in church asking for God's protection when a young migrant started his travels. When his parents announced in church that he had made it safely, the congregation also prayed to thank God. In turn, migrants' first remittances were meant for their church, as thanksgiving for the prayers and blessings. Migrants who regularly remitted to their church to support social protection activities were particularly highly respected.

Migration aspirations in Harresaw

The story in Harresaw is both similar and different. There, too, immediate wants were about a way of making a livelihood. Although not necessarily an ideal choice, migration was a way to achieve this in contrast to 'no other option, no hope'[46] in the face of drought, land scarcity and landlessness, and generally very limited local resources. As one young married man explained, 'Ideally I would prefer to live a good life here, but people [like me] only have labour to sell and don't get much for it here.'[47] People who had 'something' aspired to a 'meaningful amount of money' to start 'something better'.[48] Many young couples wanted to build their own house. They estimated how much was needed (from 100,000 to 300,000 birr, or $3,500 to $10,000, depending on location), and that it might take 'six to seven years, maybe longer depending on luck', to accumulate this sum while also covering the household's daily needs. However, there were also a number of mostly young men for whom migrating to Saudi was about 'taking part in modernisation', with modern clothes, hairstyles and so on, or who 'followed others' with no specific plan in mind.

As in Aze Debo, migration was also seen as the best way to perhaps change oneself. For some people, in the past even migration to Eritrea wouldn't allow this, whereas with migration to Saudi, there is 'half a chance'.[49] However, whereas in both communities the migrants aimed to change themselves, the desire of changing one's family was more present in the narrative in Aze Debo. In Harresaw, when parents were consulted, their ambitions were often all about their children: 'We continue to farm even though it's not profitable because we have no other option. But our children don't take things in the same way … We don't want to see our children suffer in front of us from continuously worrying about their future.'[50]

Some young people went without their parents' knowledge or nagged them for money for the trip, for which they often became indebted. Couples usually planned together, but sometimes did not agree on whether it was worthwhile to continue, such as this young woman talking about her husband:

> It [migration to Saudi] is just struggling for life and death. He migrated seven times to Saudi but he got no benefit, he lost his money for nothing. Each time he didn't work there, he was deported as soon as he arrived. My small crop trading has better benefit. I may get profits some of the time and losses some other time. But his migration is totally lost.[51]

Just as the transformative potential of migration seemed less in Harresaw than in Aze Debo,[52] so too change was defined in less ambitious terms in the former than in the latter. Parents said things like: 'We don't want millions, but reaching food security and saving for these children so that when they return they can build a house and start something that will ensure a regular income'.[53] One returnee living in an urban house built with his savings, but with little else to show for his two trips, concluded: 'I don't consider myself changed, I'm still worrying about the future and what next to do.'[54]

The social perception of migration abroad was also a lot more mixed than in Aze Debo. For some people in Harresaw, migrants just did not 'want to go through the hassle of slowly accumulating small benefits … Getting better-off takes years, [they are] not interested in that.'[55] Yet others understood migration aspirations, when there was so little else on offer. 'We advise against, but inside we know they have to go.'[56] 'We ask our youth to find their own way.'[57] 'We don't support migration but we cannot criticise them harshly. What do we have to tell them?'[58] Many parents and spouses deplored the migrants' absence (see chapter 10) and worried about them, while talking about the lack of any other choice:

> Migration is not a choice. Parents with children away are like blind people … We don't want to stay away. Nobody wants to spend life in a foreign country. When we are away, our thoughts are here. We all belong here.[59]

> People think I'm lucky, but women whose husbands migrate to Afar are the lucky ones. Their husband can come back, play with his children.[60]

The relation between religion and migration abroad was also quite different in Harresaw. As an influential institution, the Orthodox Church was asked by the government to relay its anti-migration message. However, the priests in Harresaw would not formally condemn migrants, in this way protecting them from all the social stigma such a step would attract. Like many adults, some priests thought that while migration was not desirable, the government was failing to pay sufficient attention, allocate sufficient resources, and be sufficiently innovative in addressing young people's understandable aspirations. Some deacons and priests even migrated themselves.

Two other interlinked differences with Aze Debo were noteworthy. First, while there were cases in Harresaw of people following others (most often relatives) and relying on them for support on arrival, this could not be compared with the very strong networks between established and would-be migrants in Aze Debo, with the former sponsoring the latter. As a result, most would-be migrants from Aze Debo knew what they would do once they arrived, while new migrants from Harresaw would have to find a job first. In view of the much less buoyant Saudi labour market, this had become a lot harder in 2018. Especially for young men, who were still the majority of those leaving, there were many stories of unemployment for months or having to work in harsh up-country locations.

Success also seemed to be rarer in Harresaw, and there were more sad stories. People talked about migrants or their families falling into debt when the former did not reach Saudi or were deported too soon to be able to refund the loan that most had to take to travel, or if they died on the journey or at the destination. They mentioned families not knowing the migrants' whereabouts for months, or learning about their death but being unable to repatriate the body. We heard stories of sometimes ten or more migrants from Harresaw dying on the same trip. This is not to say that the journeys to and experiences in South Africa were all without dangers. But while migration aspirations were strongly socially embedded in both localities, the 'migration cultures' were markedly different. The negative or 'feared' selves that young migrants and aspirant migrants sought to escape from were similar. But it was harder in Harresaw to believe in migration as a way to achieve the positive or 'desired' self which they aspired to become.[61]

'Glocal' ideas of the good life

In both communities, ideas of the good life were evolving, in an evolving context as well, notably as a result of increasing urbanisation. Urban–rural links were denser, especially in Aze Debo given its proximity with Durame. Internal urbanisation was also important, with a growing small centre in Harresaw, roadside urbanisation in Aze Debo, and strikingly different lifestyles between people living in these more urbanised parts and those living in remoter areas. As Pankhurst explains, electricity and the expanding reach of communications media also prompted rapid and multi-faceted changes, especially in young people's outlook, leisure and cultural practices.[62] In these contexts, ideas of the good life in Aze Debo and Harresaw resulted from a fusion, or assemblage (see the Introduction), of 'local' and 'global' elements, specific to each context, which kept evolving over time. Migration aspirations were reflected in, and were at the same time constitutive of, these 'glocal' ideas of the good life.

Again, people often first mentioned the material aspects of the good life that would come thanks to migration. Ambitions reflected the 'learned' nature of aspirations, as people observed the experiences of others and assessed what they could 'realistically' aim for on this basis.[63] This was quite different between the two communities. In Aze Debo, there were young people dismissing the possibility of starting something worthwhile with even 160,000 birr (about $5,700 in early 2018, or the cost of travel to South Africa by air with a broker-arranged visa in 2018). In Harresaw, this sum was what some migrants aimed to get so as to build their home. Local perceptions of migration as a way of achieving other, non-material aspects of the good life also differed markedly between the two sites.

Ideas of the good life in Aze Debo

In Aze Debo, at the material level, the good life meant a better house for the migrant and his or her family ('you do not find in town a house like those built here')[64] and better living standards (with TVs, refrigerators, sofas, etc.), the ability to buy or build at least one house in town, and the capital to start or invest in a business. The biggest and best hotel in Durame belonged to two returnee brothers; respondents also mentioned, for instance, a man who bought land in Durame for 1.5 million birr (around $54,000) and planned to build a multi-storey building, and another migrant with a house in Durame and also in Hawassa. The most favoured business sector seemed to be transportation, in which migrants invested for their family (buying a *bajaj* or even a minibus for a younger brother to drive) or on return (some bought Isuzu trucks or buses for close to a million birr).

Ideas of the good life associated with migration nonetheless continued to be quite strongly linked to 'home'. Although families didn't know when or indeed whether a migrant member would come back, the idea was that he could do so and send another family member to 'replace' him. Migrants who cut off links with their family seemed to be the exception. Parents and migrants relocating to town most often went to nearby Durame—not full-time or fully for those with farming plots. People continued to value highly things like a good number of cattle, and migration money made it possible to invest in hybrid stock. Dairy production, which was possible on a larger scale with hybrids, continued to be culturally important. At the same time, it had become a worthwhile investment in view of the rising demand from Durame.

This 'fusion' of global and local in what constituted the good life was also reflected in the fact that most migrants would marry locally. But in this regard as well, aspirations and ideas had evolved based on learned experience. A few years earlier there had been a trend of 'selecting' wives among the beautiful girls in Aze Debo and taking them to South Africa (see chapter 8). In 2018, some women had heard about the difficulties of living in a foreign place with husbands mostly away. They no longer agreed to go, and were waiting for their husband or fiancé to return once he had made 'enough' money.

Beyond the material aspects, the interviews clearly illustrate that being able to change oneself and one's family, being a respected member of the community even when away, being respected for one son's success, were all key elements of the good life. All of the young men interviewed saw good sides to life in the community (peacefulness, being with one's family and friends) but they were clear that joblessness, idleness, and being pitied or made shameful because of it made up 'the bad life'.

Ideas of the good life in Harresaw

In Harresaw there seemed to be two groups among migrants and families. In the first group, people's ideas of the good life resembled a scaled-down version of those in Aze Debo—and of what a few migrants from Harresaw reportedly had achieved in earlier times. As I noted earlier, this was expressed as attaining food security and something to live on, not worrying about the future; owning a 'modern' local house (standards were visibly lower than in Aze Debo), sometimes a second house or additional rooms to rent and receive a regular income of a few hundred birr for daily needs; money to marry (with 35,000 to 40,000 birr, or around $1,300 to $1,500) and start a small business locally (another 35,000 to 40,000 birr to start a barber or consumer-goods shop, a tailor's business, or a local cafe). A few in this first group were more ambitious and talked about houses in Atsbi (the district town) or Wukro (a bigger and booming town on the main road to the regional capital of Mekelle), or opening a business in Wukro or even Mekelle. But the biggest ambitions costed in the hundreds of thousands of birr and not millions.

The good life was also about changing oneself, but the idea of being respected because of success was less present in the narrative, presumably because success cases were rare and most often the level reached was quite modest.

The good life could be 'at home' for some young people, even among returnees or would-be migrants. If so, obtaining farmland was important and featured in migration aspirations, usually alongside other goals. More broadly, the 'glocal' ideas of the good life continued to value land, and this also played out in marriage strategies. However, the case for the good life at home was less clear-cut than in Aze Debo. Some respondents also suggested that migration led to 'dissimilation' on return,[65] and talked about migrants being 'rootless' and 'dis-adapted' because

> There is a huge gap between a young man returning from Saudi, who has seen many things and has had a good life or terrible experiences, and a young woman who never travelled or at most, [travelled] in the Region [and nowhere else]. This is even more difficult for young women, [on return] they no longer want to live and marry here.[66]

This leads to the second group of mostly younger men, often somewhat educated but not enough, usually unmarried, who had tried migrating but failed or returned with too little money (in their eyes) to start anything. So, they migrated again, often to fail again, and then repeated the cycle. Some people said they had become obsessed with migration. They attracted a mix of pity, disdain and anger from adults; certainly not respect.

> they gave up on life because they spent unsuccessful migration and sad return. They do not care for the community here. They quarrel and fight with their parents and force them to give them money to return to Saudi. They also fight each other in drink houses, and with the drink house owners because they refuse to pay for their drinks. When they are asked to pay, they say, 'please ask Hailemariam Desalegn [the Prime Minister at the time of fieldwork] to pay for our drink because he is responsible for our unemployment'.[67]

Some adults disliked what they saw as an unwelcome change in young people's cultural identity, clothes, hairstyles and manners and blamed them for 'consumerism' with 'lots of drinking and spending one's small money in towns'.[68] For sure, in both communities, the 'glocal' ideas of the good life differed between generations. But the difference seemed more pronounced in Harresaw. This may seem counterintuitive considering Aze Debo's greater 'connectedness', with more global ideas within reach of the younger generation there. But in Aze Debo migration abroad prompted aspirations broadly shared across generations, in which 'loyalty' to one's locality was present.[69] In contrast, in Harresaw many adults were resigned to a life from which many youngsters wanted to 'exit'. Not trusting that government would listen to their 'voice', they saw their 'exit' option as moving away.

Changing aspirations, 'glocal' ideas of the good life, and the government

There was indeed a large gap between the government's ideas of the good life for rural people, which seemed to be about reproducing rural life, and people's own 'glocal' ideas, especially among young people. This 'clash' between contradictory ideas of the good life was one of the reasons for young people to migrate. Faced with the inability or unwillingness of the government to listen when they voiced their changing aspirations, young people 'voted with their feet' by migrating.

In Aze Debo, young men watching TV in a cafe in Durame were shouting to the bar owner to 'change it', refusing to see a documentary on the dangers of illegal migration. A returnee from South Africa expressed a sentiment that many shared when he said: 'What is wrong if they [migrants] work there and come back with fortunes? What is wrong for the government to make the travel open so that they can go and work legally there rather than living with worry and deprivation here?'[70] Similarly one young man in Harresaw pointed out that 'there are many plans ... but there is no plan for the youth. We are the future of this country, but we don't know what our future will be.'[71] Those who had listened to government promises made during the 2013 and 2017 repatriation programmes explained bitterly that these never materialised, which local officials indeed acknowledged. In Harresaw, too, many said that 'government should not stop people. It is in the interest of both people and government that people move.'[72]

Conclusion

In this chapter I show how migration abroad arises from and contributes to the enlarging of young people's map or window of aspirations.[73] The chapter also reveals how, beyond immediate aspirations such as finding work and earning an income, migration is valued as transformative, allowing young people to make their future in line with extant local social norms. The examples of Harresaw and Aze Debo demonstrate how changing aspirations remain culturally embedded, as ideas of the good life as an object of these aspirations are also evolving.[74] These examples also illustrate the fallacy of thinking that in our virtually borderless world, ideas of the good life would become global; rather, these ideas evolve through processes of 'glocalisation' or fusion of the global and the local.[75] As the local is diverse, glocal ideas of the good life remain diverse too.

This chapter also illustrates that while ideas of and aspirations towards the good life 'exist in all societies', the decision to migrate to fulfil them is not just a matter of structural constraints and opportunities in contexts characterised by a scarcity of local options.[76] Migration abroad and, indeed, the very act of aspiring to migrate are manifestations of agency and, as Fernandez notes, migrants' agency is 'constructed through this desire for change'.[77] The 'beyond economic' dimension of migration aspirations and decisions is also highlighted, as is the way migration is driven by values such as 'filial piety and commitment to community' and by wants such as the desire for self-worth and recognition.[78] In this vein, even the 'drifting young men' of Harresaw are showing agency, claiming and acting the right to exit, to escape from the government's structural model they don't believe in, and to 'search for respect, dignity and recognition' just as generations of young people have done before them.[79]

PART III

MICRO-VIEWS ON MIGRATION

6

RITUALS OF MIGRATION

SOCIALLY ENTRENCHED PRACTICES AMONG FEMALE MIGRANTS FROM AMHARA NATIONAL REGIONAL STATE

Kiya Gezahegne

Introduction

She told me to call her Sara, when we were first introduced at the International Organization for Migration (IOM) emergency response centre in Metema Yohannes town, on Ethiopia's border with Sudan. Sara[1] was a cheerful 14-year-old girl born in a rural village in South Gondar, where many consider themselves deeply religious. Raised as an Orthodox Christian, Sara, together with four other deportees, was happy to make coffee as the day was the celebration of Meskel (the finding of the True Cross). As their guest, they treated me to a good Arabica coffee and the heart-wrenching story of their journey to Sudan. As we had met several times in the centre, they now considered me part of the migrant family. In the middle of our conversation, Sara asked me if I was married. I was curious as to why she asked such a question. With a smile on her face, she said, 'I do not think I will ever get married or have kids. I have had enough. If it were not for God and my preparation, I would have now been with a child.' Sara continued to describe her experience in the desert of Sudan before she was caught and deported. 'You travel well prepared. You have to convince yourself of the dangers you might face. You have to put your trust in God and have faith that things will work your way. I was unfortunate but I know the worst could have happened. When I left home, my friend and me got an injection [contraceptive] just in case … Everyone does that when they leave home. It is your insurance just in case something happens to you. If you get sick, you have your *emnet*.[2] If you get raped, you already have protection … When you get emotionally drained, you boost yourself with spiritual songs or talk to each other … Brokers in Sudan kept me as a sex slave in the camps for months. I have been through hell already and now there is nothing I fear. I am a woman now; I am no longer a child. After I go back home, I am going to get myself together and regain my strength. Then, I will come back. This time, I will be even more prepared and will make it to Khartoum. I know what to do now. Even during this journey, I knew what to do and how to act in front of the brokers. That is why I am alive and well. If I resisted or tried to run away, I would have ended up dead.' Grateful, despite her sad story, Sara kept telling how her preparation made her strong mentally, physically and emotionally. She constantly brought up how this is not just her story but also the story of many others.

This is an excerpt from one of several interviews I conducted during my research in Metema Yohannes in West Gondar Zone, Amhara National Regional State (ANRS). When analysing migration from the region there are different migration phenomena and also common trends. However, what caught my interest and what is covered in this chapter is the ritualisation of migration and the deeply entrenched ideologies that drive the migration experience.

The experiences of Sara and others, interviewed at different times during the research period, show how certain rituals are used by migrants as a strategy for coping. Their experiences also demonstrate the impact and significance of rituals in the processes of migration and migrants' life en route, at the destination and in the place of origin.

Rituals help migrants settle at their destination and at the same time maintain relations with their families and the community in their place of origin. In this regard, this chapter makes an argument for considering rituals of migration as an analytical framework within which to understand migration and mobility, a subject that, according to Pedersen and Rytter, has 'received too little scholarly attention'.[3] The relationship between rituals and migration can go both ways: the migration process can affect rituals and ritual performances can have an impact on migration experiences. It is the latter that will be dealt with in this chapter.

The discussion in this chapter is from a field study limited in spatial scope and number of informants. It is an analysis of data collected in 2013, 2014, 2017 and 2018 in three towns, Metema Yohannes, Qobo and Woldiya in Amhara region.

The study areas selected provide a good representation of the migration geography, including transit and sending areas. The two towns of Qobo and Woldiya are among the places identified by the regional Bureau of Labour and Social Affairs (BoLSA) as hotspot source points of migration. Situated in adjacent *woredas* of Qobo and Guba Lafto within the North Wollo administrative zone, Qobo and Woldiya are located along the main highway that runs from Addis Ababa to Mekelle (capital of Tigray National Regional State). As of 2006 and 2002 respectively, these two towns have officially become urban districts with the legal status of municipalities. In 2015 Metema Yohannes also became an urban district under the administration of the newly established West Gondar administrative zone. Metema Yohannes is a transit town on the main road, also known as the north-western route, connecting Addis Ababa with Khartoum, Sudan and onwards to Europe through Libya or Egypt. Few migrants from Qobo and Woldiya use this route to get to Sudan. The majority, mainly women whose destination is the Middle East, go through the eastern route using the border with Djibouti and Somalia.

In this chapter, the emphasis is on migrants' experience rather than on the places of origin and transit. Efforts were made to avoid biased generalisations about migration from Amhara region. Rather, the study looked at trends in ritual practices performed by migrants across the study sites which probably occur in the region in general.

Migration trend from Amhara region

Migration in the Amhara region, like the rest of the world, is an age-old and widespread phenomenon. Internal migration within the Amhara (mainly rural–urban and rural–rural) to other regions of Ethiopia, and also internationally, has been common. The Central Statistical Agency (CSA) population projection indicates that 38,000 individuals migrated out of Amhara region in the year 2007/08.[4] With the second-largest population in Ethiopia, Amhara has the second-highest migration rate in the country after Oromia National Regional State. The Regional Mixed Migration Secretariat reported that 17% of migrants to and 24% of returnees from Ethiopia are originally from Amhara region.[5] The number of migrants continues to increase, as more women and men migrate from the region in search of better livelihoods for themselves and their families. Table 6.1 on regular migration from the region shows the significant increase in the number of migrants, though it is not a complete picture, as irregular migrants are not included.

A study of adolescent migrants from Amhara region also showed the increasing number of migrants, especially to Middle Eastern countries such as Saudi Arabia, Kuwait, Dubai, Beirut and Qatar.[6] A considerable number of migrants also travel to Sudan and Israel from the region.[7] Many writers have documented the major waves of migration of the Beta Israel, widely known as the Falasha, from the north-western part of Ethiopia, in Amhara region. The movement that took place between 1980 and 1991, according to Kaplan and Rosen, put an end to the Beta Israel as a community in Ethiopia.[8]

There are only a few accounts of Ethiopian migration to Sudan, and almost none from the Amhara region. Furthermore, the exact number of migrants from Amhara region to Sudan is not known because of the irregular nature of migration and the lack of a centralised registration system for migrants.

The majority of migrants undertake irregular migration mainly because of restricted access to formal channels. The irregular channel is also considered to be less bureaucratic and time-consuming, cheaper and more successful in getting to destinations.[9] Prior to 2013, 40% of Ethiopian migrants, mainly women, had been leaving the country

Table 6.1: Migration statistics for Amhara region

Year	Migrants (total number)	% (from total pop.)	% from the (18–35 aged pop.)	Female migrants	% of female migrants	Female migrants as % of total female population	Female migrants as % of female population aged 18–35
2008/09	4,530	0.025	0.161	3,551	78.39	0.039	0.238
2009/10	2,213	0.012	0.077	1,952	88.21	0.021	0.128
2010/11	11,311	0.059	0.383	10,769	95.21	0.113	0.687
2011/12	66,298	0.339	2.186	62,836	94.78	0.645	3.906
2012/13	36,135	0.180	1.161	33,831	93.62	0.338	2.050

Source: Adapted from Asnake and Zerihun 2015: 23–7.

through the regular channel, mainly to the Middle East.[10] However, following the 2013 ban on labour migration to the Middle East, the number of regular migrants decreased significantly. Further, by over-staying their visa, these 'regular' migrants over time can also become 'irregular' in destination countries.

The Federal Democratic Republic of Ethiopia Anti-trafficking Council report of 2015 identified four source points of migration in Amhara region: South and North Wollo, Oromia Special Zone, North Gondar and North Shewa. The report further noted that the migration phenomenon was spreading rapidly throughout the zones and *woredas* in the region.[11]

Generally referred to as push and pull factors, drivers of migration include poverty, environmental degradation, political persecution and conflict in areas of origin, and labour demand and better opportunities in destination countries. In line with this, migration from Amhara region has been fuelled mainly by socio-economic and political factors. Unemployment, underemployment, inflation and poverty, coupled with a lack of affordable housing, poor infrastructure provision, mal-administration and lack of good governance, are among the various push factors that drive individuals into migration. Drought and soil degradation are also among drivers of migration from the region.[12]

In an agrarian economy, Kosec and colleagues argue, 'land is a unique form of wealth, and thus its impacts on physical and occupa-tional mobility are different than those of other forms of wealth'.[13] And thus, because of the acute land demand in the country and in the region in particular, scarcity of farmland, youth landlessness, fragmented landholding, land degradation and decreasing agricultural yields, land insecurities, and environmental and climate change such as drought and famine are among the major driving factors for seasonal migration out of the region. A GIZ report in 2018 indicated that about 80,000 people from Amhara region cross the border every year to work on farmlands in Sudan. Because of the high labour demand in Sudan, seasonal labour migration has become common and 'a stable livelihood basis both to Ethiopian families and to the sustainability of farming and agricultural production in Sudan'.[14] Men from the north-western part of the region are involved in this seasonal labour migration to work on farmlands in the Gadarif State of Sudan.

Amhara region is highly dependent on rain-fed agriculture and 85% of the population is engaged in agriculture. In 2012, the Ministry of Finance and Economic Development (MoFED) reported that 42.5% of the population was facing a food shortage and unable to meet their food requirements. Therefore, men leave their area in search of open spaces or work on others' farms. In addition, youth landlessness coupled with few rural employment opportunities outside agriculture is considered a primary motivation to migrate.

To overcome these economic challenges, people look for other livelihood options to diversify household income. Migration is regarded as a practical option and an effective strategy to support oneself and one's family. Remittances supplement household incomes and are considered a way out of poverty.

Political insecurity and persecution drive many away from the region and the country. According to the RMMS, the arrest, detention and killing of those opposing the ruling EPRDF regime since 2005 have resulted in political migration from the country.[15]

Many argue that a 'culture of migration' has developed in parts of the region, where the youth, mainly girls, are expected to provide for families by sending remittances and to establish a social status for the household.[16] There are, in fact, more than 180,000 Ethiopians working in the Middle East, the majority of whom are women.[17] Young women who fail to pursue their education beyond primary or secondary school have limited livelihood options except migration whereby they can earn income for their families by sending remittances.[18]

Enticements from smugglers and traffickers, peer pressure, and access to information through social media were among the factors involved in making decisions to migrate in this study. Social networks and the flow of information through social media counter the assumption that 'migrants make an uninformed decision' to migrate.

A number of pull factors are also at play, including the wage differential between Ethiopia and destination countries and the demand for labour, mainly for domestic workers in the Middle East and Sudan. For all these reasons and others, the young population of the region feels it has few options other than to migrate.

Gete Zeleke and colleagues reported that among young men in Ethiopia, those in Amhara region were the most likely to migrate because so many are landless and in search of wage employment.[19] However, following the national trend, women account for the majority of migrants from the region. According to Asnake and Zerihun, 93.62% of migrants from the region in the year 2012/13 were female.[20] In particular, female migrants dominate the eastern route to fill the demand for housemaids in Middle East countries; 95% of Ethiopian migrants in the Middle East come from rural parts of the country and are predominantly young single women.[21]

Many scholars report abuses and exploitation of migrants.[22] This occurs across all routes from departure to destination and takes place mainly on account of the irregular nature of the migration. Overcrowding, starvation, suffocation, beating, murder, drowning, verbal abuse, theft, sexual assault, and rape are common occurrences en route. Some abuse continues in host communities, particularly confinement and isolation, deprivation of sleep, heavy workloads, denying payment, confiscation of passports, sexual and verbal abuse, and physical violence. Regardless of such abuse and exposure to risks, large numbers of migrants continue to leave the country, both regularly and irregularly. It is therefore clear that the potential benefits of migration to these individuals and their families outweigh the risks. The risks, while known, are avoided or mitigated by the performance of rituals. The next section thus focuses on how the migration experience is mediated by rituals, and offers the perspective of potential migrants, migrants, and deportees and returnees.

Rituals of migration

Migration, though an age-old phenomenon, remains a new experience for those involved. When moving to a different cultural environment, migrants reflect and act upon their new situation. In this process, migration creates social, economic, cultural and religious differences between migrants and their communities. These differences, inflected by generation, destination, number of years of working abroad, and line of work, are then negotiated and dealt with through the practice of rituals.

The migration experience itself can be viewed as a ritual. As Aguilar noted,

For the individual migrant, leaving the country for the first time to work overseas is irreducible to sheer routine. The alignments of feelings may be predictable, but for each migrant the sensations are fresh. Beyond its established routines and practices, international labour migration can be viewed from the individual worker's perspective as partaking of a ritual character.[23]

As yet, scholars have failed to clearly define the concept of rituals and the subject area of ritual remains contested. For this chapter, I use the definition of ritual given by Ronald L. Grimes as 'a style of action, one that is formal, stylised, prescribed, symbolic, non-technological, repetitive, traditional and so on', at the same time acknowledging its different natures and uses.[24] The discussion within this chapter recognises the existence of rituals within migration for therapeutic purposes, conflict resolution, effecting social change,[25] and rites of transition.[26] Rather than focusing on the performative nature of rituals, this study deals with the social function and cultural context of the ritualised process of migration.

As Roy Rappaport argues, rituals make society possible by creating what is moral and acceptable and by setting out responsibilities and establishing norms. Rituals, according to Duntley, 'may be used intentionally and unwittingly to embarrass, destroy, or disturb as well as to unify, satisfy and heal' and can be further categorised as mythic (enacting the ideal) and parabolic (addressing and resolving problems or contradictions).[27]

The nature of these rituals varies according to the religious standing and socio-economic status of the individual migrant and the family. Even when they share the same beliefs, the rituals among migrants from Amhara region might differ according to their circumstances. However, there is a common feature that can be traced in all observed cases, which is the ritualisation of migration as a transition and as a reflection of the ultimate value of communities.

Eisenburch uses the term 'cultural bereavement' for situations where 'the loss of one's social structure and culture can cause a grief reaction'.[28] When uprooted and put in an unfamiliar environment, migrants experience grief and other emotions which make it difficult to get on with daily life.[29] Rituals are thus elemental in negotiating one's belonging to a community and reassuring one of a connection to home. As Bell proposes, ritual should be rethought as practice or as 'a strategic mode of action effective within certain social orders'.[30]

Another feature in this ritualisation of migration is the centrality of gender. Many have argued that migration is gendered in one way or other,[31] and so is the ritualised process within it. When we look at the practices detailed in the coming subsections, female migrants are more prescribed in their performance of rituals than male migrants. Their visibility, as well as societal expectation, puts pressure on women to abide by established socio-cultural and economic practices. As Piper puts it, 'migration is not only a spatial relocation, but a far-reaching gendered experience', and this includes ritual as well.[32]

Migration from Ethiopia is still an area to be researched in terms of the explicative economic, socio-cultural and political dynamics of the country in general and of Amhara region in particular. The mass out-flow of migrants from the region can be accounted for by a combination of factors including economic, environmental, political and social. Economic migration to the Middle East and Sudan in its current high numbers is relatively recent in many parts of the region. Previously, when the basic needs of a household could not be met, family members would move from one part of the country to another. Now, with increasing demographic pressure, landlessness and competition for scarce resources, there is a need for other livelihood sources. Labour demand in destination countries has meant that migration has become not only an option but a *sine qua non* for individuals competing for survival or to sustain themselves and their families.

Migrants from the same region have different socio-cultural, religious, political and professional profiles. But migration gives them something in common, the status of migrant. With this status, migrants enter into a different social, economic and political environment that ushers in different relationships. The socio-cultural and economic change that a migrant brings back on his or her return has an effect on the community, whether disruptive or constructive. The change is thus welcomed, accommodated, denied or soothed through what I would like to refer to as rituals performed mainly by migrants at various stages, including prior to migration.

A question then comes to mind as to how these practices are considered as rituals of migration. Rituals can be characterised from different perspectives. A common distinguishing feature of a ritual is, however, its repetitive, routinised, habitual practice, which reiterates a system of meaning. The rituals discussed here have similar features in the way they are performed repetitively among migrants and are acted out to restore, reinforce or redirect personal, social or religious identity.

Culture of migration fuelling rituals

In the study areas, migration has become a norm or a 'culture'. In each of the fieldwork areas, migration is part of the popular culture, integrated within the social structure of the communities in one way or another. As I have argued elsewhere, 'the social norm and context embellish the concept of migration and movement of people across international borders' for different reasons.[33] For Muslims living in the study areas, migration to the Middle East, particularly Saudi Arabia, is seen as a religious pilgrimage regardless of the fact that many migrants do not go to Mecca. For others, migration to the Middle East is seen as a family tradition or a norm in their neighbourhood. The easy flow of information, the existence of social networks among migrants, and their links with their place of origin encourage and motivate potential migrants to leave the country, building up over time a chain of migrants from certain places.

As the study by RMMS noted, 'where a culture of migration has developed, the pressure to migrate is intensified irrespective of the risks'.[34] School-aged young people are under social and peer pressure to migrate, mainly to the Middle East, for social and economic gain. Parents encourage and push their daughters to migrate and generate income for the household. Such pressure from family, friends, peers or other community members is also related to the notion of success and failure. Success, in most areas, can be defined as having an iron sheet roof and fully furnished house, private cars, trucks or shops. Social status and respect are also accorded to families and households with members working abroad.

Nonetheless, when embarking on a journey, there is always a calculated risk and, as Aguilar calls it, 'cross-border gambling'.[35] There is a saying that 'you are meant to go through your experience', whether good or bad. If the gamble works, the migrant returns with money and gifts for family, relatives, friends and neighbours. If not, coming home empty-handed or getting deported (locally known as *meterez*) is considered a failure, a situation that further pushes the migrant to try his or her luck once again. Staying at home means relinquishing one's newly acquired position or status within the family as the main income-earner. Some have reported being verbally abused by family members for their failure. Even though they are not expressed formally, social exclusion and disappointment on the part of family members have a damaging effect on returnees who do not live up to expectations. To avoid this, migrants put up with hardships in destination countries and transit points or stay at the border, such as in Metema, to earn money to send back home. The ritual of *hijaza*, among others, can relieve the stress and suffering of migrants. *Hijaza* is a weekly or monthly day off for domestic workers. The term can refer to their day off or to the house in which they spend this day. Many migrants who get a day off, in both the Middle East and Sudan, rent houses where they can get together and share their experiences, support each other, go out on dates, or spend time with spouses.

The culture of migration is built not only on economic success but also on factors such as freedom of choice. Young people's need for independence and their agency in deciding for themselves have driven the culture of migration in the research areas. Among adolescents, the decision to migrate is seen as the first step in making their own decisions. Going through the migration experience makes them no longer an adolescent but an adult with the independence they seek. Migration is thus seen as a transition for adolescents into womanhood and manhood with personal, economic and cultural autonomy, and in this way it becomes a rite of passage.

Rites of passage

Almost every culture in the world has rites of passage.

> During rites of passage, participants attempt to ritually move from one stage of life to another through a culturally-specific framework of actions and stages ... Regardless of the specific stages of the ritual or the level of stress placed on initiates, rites of passage are intended to transform the subject of the ritual.[36]

Arnold van Gennep's notion of rituals as rites of passage has often been used in relation to birth, puberty, marriage and death, all occasions which mark transitions.[37] As another transition, migration should be considered as a rite of passage. For some, this transition and the rituals that are performed can be seen as celebrating a new status or reclaiming a previous status. As Pedersen and Rytter note, 'rituals of migration are not only concerned with "being and belonging" but also with "becoming"'.[38] Victor Turner further explained rites of passage as a space where individuals undergo a transformation of the self.[39]

Van Gennep distinguished three stages in this process: separation, transition and incorporation. In relation to migration as a rite of passage, the separation stage commences with the departure of a migrant to the host country. The transition or liminal phase is the experience of the migrant in the host country, the experience of temporary freedom from previous social relations and networks. The incorporation stage is the migrant's return home. In this final stage, the migrant rejoins the community as a new individual with the status of returnee, now presumed to be a mature and wealthy individual. The status of 'returnee', accorded to all migrants upon their return, is given on the assumption that the individual has gone through an experience that is different from those of the rest of the community. This experience, positive or negative, with or without the intended outcome, is seen as having transformed the individual into a new person, culturally, socially, economically, psychologically and physically. From what is observed, migrants exhibit one or more of these transformations. Though the status of returnee is mainly associated with positive outcomes (economic gain and better status within the community), the transformation does not exclude those who have failed to become 'successful'. Interaction with foreign cultures and people in itself is considered to have an impact on an individual's life.

Young people use migration as a path that gives them agency to make their own decisions. It is a ritual, a journey that provides a space, especially for girls, where they have the freedom and agency to make decisions free from societal and family expectations and pressure. In some cases, girls use migration to escape forced or early marriage. On their return, girls are given a new status as part of the migrant category, in which they are financially independent and have the autonomy to make their own life choices. One such area about which migrant girls become self-determinant is marriage.

Marriage is redefined with migration in the picture. There are, however, two sides to this. Female returnees who have their own savings and property are seen as more desirable. At the same time, returnees from the Middle East are deemed 'non-virtuous', and it is believed they were sexually exploited by their employers and thus not suitable for marriage. Thus, migrants are considered marriageable for their money but at the same time are cast aside for their supposed 'impurity'. 'Whoever gets involved with them is after their money or they were in a relationship before their departure', says a male migrant from Qobbo town.

Sexual abuse of migrants is common and is acknowledged in the community. With this information, to avoid the risk of unwanted pregnancy, female migrants take a long-term contraceptive (the Depo-Provera injection) before departure. Though migrants are aware of the existence of sexual abuse and violence en route or by employers, the benefits of migration are seen to outweigh the risk and so rituals are performed to protect them from further risks such as pregnancy. In some places, such as Hara, potential migrants are married so as to undergo what is called the 'ritual loss of virginity' before leaving the country.[40] Aware that migrants can experience sexual violence, the community prefers girls to lose their virginity in what is seen as a more dignified and less traumatic manner. Through this, the family, as well as the girl, can maintain the 'honour' that might otherwise be lost during their time in the Middle East.

Another reputation these girls lose after migration is their religious purity and piousness. Working for long periods in Islamic countries or those dominated by Muslims, Christian female migrant workers are presumed to have been 'polluted' and thus, before their reintegration into the community, are obliged to undergo religious cleansing.

Religious cleansing

Religious rituals of cleansing and converting are rituals performed by migrants. Conversion to Islam or pretending to convert is a common phenomenon among Christian female migrants travelling to the Middle

East and Sudan. This is believed to help secure better job opportunities in destination countries and create positive relationships with employers. Moreover, it is common in destination countries for Christian migrants to adopt Muslim names. This form of religious assimilation is a way of keeping migrants safe from physical and psychological abuse.

Though migrants have to 'look like Muslims' if not converted, they preserve their religious traditions when situations permit. Though they take off their cross pendants to conceal their religious affiliation, migrants keep religious ornaments with them, such as crosses and prayer books, holy water [*tsebel*] and *emnet*. They are also reported to maintain a strong religious identity in their private lives, by keeping strict daily prayer and fasting schedules.

In major cities in the Middle East and Sudan, migrants are free to exercise their religion; restrictions are observed more in rural places. Orthodox churches in destination countries provide migrants with religious services. They also serve as a place where social networks can be established and as a bridge for migrants to maintain their relationship with their country and religion.

Regardless of this religious observance, upon their return, to keep their Christian identity, migrants pass through a cleaning ceremony involving the use of holy water—this is called locally *qeder*. This ritual is necessary for migrants to participate in church services. This form of baptism is a requirement of the church for those who have 'polluted' their 'sacred' bodies whether by failing to fast or by consuming meat slaughtered by Muslims.

Muslim migrants face fewer problems associated with destination communities. However, even these migrants have to acquaint themselves with some Islamic traditions not practised in Ethiopia. For some Muslim migrants, migration is not only seen as an economic venture but also a religious pilgrimage. Travelling to Saudi Arabia for work is considered to be a religious journey, similar to the *hajj* and *umrah* to the sacred land of Mecca and Medina. The *hajj* and *umrah* have in fact been used as a means to get visa access to Saudi Arabia, both by Muslim and Christian migrants.

Another example of religious ritual within the migration experience is the practice of *wadaja*,[41] widespread in North and South Wollo Zone. Specialists are called upon to perform *wadaja* for migration, to influence the course of events so that people will become more prosperous or more successful.[42] Accordingly, *wadaja* is carried out for a person migrating to the Middle East for a better future. This religious practice is mostly performed during rites of passage such as births, weddings and funerals. In this context, the religious performance marks the rite of passage of an individual to migrant status.

Formal rituals

So far, this chapter has looked at social rituals and practices performed in relation to migration to the Middle East and Sudan. In this section, I discuss formal rituals that migrants undergo when travelling legally for overseas employment.

In October 2013, following the rise in abuse of Ethiopian migrant workers (a source of concern to critics of irregular migration and the Ethiopian government), overseas employment to the Middle East was banned. Following the ban, to strengthen the mechanism for monitoring and regulating domestic and overseas employment services, the Employment Exchange Services Proclamation (no. 632/2009) was revised by the Overseas Employment Proclamation (923/2016). Aimed at regulating irregular migration and providing protection to migrants, the new proclamation demanded bilateral agreements between Ethiopia and receiving countries. Private Employment Agencies (PEAs) meeting the requirements were given licences to operate under the revised overseas employment policy. The proclamation holds these PEAs and employers accountable for the welfare of employees and requires payment of a bond for a licence. The PEAs are also expected to have a representative consular office in the destination country, able to provide temporary food and shelter to migrants upon their arrival. The PEAs are responsible for following up contracts, making sure overseas employees are paid wages, and ensuring the safety of migrants.

The new proclamation sets a minimum education level for migrants of Grade 8. Migrants are also expected to present evidence of occupational competence to qualify for overseas employment. Before migration, potential migrants are expected to undergo pre-departure and pre-employment training at technical and vocational education and training institutions (TVETs) and take a competency exam. This training provides knowledge of housekeeping, food preparation, child care and an introduction to the Arabic language. After one to two months of training and after taking the Certificate of Competency exam, migrants are then expected to register with licensed PEAs and proceed with their travel to countries that have signed a bilateral labour agreement with Ethiopia; to date these are Jordan, Qatar and Saudi Arabia. Labour contracts are then signed with the understanding and agreement of both parties. After the recommencement of labour migration to the Middle East in 2018, a number of PEAs registered to send migrants to the Middle East legally through this process.

Migrants travelling to Saudi Arabia through the *hajj* and *umrah* also used to go through a ritual of training and examination. Migrants from the research area, in particular from Woldiya and Qobbo, mentioned getting at least three months' religious teaching either from sheikhs or Islamic *madrasa* schools about the fundamentals of Islamic religion and religious practices such as *salat* (Islamic prayer). When the training was completed, potential migrants were interviewed by the Ethiopian Islamic Affairs Council and given certification as being Muslim, which then gave them the right to make the religious pilgrimage of *hajj* and *umrah*. Many, regardless of their religious affiliation, have exploited this process to travel to Saudi Arabia for work.

Concluding remarks

Pedersen and Rytter note that although rituals are imperative in migrants' experience, researchers so far have overlooked the overall ritualised process of migration.[13] From the discussion above, we can see the importance of rituals in giving migrants the ability to establish themselves in their places of destination, cope with unfamiliar or difficult situations, and help them define their place at the destination and in their location of origin. Performing such rituals helps migrants navigate through the local environment by holding onto their own identity and maintaining a link to their home town.

For migrants, survival is the leitmotif that drives them every day. The rituals they perform are essential for an understanding of their daily lives en route, at the destination and at their place of origin.

Performed at different stages of migration, from departure to return, these rituals involve not only repetitive norms and practices deeply entrenched within society but also strategies to help migrants adapt to changes and respond to risks. Prior to initiating the migration process, potential migrants have preconceived ideas about what to expect on the journey and the experience to be faced in the destination country. Precautions, which can also described as rituals, include (for women) taking a contraceptive injection before departure and early marriage to alleviate the psychological effect of possible sexual abuse and to protect the honour of the family and the girl. Cleansing oneself in church and performing religious rituals for a safe journey and some luck at the destination are also common among migrants. The ritual of cleansing oneself, mainly among Christians and particularly women, continues until a migrant returns to Ethiopia. En route and at the destination, migrants are positioned at the bottom of the social hierarchy, with few rights and usually living in abject poverty, making them particularly vulnerable to violence and physical and sexual exploitation. They are far removed from their place of origin and thus left to deal with any abuse or risk they face alone. In some cases, especially en route, they cannot satisfy their basic needs for food and water. In such situations and many others that put them at risk, migrants develop coping mechanisms to protect themselves.

By looking into these migration rituals, this chapter makes the case for analysing the agency of migrants at different stages of migration. The rituals performed transfer decision-making power, and thus agency, to migrants either at their place of origin or at the destination. In the meantime, the rituals mitigate the risks and accommodate changes experienced in foreign lands.

In a region where youth migration has become commonplace, it is important to give migrants agency to define their experiences. Rather than focusing on push–pull factors and the victimisation of migrants, this chapter has examined how migrants manage and attempt to define the outcomes of migration, both negative and positive, by engaging in rituals. I would like to conclude by suggesting that there is a need to look further into migration through the prism of ritual because of the detailed insight it gives into how migrants go about their daily lives, which is essential for any programme or intervention aimed at them.

7

IRREGULAR MIGRATION AMONG
A KAMBATA COMMUNITY IN ETHIOPIA

VIEWS FROM BELOW AND THEIR IMPLICATIONS

Mulugeta Gashaw Debalke

Introduction

A single, unified theory of migration or international migration does
not exist; rather, there are groups of theories propounded by different
scholars.[1] Many rightly agree that because of the inadequacies of individual theories, a better understanding and explanation of the phenomenon requires 'an integrated approach' or 'a complex theory' to grasp
the complex, multivalent, multi-perspective and multi-level nature of
the phenomenon.[2] Hence, such an integrated theoretical approach is
more appropriate to better study irregular migration as a variant of
international migration. Accordingly, to address this complexity, a
number of theoretical strands inform this chapter, based on empirical
data drawn from one community.

The different theories put forward thus far have important aspects relevant to understanding the complexity of irregular migration. However, most of them also have a common aspect, which is reliance on the perspective of 'Western' elites and 'Western' scientific knowledge, while disregarding local elites and traditional knowledge or ethnoscience. Critical migration theorists have challenged this epistemological hegemony with some effect but still have to open a new path to bring on board 'the views from below'. This kind of understanding generally serves as a loose theoretical frame of reference in this study. The chapter may serve as an additional case study to expose the limitations of the standard approach. It also provides new details revealing the increasing agency of individuals, their families, and networks in the process of irregular migration whereas the place individuals hold in the socio-economic structures of their communities and networks within and outside the country plays its own role.

The central argument of this chapter is that official narratives of irregular migration emanating from receiving countries and largely echoed by sending countries, though useful in some respects, miss out a number of insights, experiences and outcomes. The data for this study is drawn from a Kambata community in Aze Debo *kebele*, Qedida Gamela *woreda* of Kambata and Tambaro Zone in southern Ethiopia. Located 359 kilometres south-west of the Ethiopian capital, Addis Ababa, Aze Debo is situated four kilometres from the zonal seat, Durame. The zone constitutes one of the most densely populated areas in the country, where, historically, labour outmigration to different parts of the country has been a longstanding reaction to land scarcity.

Aze Debo's economy is based on mixed-crop and livestock agriculture, focusing on coffee and the drought resistant crop, *enset*, but also including cereals, pulses, fruits and vegetables. Livestock kept include cattle, sheep, goats, chicken and, to some extent, horses and donkeys. The use of cross-bred dairy cows has boomed recently, with about 80% of households owning at least one cross-bred cow.[3] Farming is rain-fed and affected by drought. A few small streams and shallow groundwater make irrigation possible, though this is being done without major government support. The economy of households is also increasing through the cultivation of eucalyptus trees and some surviving indigenous trees and non-farm activities such as petty trading in grains and livestock and shopkeeping. Remittances from migrant family members have also become a significant part of the income of a growing number of households, poor and rich. Aze Debo *kebele* is among the chronically food-insecure communities in the country targeted for the receipt of government aid, even though the number of households seeking assistance has been decreasing over the last five years.[4]

Aze Debo *kebele*, and Kambata and Tambaro Zone in general, are areas where rural–urban labour migration and irregular migration, particularly to the Republic of South Africa, have been common for decades, making Aze Debo an ideal location for this research. The other reason for choosing this area is the social contacts developed during work on the WIDE Ethiopia project (see Introduction) for several years until this research was begun in March 2018. The study was mainly synchronic, focusing on local perspectives on the causes, consequences and experiences of irregular migration of young men (to South Africa and Sudan) and young women (to Sudan and, to a limited degree, the Gulf States). Data was generated by conducting in-depth interviews with 33 respondents—returnees, migrants' families, would-be migrants, non-migrants, and local government officials. As much as possible, I withheld personal judgements and my epistemological inclination is towards what is local, vulnerable and less powerful, owing to my training in anthropology.

The dominant global, governmental and media portrayal of irregular migration renders it a practice of the subaltern and the underworld in response to proverbial push factors related to safety and security concerns as well as economic and social burdens.[5] Moreover, the dominant public opinion in destination countries is that illegal migrants are a threat. Sending countries treat migrants with a similar negative attitude and assumption of criminality. In both cases, there is 'a grave lack of knowledge about their motivations, aspirations and about the journeys and process'.[6] In the face of this, there is an emerging critical perspective, a new outlook investigating the complex and nuanced personal, familial, social, economic and cultural dimensions of irregular migration and the contexts in which it takes place.[7] Similarly, this chapter aims to unravel some of the detailed and dynamic 'realities' of irregular migration from the perspective of the returnees, their families, would-be migrants and the community. This perspective is mindful of the fact that the official, receiving-country-dominated discourse, adopted by sending countries, has overlooked views from below.

It is necessary to consider the interplay of the multiple factors influencing migration rather than a simplistic framework of causes and consequences of migration to get a full picture of the complexity. In so doing, the chapter also argues that the exclusionary and top-down standard official discourse needs readjustment based on local experiences and views.

In the composite theoretical approach adopted in this writing, economy is just part of the complex of causes and outcomes of international migration. People's philosophy and life objectives, mediated by factual and symbolic processes and interpretations, do matter in the causation and outcomes of irregular migration. Investigating migrants' 'lived experiences, their interpretations and subjective experiences and their social and structural context, [which] necessitate[es] theoretically informed empirical studies', is at the centre of the methodological and theoretical stance of this study.[8] The theoretical framework behind this chapter is also informed by some theoretical stands from dual labour market theory, which segments the market into formal (primary, high-skilled, capital-intensive) and informal (secondary, low-skilled, labour-intensive) sectors, and the new economics of labour migration focusing on remittances, the positive difference remittances bring to the position of a household relative to those in the larger society, and the sense of relative deprivation this creates in households whose members have not migrated.[9]

The chapter has five sections. The next section explains why young people migrate and why irregular migration is sustained. The third focuses on the consequences of irregular migration. The fourth sets out the experiences and local interpretations. The last concludes the chapter.

Drivers of migration: Poverty, obligations, status, networks and history

Poverty pervades the literature as a major driving force of irregular migration.[10] Likewise, the data from Aze Debo reveals that many young people from poor families have irregularly migrated, seeking jobs and better life opportunities, fleeing economic hardships, unemployment or underemployment. Landlessness and lack of farming opportunities, limited opportunities for employment in government and the private sector or for self-employment force many youth (including those who have completed school grades and college or university graduates) to live in poverty or with an extended dependence on their parents. All these reasons come together in the phrase 'to change my family and to change myself', the most common answer to the question why young people go abroad seeking employment. There are also many cases of young people from rich and middle-income families migrating to seek employment or better employment abroad. A young woman returnee from Kuwait said, 'My advice is for people to go and work where there is a job, whether in or out of the country.' She added that 'then young people would not have to ask their parents for money to replace their worn-out shoes'.

Even though it is difficult to state a minimum monetary threshold that is considered acceptable, the youth principally seek opportunities that can earn them 'substantial' amounts of money in a relatively short time. The aim is not only to allow them to support their family, but also to build a house or houses, own modern assets such as cars, save, invest, and live a good-quality life. Many successful migrants regularly remit money (see chapter 9), letting their families lead a comfortable life by local standards.

The need to be wealthier, not merely to survive or help the family, is at the heart of migration from middle-income and rich families. The life aspirations of youth brought up in such families cannot be fulfilled by most local opportunities. For example, a young woman who returned from Sudan stated that she could not understand how one could live on 50–60 birr (US$1.80–$2.10 at the time when the data was collected) per day, the average salary at a local coffee-processing plant. Although many aspire to this income, she was contemplating going back to Sudan. Self-employment, through which one can earn a higher income, was also viewed as problematic, in view of such deterrents as the formalisation requirements and the costs of business registration, licensing and 'very high' taxation.[11] A young female returnee from Kuwait stressed that these challenges meant that she had to shut down her shop in Durame after six months, increasing the likelihood that she would remigrate.

Poverty and unemployment as factors that encourage irregular migration are also better understood in relation to education. Those who complete school grades, as well as college and university graduates, find it difficult to get jobs, let alone decent jobs.[12] This has created disillusionment among parents and young people about the value of education as the gateway to employment, economic success and social status. As a result, many youth have dropped out of school and migrated, even though many wished to complete primary school (Grade 8). Many expressed pity for high-school and tertiary-level graduates who had no job and were forced to sit idle in their villages, further burdening their families. An example of this is the case of one returnee from South Africa. Before leaving for South Africa, he graduated from a four-year programme at a government health college and was working in a nearby district town for a private health facility. His salary was not enough to support himself, let alone his parents.

The case of a migrant living in Addis Ababa is also illustrative. It is three years since he left for Addis Ababa. With a diploma in pharmacy, he is upgrading to a degree while working for a national NGO. Getting a degree and paying for his education meant that he was not able to assist his family until he finished. Despite this, his family survives thanks to regular remittances from two sons working in South Africa. Another man who has a son working in South Africa lamented, 'I educated my child to become a doctor, a director and nothing else when I raised him hoeing the land.' He added, 'I sent them to school to live a life better than mine; but he was not successful.' This disillusionment about the utility of education is not only because many young people have difficulty getting jobs but also because the jobs do not pay enough for the employee to support himself or herself, let alone the parents, and become financially independent to establish a family and transition into adulthood (see chapter 4).

According to many respondents, the parent–child bond is very strong in the community and Kambata children have a deep sense of obligation to help their families and improve their economic position. This bond and obligation to family have to do with the extent of 'deep poverty', in the words of some informants, that was experienced while growing up. Hence, extricating one's family from poverty or assisting them in any way is a prime objective of the youth. Findings show that this family commitment runs in both ways. Parents, even those who do not have savings, go to great lengths, by selling productive assets, including their most prized land, to finance a child's migration. Failing to do so would create a sense of disgrace or humiliation. This subtle moral obligation for parents turns into a necessity in the face of other parents fulfilling it. In turn, when working abroad, the youth will remit money to repay the loan and reclaim property that has been mort-gaged. Both young women working in Sudan and Gulf Arab states and men working in South Africa (and a few young women joining them as wives) regularly remit to their parents and families even before having accumulated enough for themselves. In many cases this decreases after the young person is married in the destination country. Migrants not supporting their families are equally a disgrace for all. Therefore, affec-tion, social approval and disapproval interact and push young people towards irregular migration.

This two-way obligation creates in both youth and parents a sense of competition, albeit a positive one. Accordingly, the youth compete, not only to migrate, but also to make good fortunes to fulfil their com-mitments. This tallies with the findings of another study made in Gondar and Kambata and Tambaro about young people migrating to Europe and South Africa.[13] The expression used by would-be migrants goes something like this: 'If someone in the neighbourhood or some-one I know of has gone elsewhere and has succeeded, then why not me?' Similarly, for families, there is the feeling, 'Why not our child; why not my sister or brother?' It is this intrinsic desire that induces many youth, their parents and close relatives to decide in favour of migrating and paying fees, which have gone up from about 5,000 birr (about $185) in the late 1990s to 150,000 birr (about $5,555) in 2018 per migrant. Poverty, the desire for economic prosperity and a better life, coupled with affection and moral obligation, are powerful drivers to migrate.

Not many local households can raise the required amount of money to finance the outmigration of an individual. Among the issues that need to be noted here is that most migrants are sponsored through a loan arrangement with a prior migrant from the (extended) family who is successfully working abroad. The migrants will pay the loan back, by working for an agreed time period just for food and residence (see chapter 8). Second, there are 'rich' families who are able to afford to finance one of their members. In one case, a father put all the 120,000 birr (about $4,444) he received in compensation for some land he lost to an expanding highway towards one of his children's migration project. Third, such high figures as we have cited are regarded by many, if not most, young people as too small to furnish the capital to establish a profitable venture in Ethiopia.

Young women describe having specific, more subtle, culturally defined or imposed demands, like wearing new or fashionable clothes, shoes, ornaments and hairstyles, to present themselves in an elegant way, all of which need finance. A female respondent remarked, 'This is part of the challenge of being a woman.' These demands are further illustrated by the experience of a female returnee, who had been to Sudan and Beirut. She reported that as there was nobody around to help her financially, she was in difficulty and did not know what to do while attending a three-year TVET training course. She discontinued her training after one year. She recalled, 'I did not have clothes; I did not have shoes. I was wearing worn-out clothes. I was confused about what I could do; my parents were poor and my father was sick and blind.' She added, 'Unlike me, my classmates were well dressed and that used to trouble me.' She left for Sudan against the advice of her father, who insisted she should finish her training. After she threatened to leave them, her father eventually yielded and financed her travel by mortgaging some of their farmland for 3,000 birr (about $110) and selling a bull he had helped rear for an additional 1,250 birr (about $46). The broker in a nearby *woreda*, who demanded 4,000 birr (about $150), was willing to take 3,000 birr (about $110) on condition that she would pay the balance from Sudan, which she did. At the time I interviewed her in March 2018, she was a happy, thriving, single young woman. She was living with her parents, running a small shop in a room in her parents' compound, a big villa she had constructed for them with a 70,000 birr (about $2,590) remittance she had made in Beirut, to which she travelled after working in Sudan. She was not intending to go back even though her employers were expecting her.

There is also much networking and social learning that takes place in the course of the migration process. International phone calls, made possible by mobile phones, the exchange of images and messages through social media, the positive impacts of remittances, the changed (and envied) styles of returnees and migrants coming back for visits, are all socially important labour migration outcomes, adding momentum to migration dynamics. Social approval of irregular migration by parents and community members reinforces this learning, turning irregular migration into a necessity that is at odds with the government position, which discourages it. These aspects may be seen as part of what Flahaux and De Haas have called increased 'capabilities and aspirations to migrate', which are 'driven by (ongoing) processes of development and social transformation': this negates the conventional interpretation of African migration as inspired by poverty,[14] a driver which is also underlined by the United Nations Economic Commission for Africa.[15] The phenomenon of young women migrating in large numbers within and outside the country can also be understood in this developmental sense, the result of 'the will to change', and it stands in contrast to their static or subservient status some three decades before, as described by elderly informants.[16]

For both men and women, direct peer pressures or social stimuli come from close and distant relatives and friends. Social support, given by successful migrants in South Africa to poor community members and orphans back home, sets them up as heroes, earning them envied fame and respect, which are even extended to their parents. In this way, both returnees and migrants set an example for young people to migrate, whether they are from poor or rich families. They do this through family and community remittances, investment, and improving the living standards of the neediest. As a result, they render international migration a sought-after livelihood path among the options young people can consider not only to escape poverty and successfully transition to adulthood but also to acquire their fortunes, and seek fame and status in their communities and beyond.

Returnees are also spurred on to further migration, partly as a result of their status back in the community, be it through successful investment and a better life back in Aze Debo, or because of difficulties in getting a job, working productively and reintegrating. The case of a young female returnee from Sudan is illustrative. She went to Sudan in 2013 and came back in 2018. At the time of this study, she was living with the family of her younger brother, as both of her parents had died.

After her return, she did not earn any income and, even though she had not been back long, she had a negative attitude about the possibility of making a living here. She used the money she earned in Sudan to build a small house and bought a local breed of cow for 5,700 birr (about $210) from relatives. Although she intended to give the milk to her brother's children rather than sell it and other products, the cow was not pregnant as expected. On top of this, she had to abandon her plan to open a shop. She was supporting the basic needs of her brother's family, who could not make ends meet from farming the less than a quarter of a hectare of land they owned. Thus, she was contemplating remigrating, and her friends were encouraging her, although she had run out of savings to finance her journey. She stated, 'When my friends ask me to go back to Sudan, I tell them not to come back to Ethiopia', adding that in the future, 'if it is the will of God, I will go back'. This supports the evidence that shows that poverty, apart from being a driver of irregular migration, can also serve as a deterrent for young people with poor networks and poor relatives to finance their migration, adding to the complexity of the phenomena of migration.

For the Kambata, social networks have turned into innovative and instrumental platforms, serving as social capital for undocumented travellers and immigrants, both in Aze Debo and in destination countries.[17] For irregular migrants, these networks provide reliable information, facilitate hosting, and organise parties to initiate and mobilise funding for migration expenses. As already outlined, there were instances of travel payments as high as 120,000–150,000 birr (about $4,444–$$5,555) and possibly more for a single direct flight to South Africa. Once there, the new immigrants work for their financiers just for food and lodgings for one year to pay them back.[18] According to a 16-year-old would-be migrant, who had been promised by his uncle working in South Africa to cover his expenses of 160,000 birr (about $5,925), the migration expense is not considered high: that amount would only be enough to open a shop commonly found everywhere, and it would not likely lead to moving up the ladder of wealth. This is a common attitude of Aze Debo's youth, and is likely to affect youth entrepreneurship and job creation programmes in the future. Getting loans and raising support from families, relatives and friends are not as easy when starting a self-employment initiative, as there is some reluctance to contribute, suggesting that compared with irregularly migrating out of the country, local entrepreneurship in its current shape carries less value.[19] All these drivers seem to have resulted in what has been termed 'the culture of migration', creating yet another collective driver, which further sustains this form of mobility.[20]

The beginning of modern education in Kambata, started towards the end of the 1940s by Western missionaries, was an important historical driver of movement out of the community. According to the elders interviewed for this chapter, at that time some men and a few women left the area for the capital, Addis Ababa, and other big towns for higher education and employment after graduation. Following this, other historical events opened the way for uneducated and less educated people in Kambata to move out for work and relocate to other places. Most important was the establishment of the Wonji, Shoa and Metehara sugar factories in the early 1950s, 1960s and 1970s, respectively. Many people, mostly young men but also some young women, left for work in these places and were able to attract relatives and friends in the process. The positive outcomes for the early migrants served as a stimulus for others to follow suit. Later, the expansion of commercial and state farms in the Rift Valley opened up more opportunities for the less skilled or uneducated to go out and engage as farm labourers for payment in cash. Hence, by the time migration to South Africa and then to the Gulf States emerged as a livelihood option, the practice had already taken roots as a cultural form among the Kambata. Even though some young respondents mentioned that at the beginning there was fear about AIDS in migrating to South Africa and talk of a less restrained culture of sexual relationships, this was not strong enough to deter them from going, and migration has escalated over time.

Migration outcomes: Remittances, investment, social remittances and risks

Economic impacts are the most conspicuous outcomes of irregular migration. Remittances are made to churches, parents, spouses and children, other family members and poor community members, including orphans. In all cases in this study, the first remittances made by migrants went to churches as a way of giving thanks for the prayers made for them before departure. A young woman who migrated to Kuwait first sent 1,000 birr (about $37 in 2018) to the church and, on her return three years later, donated a further 1,500 birr (about $55 in 2018). A father with three sons in South Africa said that two of them together remitted 20,000 birr (about $740 in 2018) to the church. In another case, a young man living in the United States, with two brothers in South Africa, had erected and donated two flour mills to the church as a means of income generation to help preach the gospel (he also put a grain store for his family next to the mills). The fulfilment of these thanksgiving and spiritual obligations is a source of great satisfaction for the migrants and their families, and also earns them high social status. These blessings and prayers by Protestant churches are also reported in Durame *woreda* and Hosaena town as common practices.[21] Spiritual fulfilment as one outcome of irregular migration is very likely also a driver of migration in this community where people pay attention to their religious life. Such intricate causations are neglected in official and scholarly explanations, which are largely framed by the thinking of policy-makers, scholars and donors from the Global North and mimicked by their counterparts in the South.

Regular remittances to parents are very common. Among the parents of migrants and returnees interviewed, we did not hear of any case of a non-remitting migrant, although complaints about the frequency and amount being remitted were raised in some cases. Cash is regularly sent through formal and informal channels. A resident remarked, 'Once they have reached there, they change, and send remittances to their families.' Remittances are used to pay for everything, from basic needs to more luxurious items, the repayment of loans (such as those taken to finance one's migration), savings, investment, and the financing of the irregular migration of a sibling, relative or friend. Remittances made to richer families were more substantial, suggesting that the children from richer households have a better chance of migrating to better-earning destinations, typically South Africa, by means of expensive but safer air travel. Most migrants had built new modern houses for their parents: tin-roofed, well plastered, magnificently painted, and equipped with modern furniture and luxury items such as TV sets. In such cases, irregular migration to lucrative destinations can be better understood as the monetary manipulation of physical distance and legal constraints to invest one's resources for a higher and quicker return than can be earned in one's own locality or country.

Others have built houses. Prices in Durame are higher than in average rural settings, with a house costing about 200,000 birr (about $7,407 in 2018), and a 200-square-metre plot of land for residential purposes costing about 80,000 birr (about $2,960 in 2018). There are cases of more expensive sites, the most cited being one bought in a 'strategic location' in Durame's centre for 1.5 million birr (about $55,555 in 2018) by a young man who had worked for a decade in South Africa. It is said he intends to build a multi-storey building, in addition to the residential houses owned by his parents and himself. In Aze Debo as well, the traditional rural residential landscape, which was once dominated by thatched and mud-walled houses, has given way to modern housing structures, thereby changing and enlarging the built environment.

All migrants have, at the very least, built houses of moderate size, often in their parents' compounds. Others have built or purchased houses or buildings in Shashemene or Hawassa, and a few also in Addis Ababa. The biggest hotel in Durame is said to have been bought by two brothers with money earned in South Africa. These successful young men serve as symbols of success from irregular migration and nearly everybody in their communities knows of what they have achieved.

Other than fixed assets, many migrants, returnees and migrants' families have savings in banks. Some own three-wheeler Indian auto-rickshaws (*bajaj*), minibuses or trucks, operating within and outside the Kambata Zone. Remittances made on the death of a family member to serve refreshments for mourners are gaining prominence as status markers. Remittances provide the means to offer high-quality food and bottled water at funerals and condolences, as is the custom in towns, and it is now becoming common among families of migrants. This earns a good name for the family and the remitting child, also encouraging others to send their children to work, preferably in South Africa, where potential earnings are higher. Remittances to finance the mourning of a family member may relieve other community members, mainly the members of the *idir* (self-help association), of the need to make contributions. News circulates that the child of So-and-so has spared the community from such a contribution.

Social remittances to vulnerable groups, such as orphans and poor households, represent the most philanthropic outcomes of international migration from Kambata. Such assistance is made through churches and migrants' families. Successful young men in South Africa buy school materials for orphans and children from poor families. Some migrants working in South Africa remit money, especially for the Meskel festivity (celebrating the finding of the True Cross), to buy bulls or oxen to be slaughtered and distributed to poor community members and, sometimes even, for neighbourhoods at large.[22] A returnee woman from Sudan said that two years earlier, 'My eldest brother living there [South Africa] had once contacted the *kebele* chair to get the list of destitute people for whom he remitted money for their Meskel festivity. What is more, every year he buys an ox for poor households to be slaughtered for this event. He had also remitted money for 70 needy people; giving each of them 300–500 birr [about $11–$19 in 2018].' Social remittances such as those for Meskel are made on a yearly basis while others are likely to be made occasionally throughout the year. While remittances are high on the agenda of the conventional literature on (irregular) migration, such nuanced, socially meaningful economic impacts and other shades of meaning presented in this chapter are rarely, if ever, covered.

Increasingly, it is families of migrants who provide credit or free support to others in times of need. In fact, this is part of an informal system of social protection, in some ways easing the burden on the formal and donor- and state-financed social protection services even though there is a reluctance to acknowledge this in the official narrative. The fact that the number of vulnerable people seeking formal social protection in the community has decreased over the last five to seven years may, to some extent, account for this factor.[23] In fact, as many informants have said, households with migrant family members cannot access government social protection as they are considered self-sufficient.

Besides these positive outcomes, there are negative consequences of irregular migration which all informants acknowledge. Some married young women have migrated, mostly to Sudan, leaving their children and husbands behind. Similarly, some married young men have gone to South Africa and Sudan, leaving their wives and children, mostly with the men's families. When married men go, the responsibilities of raising and educating children, and doing other work, fall on the wife and, to some extent, the grandparents. Despite these burdens, it is believed that women may benefit if the migrant husband remits sufficiently and regularly. If this does not happen, for whatever reason, the women and children left behind will be disadvantaged. There are also cases of some men secretly marrying a second wife, and of female migrants secretly marrying. The families of migrants who die en route or at the destination or who are detained or disappear are seriously affected. Consequently, migration may strain family relations and lead to family disintegration, often with dire consequences, especially for the children and parents of migrants.

Migration can be a dangerous experience, leading to hardships, physical injuries as well as death. Many migrants have died en route to South Africa from suffocating in containers and gas tanks, as well as from disease. Some young people returned after detention and imprisonment. Hunger, thirst, fear and tiredness are part of local migration narratives. In South Africa, both those who vend goods and those who run their own stores are exposed to beatings, stabbings, shootings, and looting by robbers who target their hard-earned money and property. In the Gulf States, some young women were abused and had their wages denied or misappropriated by brokers. Beatings, misappropriation of money, and demands for a bribe from the police were also reported in some cases.

Migration aspirations and decision-making

The experience of irregular migration starts with the aspiration and then the decision in its favour. Most migration decisions are made in close consultation and agreement with family. A female returnee from Sudan asked, 'When someone goes against the will of his family, where does he get the money for travel? He will be forced to stay with his disappointment.' She added, 'They do not go even to Hawassa without a friend there; where do they spend the night?' However, it is not always the case that the decision to migrate is consultative or spreads the risk. There are instances in which parents are presented with the decision as a fait accompli, especially in cases of destitute parents whose blessings are, nevertheless, sought before departure. Some migrants threaten to leave their parents if they are not financially supported to migrate.

Migrants and their families have a trusted source of information in relatives and friends. Official advice, clamour and appeals to listen to the law have mostly fallen on deaf ears. In this respect, one informant said, 'Even if they [prospective migrants, the youth] find information from other sources, it is not going to be useful for them ... they do not have trust in it.' Relatives, siblings, friends, and friends of friends are the major trusted sources of information about where to go, how to go, who to meet at the destination, and which broker to contact for reliable, quick and efficient service. Accordingly, migration has become a way of utilising valuable social capital for the better rather than purposely negating government policies. Some of the migration stories reveal the ordeals migrants undergo. On the one hand, there is fear, despair, hunger, thirst, robbery, mental and physical stress, detention, arrest and even death. On the other, there are cases of kindness, mutual support, and other humane behaviours and deeds experienced by migrants, especially from women they had come across while passing through various countries to reach South Africa. However, none of these difficulties and tragic consequences have stopped people from migrating. The aim of the official discourse to stop irregular migration needs to be reframed to reflect the hopes and despair of migrants, their families and their communities.

Young men and women experience different migration routes, destinations, stories and types of jobs. Those who had migrated to South Africa were young men, except for a few young women joining their fiancés in wedlock. The reasons for this include the long, physically arduous, risky and sometimes fatal journey by land or sea, and also the risky nature of work and life in South Africa, which can involve robbery, beating, stabbing, killing and even the kidnapping of women to gain a ransom from their husbands.

Those who migrated to Sudan were mainly young women because of the ample job opportunities in cooking and housekeeping, mostly for individual households. For many young men, too, there is work in factories and on farmland, where the pay is comparatively attractive, going up as high as 800 Sudanese pounds (around $114 per month before their currency devaluation), for those who are willing to risk the hardships of the desert and a lonely life. In the Gulf States young women mostly work as domestic servants, while men go there in insignificant numbers. Here, it is important to note that the market structure is divided not only into skilled and unskilled labour, as dual labour market theory holds.[24] The division is also one of gender, which is based on cultural notions of who should do what.

Migration experiences and accounts that restrain people from further migration are limited in number. Useful insights can be drawn from them, however. A young woman of about 20, who does not want to join her fiancé in South Africa, observed, 'I hear at school and from the families of those who have gone, about the travel in the jungles, passing the nights there. I advise others in the name of good health and peace that young people can work in freedom where they live. Women who go abroad do not have respect.' She added, 'When they are married too, there are couples who do not respect each other because of that [their migration experience]. You know, it is not good for marriage when they [young women] spend nights travelling long distances with [male] brokers and others [males].' Furthermore, 'There is the problem [risk] of health as well. There is also HIV, which is a threat to the human race.' However, she stated that people are not even afraid of death, because of poverty. She went on to add, 'If a person does not find something to eat, drink and wear, he does not care for the hurdles lying ahead to fulfil these necessities.' Her reflections seem to represent those of most community members. However, it is also important to mention that the desire for greater wealth by the relatively better-off is also a factor.

Poverty and, to some extent, risk management pervade the literature as major driving forces of irregular migration, including refugees from conflict-ridden countries such as Syria and Iraq.[25] Likewise, the data from this research reveals that many young people from poor families have irregularly migrated. However, young people from rich and middle-income families have migrated as well. The richer migrants mostly travel by air, whereas the poor use a riskier mix of foot, car and boat, while some cover part of the journey by air and complete the rest by other modes of transport. The wealthier largely go to South Africa, a more lucrative destination, while the poorer mostly go to Sudan. In the case of women, the rich choose to fly to the Gulf States. Rising aspirations and expectations of better income opportunities and lifestyles create a feeling of relative poverty, serving as a reason to migrate for many.[26]

As a result, the arrests, injuries, suffering and even deaths mentioned in the rising anti-migration discourse have had little effect as a deterrence on irregular migration at both the personal and the community level. A young man, who returned after serving two and a half years under arrest in Tanzania, said young people would often ask, 'Do you think I would not be successful if you were not?' He has been facing this challenge, sharing his negative experiences, giving lessons so that others do not venture on irregular migration. But the perception that 'you cannot avoid death by being at home' is very common and strong. The official discourse is incapable of dispelling this justification, which is anchored in people's belief system. In addition, local views extract success stories out of what is otherwise a failure in the migration literature. The saying 'You would leave a good name dying en route to South Africa rather than sitting idle here' is far from a mere linguistic expression. This favourable evaluation of failures or mishaps, contrary to the official narrative, further reinforces and sustains irregular migration. Hence, local conceptions of success and failure are at odds with the official understanding and serve as additional reasons to emigrate. It may be confusing to see young people shy away from describing their bad migration experiences as failures. But as the quotation shows, for every bad migration experience, there is a positive interpretation that carries more weight. Among the returnees interviewed, no one regretted going. Each individual migrant is considered a distinct creature with a different destiny, even though they have shared values and objectives in migrating. Whether migrants make a financial gain or loss, experiencing air travel and a foreign land is a success in its own right. Such nuances are probably unknown even to far-sighted policy-makers, leaving the gap between the official and the local narratives and 'realities' unfilled. Locally informed studies, as in this book, are important to address this deficiency.

The laws and lessons of education that aim to deter irregular migration have not succeeded.[27] Hence, alternative strategies and policy instruments 'that rely less on deterrence' are necessary. Strategies focusing on deterrence have resulted in negative side effects, have not been effective,[28] go against the 'fundamental non-criminal nature of migration',[29] and, in the example of border control, have increased the intensity of smuggling and the death of migrants.[30]

Overall, the case of Kambata shows that irregular migration has developmental impacts on migrants, their families and the community at large. Those who fail to fulfil the personal, familial and collective goals set for irregular migration, and for migration in general, are small in number and not enough to discourage this socio-economic practice. A returnee reflected, 'There are young people who are not working even after going to Sudan. The men just stroll and the women start affairs with the police. These are the ones who are not remitting money to their parents.' The results of migration are mixed, but the positive ones predominate.

Conclusion

This chapter argues that global narratives and orthodoxies about irregular migration need to be challenged and corrected. The complex and subtle drivers as well as impacts need to be further unpacked. The economic sphere needs to be rescrutinised and supported by insights from the personal, psychosocial, and moral and religious perspectives of migrants, their parents and their communities. Such a practice also needs to consider the micro-politics of families and gendered power relationships. Irregular migration is a field of economic as well as political intercourse taking place at different levels of human organisation. Practising this needs a rethinking of the global imbalance between the economically and politically dominant North and the dependent and struggling South, and how this imbalance has been formed historically and sustained.

This chapter has argued that there are multiple and nuanced drivers of migration, rather than a simple linear causation based on an economic model, anchored in poverty, that fails to capture the full picture of irregular migration. This argument is based on a detailed examination of the drivers, experiences and consequences of irregular migration from the viewpoints of the people directly and indirectly involved in this form of mobility. Lack of employment, poverty, relative deprivation, better labour markets in destination countries, and the global ideals of a good life or desire for improvement, both at the personal and familial levels, are among the major drivers of irregular migration. However, explanations, largely or solely based on poverty or economic deprivation, are inadequate. There are also social factors, such as competition, networks, and the desire to prosper and to support one's family even when they are economically well-off. The moral obligation of parents to finance a child's migration project and of migrants to support their families; perceptions and changing notions of status; and religious interpretations of migration experiences are also important facilitating factors. All these factors are inadequately understood by officials and many experts concerned with irregular migration.

The chapter confirms the risks and dangers taken by irregular migrants en route and once in their 'dreamland'. It is important to focus on how these risks and dangers are perceived and interpreted by migrants themselves and their communities. What is perceived as a failure by experts and policy-makers can be seen as a success in the local purview, or just a part of the unfolding of the inevitable destiny of an individual. What is more, when migration risks and dangers are compared to staying back home, the comparison renders migrating better than staying. Accordingly, leaving is interpreted as a move to resolve one's problems and those of one's family, with little consideration of its legality. Consequently, government intervention schemes, such as awareness creation and job creation, fall short of inducing the desired perceptual and behavioural changes.

Despite differences in interpretation, there are negative consequences of irregular migration, which the Aze Debo community unanimously acknowledges. The negative consequences seen as the most significant are non-attention to family responsibility and the breakdown of families in some cases. However, significant economic gains, changing the lives of migrants, their parents and the community, pervade local stories of the consequences of irregular migration. In fact, some respondents complained that the government does not recognise this dimension and offers no entrepreneurial support to the parents of successful migrants and successful returnees engaged in investment works.[31] This probably explains why most investment decisions by successful migrants and their parents are in real estate and transportation, relatively less risky and common types of options. When one considers that migrants' families are not eligible to access government social protection, on the assumption that they are self-sufficient or well-off, one may concede that they have a complaint. Individual remittances are of considerable size and result in savings and investment in food-processing, housing, transport and other sectors. Remittances are also employed in social and moral ways (for churches and for support of the poor) that have not thus far been captured by the mainstream literature on irregular migration or international migration at large.

8

GENDER RELATIONS IN A TRANSNATIONAL SPACE

ETHIOPIAN IRREGULAR MIGRANTS IN SOUTH AFRICA

Yordanos S. Estifanos

Introduction

This chapter examines how the irregular migration of Ethiopian women impacts on gender relations in the context of South Africa's informal economy, in which Ethiopian irregular migrants engage. It further examines how the feminisation of migration affects relationships between migrant households in Ethiopia and South Africa.

There is a growing understanding that female and male migrant networks have different influences on migration outcomes and on linkages between origin and destination households and communities.[1] In part, because men and women experience different barriers to moving, maintain different relationships with sending families and villages of origin, and experience completely different opportunities and constraints in places of destination, gender inevitably influences the quality of social networks.[2] In this regard, the chapter examines how gender in the con-

159

text of international migration affects the quality, content and character of migrants' relationships with their families and communities.[3]

The findings in this chapter contest the argument that, through providing opportunities for economic independence and granting social space for emancipation, migration empowers women. On the contrary, upon migrating, the relationship between Ethiopian men and women immigrants morphs from a benevolent into an exploitative one. One reason for this is that Ethiopian male migrants who work in South Africa's informal economy control the social and economic space in which migrant women find themselves. Structural, socio-cultural, and personal factors also conspire with the former to increase the risk of exploitation of recent women immigrants. These preclude migrant women from realising the liberating and emancipatory potential that migration can offer.

The data for this chapter was derived from two studies: the first phase of fieldwork was part of my MA thesis research in 2014 and 2015. It was carried out in South Africa and Ethiopia. Accordingly, 20 Ethiopian migrants in Johannesburg and its satellite informal townships were interviewed. Moreover, 15 interviews were held in Addis Ababa and Hosaena. Of the 35 interviewees, 5 were female (all in South Africa). The second phase of fieldwork was part of the 2018 Migrating Out of Poverty Research Consortium (MOOP) study.[4] The MOOP study relied on 40 key informant interviews conducted in South Africa (Johannesburg and Durban) and Ethiopia (Addis Ababa and Hosaena) between August and December 2018. Of these, 33 were done in South Africa and 7 in Ethiopia; and 7 were with women. The lower proportion of women informants is consistent with the male-dominated nature of migration to South Africa. Furthermore, field notes, informal and formal discussions, observations, a transect walk, and a literature review informed the research. In both rounds of interviews, informants gave verbal or written consent. If and when mentioned in the chapter, informants' names are pseudonyms.

The remainder of the chapter is organised as follows. The second section provides a brief history of Ethiopian migration to South Africa. The third section elucidates the increasing trend of feminisation in international migration and the associated changes in gender relations. The fourth section discusses how women migrants are exploited in

South Africa, while the following section examines the wider context in which the exploitation of women happens. The sixth section examines the role that female migrants play in connecting migrant households and communities in Ethiopia and South Africa. The chapter ends with concluding remarks.

Ethiopian irregular migration to South Africa: A brief history

Unlike the migration of Ethiopians to Europe, North America and the oil-rich Arab countries, that of Ethiopians to South Africa is a relatively recent phenomenon. Beginning in the early 1990s, it coincided with regime changes in both countries. In South Africa, the African National Congress-led government introduced progressive asylum laws that provided for temporary status or asylum with the right to work and study. With the end of apartheid, South Africa allowed freedom of movement and ended the requirement of non-white South Africans to carry a so-called pass book when travelling to cities.[5]

In Ethiopia, there was also regime change in 1991. After assuming state power, the Ethiopian Peoples' Revolutionary Democratic Front-led government lifted the requirement for citizens to secure a 'pass' when they moved from one part of the country to another.[6] The new government also eased international mobility by allowing citizens to have access to passports and travel documents. Unlike labour migrants from neighbouring southern African countries who migrated to work in South Africa's mining, manufacturing or domestic economy, Ethiopians were among the first African immigrant entrepreneurs in South African metropolitan areas and small towns. Today, tens of thousands of Ethiopians live and work in South Africa's cities and townships.

Ethiopian migration to South Africa happened in three major waves. The first wave was from the mid-1990s to the beginning of 2000. The first groups of migrants were men who were refugees fleeing the civil war of the 1980s and the repressive mobility policies of the pre-1991 military government (the Derg). Some of the migrants during this wave were members of the Ethiopian army, which was in disarray and was later officially disbanded in 1991. These groups of migrants also initially sought refuge in Kenya, before migrating to South Africa. Many of these migrants sought to use

South Africa as a transit stop on their way to preferred destinations—North America and Western Europe.[7]

The second wave of migration (2000–10) coincided with the appointment of Ethiopia's ambassador, Tesfaye Habiso, to South Africa in 2000/01, and the violence that followed the 2000 and 2005 elections. The ambassador is originally from Southern region; many claim he has a Hadiya and Kambata ethnic background. Migrants in this wave originate in particular from the towns of Hosaena and Durame. The ambassador's role in helping the first round of migrants from the two towns is widely acknowledged, while some informants as well as a study noted that the ambassador arranged job opportunities for a handful of migrants from the two towns.[8] In my interview with him, the ambassador gave a different explanation. According to him, his assignment as Ethiopia's ambassador to South Africa inspired confidence among migrants; many of them felt psychologically secure since he was from their place of origin.[9] Moreover, smugglers used his presence in South Africa as a cover to recruit and smuggle in migrants from southern Ethiopia.[10]

The third wave of migration occurred around the time of the 2010 FIFA World Cup hosted by South Africa. In the years preceding 2010, the promise of job opportunities associated with the construction of infrastructure for the World Cup attracted large numbers of migrants to South Africa. Smugglers also used the event as a tactic to recruit migrants.[11] During the 2010 games and the years that followed, large numbers of migrants headed to South Africa in the hope of taking short- or medium-term advantage of the trading opportunities that were expected to arise from the consumption associated with the World Cup.[12] Indeed, the 2010 event generated commercial opportunities for Ethiopian migrant entrepreneurs in South Africa, mainly from the sale of World Cup apparel.[13] Their migration was facilitated by smugglers, who exploited the prospect of opportunities for trade and for relatively easy movement during that period in their recruitment strategies.[14]

In addition to the increase in the absolute number of Ethiopian migrants during the World Cup and thereafter, there was a diversification of migrants in terms of gender, age, origin, and socioeconomic status. The initially male-dominated migration of

Ethiopians to South Africa since 2010 induced the migration of prospective wives, particularly from southern Ethiopia, which has become a key migrant sending region to South Africa since 2000.[15] As a result, the irregular migration of women from Ethiopia to South Africa for marriage or work or in transit to a third country can be considered as the fourth wave of migration.

Gender power relations in transnational space

Migration is inherently age- and gender-selective, in that younger and male migrants have a higher tendency to migrate. This tendency is augmented in the case of irregular migration, which involves multiple risks and challenges en route as well as during settlement.[16] This is one of the main reasons why young males, who have to pass through multiple transit countries, dominate the irregular migration of Ethiopians to South Africa.[17] However, the number of female Ethiopian migrants to South Africa is increasing, partly triggered by the demand for labour in the informal economy and for marriage by earlier Ethiopian male migrants.[18]

The feminisation of migration is usually expressed in terms of an increase in the absolute number of female migrants and the growing importance of independent female migration.[19] This feminisation, however, has complex impacts on gender relations. Indeed, in the context of increasing feminisation and the changing nature of female migration, the question whether transnational migration reproduces or challenges hierarchies of power and privilege is highly contested.[20] Gender relations are mediated and reconfigured by transformations in men's and women's roles. This transformation of roles is affected by transnational mobility, as change in the physical space reconfigures the social space that men and women share and their relationship within this space.[21]

Networks of exploitation

The transnational social networks that help Ethiopian migrants to participate in South Africa's informal economy engender latent exploitative relationships between Ethiopian migrants. Although recently arriving Ethiopian male migrants are also victims of such exploitation, it is especially visible between recent female migrants and their husbands, who are usually more established male migrants, and it occurs through the inclusion of females in business or in marital relationships.

Exploitation through business relations

More Ethiopian women are now entering South Africa as migrants. Although a few enter independently, many follow established migrants in South Africa to seek work. There are also cohorts of women from southern Ethiopia who migrated to South Africa via illegal channels as prospective wives for Ethiopian men who had already established themselves in that country. As indicated elsewhere, recent migrants and migrants' families can no longer afford the high smuggling costs.[22] Moreover, since female migrants take safer modes of transport, which require longer preparation time and more money, the financing of recent female migrants is mostly done from the South African side.

Unlike the relationship between established male and recent male immigrants, which is often transitory, that between established male and recent female immigrants may be a lasting one.[23] This is because labour relations are at times linked to long-term relationships, including marriage. Such relationships are replete with female exploitation. This does not mean that prospective wives have no agency in their migration. The very act of migrating may be an expression of their agency in further building their capabilities in expectation of a 'better life.' Many female Ethiopian migrants hold dual responsibilities as wife and worker, taking care of household chores and looking after children, as well as managing businesses such as tuck-shops. While managing the shops, they also assume the role of overseeing shop employees (who are mainly from Malawi and Zimbabwe).

Meanwhile, the men make business deals, stock the shops, supervise and do the accounts. A wife in Johannesburg, Meskerem Birhanu,[24] summarised the routines of most married men, originating from cities and urban areas in Ethiopia, as follows:

> A husband would get up in the morning and go to town to meet and have breakfast, usually *dulet* [minced meat], with his friends. Then he

would go to China Mall [Dragon City] to stock for the shop, which his wife runs. [Afterwards] he goes to McDonald's to have coffee and chitchat with his friends. Most males, including my husband, are just like that. If there is a husband in Johannesburg who is working from his counter in the shop, it is highly likely that either his wife has gone to Ethiopia or his kids are sick [and his wife is taking care of them]. Here, in Johannesburg, it is the females who take care of the males: not just the wives but sisters too. She would get up early, open, and run the shop. When the shops are closed and the wife arrives home, she will have to take care of the household chores and look after her children.

The majority of male informants also agreed that the arrival of female migrants in South Africa had boosted their businesses and that Ethiopian female immigrants contributed positively to their business success. This finding is endorsed by Hagan, who argues that women receive few of the benefits experienced by male co-ethnics, thereby emphasising the negative human capital returns for female workers.[25]

Furthermore, when females are entrusted with their husbands' businesses, they become responsible for their everyday operations. This translates into long working hours for females, depriving them of time to spend outside work. The men, meanwhile, spend most of their time in venues where business ideas are discussed and conducted such as restaurants, cafes, coffee shops, barbershops, and other open spaces, enjoying the opportunity to meet and socialise among themselves, which strengthens their social networks.

This reversal of roles, whereby females take what amount to managerial positions while the males socialise, has weakened women's social capital. One of the outcomes of migration to South Africa, therefore, is the role reversal of males and females in a transnational space: Ethiopian men have taken over social processes while women have taken on the role of business management, traditionally a field for men.[26] Over time, this role reversal has favoured males, as they build their social capital and widen their business networks, consolidating the power and privilege of males over females and intensifying the existing gap in social mobility. In sum, gendered relations and social institutions imported from home seem to reinforce the exploitative conditions for female migrants, who assume the dual role of wife and worker.

Monetising socio-cultural institutions

The perceived success of immigrants in South Africa is transmitted back home by means of goods, remittances and images, including videos of extravagant wedding ceremonies. This perceived success is also manifested in the actual success of returnees and their pretensions. Perceived and actual opportunities available in South Africa are transmitted to non-migrants and migrants' families in Ethiopia using social media platforms such as Facebook, YouTube and Imo. The smartphone age has made possible a seamless flow of information.[27] However, messages and images transmitted on social media platforms often exaggerate the bright side of things, while concealing the dangers and risks.

Such factors partly explain the increase in the number of Ethiopian female migrants heading to South Africa.[28] In this regard, another form of female exploitation was noted in the migration of prospective wives, which involves the monetising of socio-cultural institutions, in this case the wedding ceremony, which is often preceded by a welcome ceremony.

The welcome and wedding ceremonies are profit-making events. The ceremonies are connected to imported socio-cultural institutions such as *mahibers* (social clubs) and *idirs*,[29] which are modified to accommodate migrant and entrepreneurial needs in South Africa.[30] Amel noted that in living in South Africa, Ethiopians have been forced to prioritise other aspects of their lives over elements of the social processes that once governed them in Ethiopia.[31] Moreover, in an informal economy that increasingly involves fierce business competition, the social capital of Ethiopian immigrants has waned and is being replaced by financial capital.[32] Furthermore, social institutions that men import and control reinforce the exploitative conditions for female immigrants.

As major actors in social processes and as importers of social institutions, men have adjusted *idir* and *mahiber* institutions to their advantage. While these institutions are considered mainly as socio-cultural institutions in Ethiopia, they are reinvented by migrants in South Africa to support their needs and economic motives. These institutions are thus modified into business arrangements.[33] But their modification to accommodate primarily financial needs undermines the social capital of Ethiopian immigrants, particularly that of women.[34] Put another way, Ethiopian men, who mainly import and control these institutions, now claim the foreground in the area of social institutions, as they have more free time and are, as men, constrained by fewer restrictions.[35]

The migration of a prospective wife is dependent on the presence of an able and established male immigrant. A wife is recruited, often from the man's home town or village (in my fieldwork, this was mainly in and around Hosaena and Durame). Little is known of women's agency in their migration as prospective wives. However, many female teenagers, including high-school students, have their passports ready and are desperate to migrate and marry a compatriot in South Africa.

In addition to the desire for loving partnerships, exploitation appears to be a factor in men's willingness to finance the migration of wives. In this regard, complicated forms of exchange and reciprocity manifest in the welcome and wedding ceremonies. Such migrations are often accompanied by significant gifts which informants believe are intended to stabilise the financial situation of the man. In informal discussions, a male migrant, Yohannes Teshome, recounted his marriage in monetary terms: 'I made this much money out of [marrying] her.' Another female interviewee, Asnaku Fisseha, based in Durban, alluded to the premeditated exploitation of younger women, saying that male migrants in South Africa were recruiting adolescent women who are perceived to be more easily manipulated than mature ones:

> More recently the females that are being brought are teenagers. There are few cases where husbands bring in those females in their early twenties, as they prefer the teenagers. Otherwise, they don't want to marry mature ones. And those teenagers only see the extravagant and superficial welcome and wedding ceremonies and the amount of money their prospective husbands send them when they are in Ethiopia. Some migrants, who intend to profit from the welcome and wedding ceremonies, would save or even borrow and send money to the girl whom he plans to marry. Some of them tell utter lies to lure the girl and her family. When the girl's family hear rosy stories about South Africa and receive some money, they put pressure on the girl to migrate to South Africa without even researching the boy's background. And the teenager will have to suffer the consequences, one of them being divorce.

The practices of reciprocal socio-cultural institutions, with a quid pro quo business arrangement, blur the boundaries between socio-cultural and business relations. In these rotational savings clubs (*ikub*)

167

and social institutions (*mahiber*), members are socially bound to support one another. In the case of marriage migration, all members of a *mahiber* are obliged to attend and contribute to the welcome and wedding ceremonies. During these gatherings, every member offers a gift, generally cash, to the bride and bridegroom. The implicit understanding is that everyone who is contributing has either received payment before or does so with the expectation of similarly receiving money for a future venture—of a greater value than one gives. The bridegroom keeps a record of who attended the ceremony and what amount each person gave. Pecuniary contributions aside, close relatives and intimate friends also give presents in kind. An excerpt from an interviewee in Johannesburg, Petros Ayele, describes the generous scale of gifting:

> I brought in a girl from Hosaena and we made promise in a church and stayed together for a while before we officially got married. Once we sorted out things, we prepared a wedding ceremony. The ceremony alone cost more than 200,000 rand [US$13,440] including hiring cameraman, limousine, hall rental, catering and clothing. On the wedding day, however, I received gifts in cash. The individual gifts fall in the range of 300 [$20] to 10,000 rand [$672]. I keep record of that for I am expected to pay it back someday. The cash gifts I received more than covered the wedding expenses, leaving me with profit. Cash aside, my brother and my uncle, together with other close relatives, gave me a 2010 model car. We also received another car from the bride's relatives.

Contributions operate more like a loan than an extension of support. In some cases, cultural rituals are monetised and wives are used as a means to profit from marriage ceremonies. A female interviewee, Aberash Edossa, said: 'Sometimes, some married people even bring another woman for marriage to make money out of them. There will be a welcome party on the second day after she arrives. And they will make a lot of money from it.'

Marriage ceremonies may also finance, albeit retroactively, the migration. In these cases, brokers and smugglers receive their fees after the ceremonies. An Ethiopian female migrant in Durban, Helina Misganaw, described the process in the following words:

> There is a welcome party when they bring a wife here. And they will get a lot of money from the party, they could make as much money as

300,000 birr [$9,354] and they use the money to pay for the smuggler who brought her. The person who would smuggle a potential wife would make a deal with the smuggler to pay the smuggling fee from the money he would profit from the party. The smuggler would wait until the party is over and he takes his cut.

It is important to consider women's agency within these processes. Yet the phenomenon of women combining their migration with marriage and, in the process, managing their husbands' businesses is commonplace. Some women may migrate voluntarily and with substantial information about their possible fate in South Africa. But many are likely to know less about their potential groom than he knows about them. Another female interviewee in Johannesburg, Sophia Arega, said: 'Some of the men do background research about the girl's and her family's socioeconomic status before they bring in a prospective wife. They also research about the wealth status of her relatives in South Africa. This is to benefit from the presents and gifts during the welcome and wedding ceremonies.' Our informants indicated that many of these women originate from remote rural areas of southern Ethiopia and do not speak English or other official languages of South Africa, nor have they had exposure to an urban way of life. The unfamiliar lifestyle and high crime rate in South Africa force them to become dependent on their husbands.

Venues of exploitation: Irregularity, informality and timing

Irregular migrants' socio-legal status, their lack of the right to work, and lack of access to welfare make them susceptible to exploitation.[36] Macro-level structural and micro-level individual factors further intensify the exploitative relationship between established males/husbands and recent female immigrants/wives. Although female migrants enter the migration experience in a country where women's legal and social rights are more established than those in Ethiopia, they do so as subjects of established male immigrants. This is because of their migration status, the nature of the business, their time of arrival, and their lower socio-economic position.

In the case of Ethiopian immigrants in South Africa, the risk of exploitation is attributable to a change in the immigration and labour market policies of the country, which have become increasingly restrictive and rigid. While earlier immigrants could easily obtain permit papers and also benefit from a relaxed business environment in the informal economy, recent immigrants encounter the opposite. The South African state has been scapegoating and criminalising immigrant entrepreneurs who are contributing positively to the economy even though they have the right to trade in the informal sector and public space in South Africa.[37] If approved by parliament, the government's draft White Paper on International Migration will take away immigrants' right to work and will leave them in a more precarious situation.[38] There are also draft business policy provisions that seek to limit the rights of foreigners to trade.[39]

There is also widespread corruption, increasing raids against immigrants' businesses, and growing xenophobic sentiment. Even before approval of the draft White Paper and other policy provisions on informal business, immigrants experienced assaults on their livelihoods through the confiscation of goods, police corruption, and the removal of their right to trade in Johannesburg.[40] In recent years, government policies and practices have increasingly targeted immigrant businesses. South African government departments like the South African Police Service (SAPS), South Africa Revenue Service (SARS), Johannesburg Metropolitan Police Department (JMPD), and Tactical Response Team are increasingly storming migrants' businesses under the pretext of confiscating counterfeit goods. Moreover, growing levels of violence and crime, mainly in Johannesburg, have also negatively affected recent immigrants' businesses and limited opportunities to widen their social and business networks.

As shopkeepers and business managers, female immigrants shoulder a disproportionate share of the problem. Consequently, many female immigrants feel not only that their lives are at risk but also that their physical and social mobility is inhibited. Because recent immigrants encounter these violent state approaches and a hostile political discourse that scapegoats immigrants and criminalises their businesses, they are at high risk of exploitation.

The vulnerability of recent immigrants is also attributable to inefficiency in asylum claim processing at the Department of Home Affairs. Many immigrants, including those who have lived in South

Africa for as long as twenty years, still hold an asylum-seeker permit. This permit paper is meant to be a temporary document. The South African law insists that asylum cases should be resolved either by rejecting or granting refugee status. Many informants lamented that their applications have been held up for many years. South Africa has the highest number of unsettled asylum-seeker claims in the world.[41]

In a nutshell, recent migrants face the intersection of restrictive immigration and labour market policies, risks associated with working informally, and the precarity of their political asylum-seeking status, which is renewed for periods as short as a few months, after which they are treated as illegal migrants until the status is renewed again. Owing to such inefficiency, immigrants oscillate between being illegal and legal migrants. This means for instance that they cannot open bank accounts, thus forcing them to depend on cash transactions, which in turn increases the risk of violent crime. This creates situations where established immigrants are able to protect themselves from risks while the violence leaves recent migrants vulnerable to exploitation.

A combination of these factors intensifies the hierarchies of power and privilege between established male and recent female Ethiopian immigrants.[42] The case of John Melaku and Betel Tariku mirrors the experience of many female informants. John Melaku migrated to South Africa in 2002 and he smuggled Betel, his wife, from Ethiopia in 2012. Because he arrived earlier, he managed to obtain a status permit. His wider social and business networks also enabled him to expand his businesses as well as to establish contacts with immigration and other officials in South Africa. Over time, John managed to convert his status permit into a travel document, enabling him not only to constantly travel between Ethiopia and South Africa but also to travel to other countries, most importantly China. However, Betel is stranded in South Africa with a limited right to mobility. Owing to changes in the immigration policy, she only managed to obtain an asylum-seeker permit paper. On top of this, because she assumed the dual role of a wife and a worker, she has limited scope for widening her social capital.

Contrary to her expectation of enjoying better life prospects, she was stranded in a marriage that was potentially exploitative. Her limited social capital, restrictive migration status, and dual role as a wife and worker, as well as the violence in the city, have constrained her agency. Betel felt that she was in a disadvantaged position in South Africa and she is considering returning home. On the flip side, John is in a privileged position and he would rather expand his business in South Africa than return home. Here is what she said:

> Honestly speaking, all I want is to go back home at any time. I want to go because I would live better in Ethiopia than the life I am living here. That's even without being stressed and encountering risk. Here, every day is a struggle. Here, everything is stressful. I am tired of this! I will stay here only under one condition: if I could obtain the right paper and be able to move back and forth [between Ethiopia and South Africa] to do business and get the chance to see my family and relatives. There are better opportunities in this country, but I need the right permit to exploit those opportunities. Let alone Residence Permit, it suffices to have Travel Document. But, securing that is a huge bottleneck ... I am stuck for eight years and fatigued by suffocation. It's too much.

The increase in the size of the immigrant population (particularly after the 2010 World Cup) and a slump in business opportunities following the 2008 financial crisis have tended to reinforce or reproduce the exploitation of recent immigrants. The case of Kassech Adugna illustrates the presence of female exploitation outside the marital relationship as well. Kassech moved to South Africa to work for a friend of her brother whom she met at her brother's house in Addis Ababa. Her brother's friend welcomed Kassech in Johannesburg, where she started working in his shop. She worked for two years but she felt exploited—a feeling shared by many recent immigrants. Keen to start a business, a desire shared by almost all Ethiopian immigrants, she stopped working. Unfortunately, the business environment was not as favourable as it used to be. She remained unemployed and became a target of exploitation by established migrant entrepreneurs with whom she socialised after her arrival. During the interview, she explained the state of limbo she occupied:

> I failed in my previous [restaurant] business in Ethiopia just before I moved to South Africa because of the heavy tax, protracted bureaucracy in opening and closing small businesses, and demolition of my small business for urban redevelopment purpose. [So] I don't think I would succeed if I return. Also, if I am to leave South Africa once, to even assess the business environment in Ethiopia, I can't return because of the nature of my migration status. I don't have the right papers to move

around and work here either. I am stranded here for eight years and found myself in a state of limbo ... There are a whole lot of things to do here: I have a lot of business ideas in my head, and I get a new one now and then ... The permit is the main obstacle that's holding me back.

Female migrants' role in smuggling networks

Curran and Saguy argue that female migrants tend to maintain stronger transnational ties with families and relatives back home than their male counterparts.[43] They also note that female migrants are more reliable remitters than male migrants. Lindley indicates that while female migrants remitted more frequently, the amount sent by males is higher.[44] Our findings show that female Ethiopian migrants in South Africa tend to remit money to their families on a more regular basis than male migrants while males send larger amounts of money. They also tend to maintain better relationships with families, relatives and friends in Ethiopia and other countries of the world than male immigrants. In so doing, they contribute indirectly and positively to sustaining and per-petuating migration to South Africa by other relatives or friends. A male migrant from Johannesburg, Mikael Teffera, described the position of many of the male and female informants in our study when he noted:

Almost all female migrants here are closer to families and relatives in Ethiopia than male migrants. They are always eager to call home and also force their husbands to do the same. However, as it is believed that those of us who are abroad are in good positions, there is always some kind of request for support attached to such communications, including the smuggling of siblings or other relatives to South Africa. Some wives also use their emotional intelligence[45] to persuade husbands to smuggle in her siblings or relatives; and the husbands usually agree to do so.

A female Ethiopian migrant, Genet Aschenaki, who shared a similar view, said:

Female migrants here are more concerned about families and relatives back home. Maybe it is because we arrived recently, but we are posi-tioned better to understand the situations of people back home better than the male migrants. However, male migrants are not that hard-hearted ... if he is in good economic position, he smuggles his or his wife's siblings.

In terms of sustaining and perpetuating migration to South Africa, female migrants in South Africa appear to do a better job. One way in which they do this is by introducing their friends in Ethiopia as prospective wives to migrant men in South Africa. Owing to the dearth of female Ethiopian immigrants, those who are in South Africa may initiate or match-make potential couples through social media, through mutual acquaintances or relatives of either party. However, the practice of this type of match-making is limited to immigrants originating from urban areas in Ethiopia. Match-making in respect of women from rural areas is embedded within their social and cultural institutions and practices, and often involves protracted social and cultural rituals including confirmation by parents, relatives and village elders.[46]

Conclusion

The male-dominated migration from southern Ethiopia since the mid-1990s has induced a chain migration of female irregular migrants in recent years. In many cases, these women migrate in a relationship of dependency, including through nuptial migration. Often, the role of social networks has been exaggerated, highlighting the boost it gives to migration and settlement processes of irregular migrants by providing information, reducing migration costs and risks, and extending emotional and recreational support. However, as the stories in this chapter indicate, social networks can also be exploitative of recent migrants. Female immigrants are exploited through assuming a dual role of worker and wife. In this regard, the argument that social networks provide 'protection from below' should be questioned. The findings in this chapter do not support the argument that migration empowers and boosts the agency of migrants, as the exploitation that female immigrants endure outweighs the limited agency they enjoy in managing businesses.

The interplay between multiple factors at macro-, meso- and micro-levels reinforces or reproduces the power and privileges of established male immigrants over recently arriving female immigrants. A combination of factors weakens the emancipatory and liberating potential of migration for recent female Ethiopian immigrants. Many recent female immigrants have arrived in South Africa at a time when the size of immigrant populations has increased and business opportunities have dwindled. Many of these migrants, who originate from rural areas, are in their teenage years, lacking essential skills, financial capital and business networks, which are important factors in settling or establishing a business. The default option they have, therefore, is to depend on established male immigrants, who have often financed their migration. In so doing, most assume a dual role as wife and worker and, later on, an additional role as mother, leaving them with little or no time to socialise and expand their social capital or business networks. The irregular status they hold and their engagement in the informal economy also limit their mobility. Moreover, male immigrants control the smuggling business. They also import and control cultural rituals and institutions from home, enabling them to monetise these institutions, including the welcome and wedding ceremonies.

The arrival of female immigrants in South Africa also coincided with policy modifications, changes in the attitude of local politicians towards immigrants, and increasing crime rates in the informal economy of South Africa. In recent years there have been recurrent violent attacks on immigrants by vigilantes. Moreover, the South African government is tightening its immigration and labour market policies. These changes do not only expose immigrants to additional risks but also leave them in vulnerable and precarious situations, exposing them to various forms of exploitation.

PART IV

IMPACTS OF MIGRATION

9

REMITTANCES AND HOUSEHOLD
SOCIO-ECONOMIC WELL-BEING

THE CASE OF ETHIOPIAN LABOUR MIGRANTS
IN THE GULF COUNTRIES AND SOUTH AFRICA

Asnake Kefale and *Zerihun Mohammed*

Introduction

This chapter is concerned with the examination of two questions regarding the remittances that Ethiopian labour migrants to the Gulf countries and the Republic of South Africa send back to their home country.[1] The first is why migrants choose informal channels of transferring remittances over formal ones. The second is what contributions remittance money makes to household well-being and asset-building.

One of the key outcomes of international migration is the flow of resources to the home countries of migrants. With the rise of international migration from Ethiopia, remittance flows have recently become significant in terms of total volume and their impact on household income and the national economy. According to the National Bank of

Ethiopia, the amount of remittances to Ethiopia has increased from $3.04 billion in 2013/14 to $3.99 billion in 2015/16, outperforming the export sector in the last few years.[2]

However, a substantial amount of remittance money to Ethiopia bypasses the banking system and enters the country through informal channels. The informal transfer of remittances is disliked by international actors and national governments, including the Government of Ethiopia (GoE), for a variety of reasons. Governments of recipient countries (like Ethiopia) are keen to regularise the system so that they can gain access to hard currency. International institutions and Western governments fear that the informal transfer of money across national boundaries is used for criminal activities and to finance terrorist organisations. In spite of the growing importance of remittances, there is limited understanding of the impact of remittance flows on household well-being and the channels that migrant workers use to remit money to their families, relatives and friends.

The data for this study was collected from ten systematically selected *woredas*,[3] two from four of Ethiopia's larger regional states and the city of Addis Ababa: Adigrat and Mekelle from Eastern and Southern Zones of Tigray; Kombolcha[4] and Wereilu from South Wollo and North Wollo Zones of Amhara; Shashemene and Kofele from South Arsi Zone of Oromia; Hosaena from Hadiya Zone, and Halaba Special *woreda* from the Southern Nations, Nationalities and Peoples' Region (SNNPR); and Addis Ketema and Kirkos sub-cities from Addis Ababa City Administration. The *woredas* were selected based on a high prevalence of labour migration to South Africa and the Gulf countries.[5] Research teams were deployed to each of the study *woredas* to collect primary data for a period of six weeks (between 15 January and 30 March 2018). Different methods of data collection were used to gather primary and secondary data from various sources. The primary data collection methods were surveys, key informant interviews, and FGDs. The research team also collected secondary data from *woreda* administration offices, Labour and Social Affairs offices, the National Bank of Ethiopia (NBE), and the Central Statistical Agency (CSA).

Two separate surveys were used: one for returnee migrants and another for migrants' families. The first survey was designed for those who had returned to their villages after migrating to either a Gulf country or South Africa. We decided to approach returnee migrants, as it was impractical to include migrants who at the time of the survey were abroad. A minimum of two years working as a labour migrant in the destinations was the sole criterion for the selection of returnee migrants. On the basis of lists of returnees provided by Labour and Social Affairs offices in the study *woredas*, a sample of 25 respondents was drawn from each *woreda*, making a total sample of 250 returnee migrants.

The second survey was designed for household heads of families that, at the time of the survey, had migrant family members in the Gulf and in South Africa. This survey was designed to understand the socio-economic impacts of remittances on the well-being of the recipient households. These respondents were identified by local officials at the *kebele*[6] level. Accordingly, 20 households were selected from each *woreda*, making a total of 200 respondents.

This study is limited to migrants to South Africa and the Gulf countries, destinations that attract a large number of Ethiopian migrant workers. We believed that focusing on these two regions had the potential to reveal migrant workers' choice of remittance transfer channels and the way the funds were utilised by their families at home. The study did not cover Ethiopians and people of Ethiopian descent who live permanently in other parts of the world.

Apart from this introduction, the chapter contains four sections. The first section gives an overview of recent trends in remittance flows to Ethiopia. In particular, it considers the growth of the flows and the different total volume of remittances estimated by various actors. The second section examines how remittances are transferred to Ethiopia and the factors that motivate migrants to use informal transfer channels rather than formal ones. The third section considers the impact of remittances at the household level. Finally, the chapter provides some concluding remarks.

Recent trends of remittance flows to Ethiopia

Recently, remittance flows to Ethiopia have become significant. Although there is some variation in the exact volumes reported by different institutions, all evidence suggests that there has been a substantial increase of remittance transfers to Ethiopia in the past two decades (see Figure 9.1). The World Bank reports that remittance flows to Ethiopia increased from US$27 million in 1995 to $53 million in 2000 and reached $387 million in 2010, averaging 1.3% of GDP in 2009.[7] In 2012, the NBE reported that remittances reached $1.74 billion, surpassing the $1.6 billion of export earnings for the same year.[8] This amount seems to have increased significantly in the following years, as NBE reports that 'net private individual transfers' amounted to $3.04 billion, $3.7 billion and $3.99 billion for the years 2013/14, 2014/15 and 2015/16 respectively.[9] That made up 7.4%, 7.6% and 8.3% of GDP for the aforementioned fiscal years.[10]

The data in Figure 9.1 shows a small increase in remittance flows from $5.21 million in 1990 to $27.35 million in 1995 and $46.45 million in 2003. In 2004 the figure jumped to $133.74 million, rose to $386.69 million by 2008 and then climbed sharply to an all-time high of $1.79 billion by 2014, after which it shows a decline. The data in Figure 9.2, which contains 'individual private transfers' as reported by the NBE, shows substantially higher figures.

These NBE figures for individual private transfers show that remittances surpassed $1 billion in the 2006/07 fiscal year, reaching close to $4 billion by 2015/16. Individual private transfers, as defined by the NBE, incorporate three sub-categories: cash, in-kind and underground private transfers. This explains why NBE figures are substantially higher than other estimates, including the World Bank estimates in Figure 9.1.

Figure 9.1: Remittance to Ethiopia 1990–2016 ($ millions)

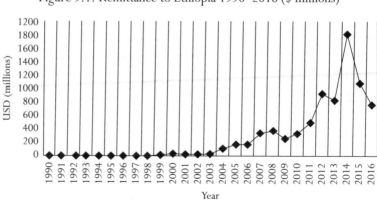

Source: World Bank 2016b.

Figure 9.2: Individual private transfers to Ethiopia (2006/07–2015/16; $ millions)

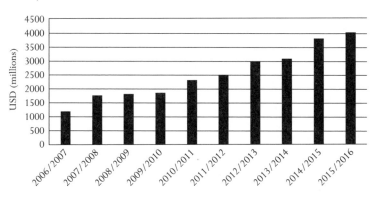

Source: NBE reports for various years.

While cash refers to official transfers, underground private transfers refer to estimates of informal individual transfers. For instance, in 2009/10 individual private transfers amounted to $1.85 billion (see Figure 9.2). Of this, cash (the official transfer) was only 42.8%, while 'underground private transfers' (informal flows) amounted to close to 52%. The remaining 5% or so was in-kind transfers.

Three comparisons can help us understand the importance of remittances to the Ethiopian economy. First, the remittance-to-GDP ratio, which tells us how much remittances are contributing to the overall economy. Both the World Bank data and NBE data show that this ratio has been rising steadily. NBE data shows that remittances have accounted for, on average, 7% to 8% of GDP since the 2013/14 fiscal year. Isaacs estimated that remittances accounted for 5% of GDP in 2015/16.[11] Second, there is the comparison of remittances with export earnings. For the past two decades, remittances have at least equalled export earnings and, in recent years, have consistently outperformed them. Third, there is the comparison of remittances with other capital flows to the country, such as Foreign Direct Investment (FDI) and Official Development Assistance (ODA). In 2010, remittances to Ethiopia were $387 million, higher than FDI of $100 million according to World Bank figures. ODA was $3.3 billion.

From the above discussion and figures, it is possible to deduce that the majority of remittance inflows to Ethiopia are informal, which is why they are not captured by World Bank official figures. Isaacs argues that while the GoE has managed to increase formal flows of remittances in recent years, informal channels are still the main means for Ethiopian migrants to send money home, and estimates this flow to be as much as 78% of total remittance inflows.[12]

The methods for informal transfer of remittances include sending cash through returning family members and friends and the use of *hawala*[13] services, which are seen as cost-effective. Isaacs defines informal remittances as 'remittances that do not pass through officially-regulated businesses at both the sending and receiving ends of a transaction' and involve informal methods of transfer like 'hand-carrying foreign currency, giving foreign currency to someone travelling to Ethiopia, using an unregulated money transfer operator (often known as *hawala*), or sending physical goods'.[14] This is not a uniquely Ethiopian phenomenon; substantial flows of remittances pass through informal or underground channels throughout the world.[15]

Remittance flows from the Gulf and South Africa

Ethiopian migrant workers in the Gulf countries and South Africa regularly send money to their families. In fact, remittances are highly important to these migrants, as their primary motive to migrate was to find employment that would enable them to change their and their families' lives for the better. Consequently, the majority of migrants send remittances home as soon as they make money. As shown in Table 9.1, the vast majority (close to 96%) of the returnee migrants reported sending money to their families, and 91.5% of household heads of the migrants' families reported receiving remittances.

As shown in Figure 9.3, 34.3% of the returnee migrants said that they regularly remitted money, and 36.0% of migrants' families said they regularly received remittances. In addition, 36.3% of the returnee migrants and 31.5% of the families said that they respectively sent and received remittances when there was a need like illness, paying children's school fees, purchasing seed and fertiliser, and building or maintaining houses. Typical amounts of money sent on demand ranged between 5,000 and 10,000 birr (about $185–$370).

Table 9.1: Responses of returnee migrants on sending/receiving remittances

Category	Question	Yes		No		Total	
		Freq.	%	Freq.	%	Freq.	%
Migrant/ returnees	Were you sending money back home when you were abroad?	239	95.6	11	4.4	250	100
Migrant families	Do you receive remittance from your family member living abroad?	183	91.5	17	8.5	200	100

When we look at the regularity of remitting, out of the 86 returnee migrant respondents who indicated that they were sending money to their families, 55.8% sent money quarterly, 40% intermittently and 3.5% sent a larger sum yearly. In terms of amount, 37.2% regularly sent between 1,000 and 5,000 birr (about $37–$185), while 32.6% sent between 5,001 and 10,000 birr (about $185–$370). Holidays such Easter, Christmas, Eid al-Adha and Eid al-Fitr were times when sizeable remittances were made to families.

Channels of remittance transfer

Remittances are sent using formal and informal channels, which have their own advantages and disadvantages for both senders and receivers. Returnee migrants were asked which transfer channels they used most to send remittance to families. Half said that they used banks

Figure 9.3: Occasions when migrants send remittances to their families back home (as percentages)

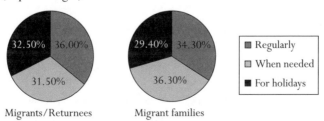

Migrants/Returnees   Migrant families

and money transfer institutions (such as Western Union and MoneyGram), and half said they used informal *hawala* and individuals travelling to the country.

Table 9.2: Most-used channels of remittance

Channels of remittance transfer	Returnee migrants		Migrant families	
	Frequency	Percentage	Frequency	Percentage
Bank/money transfer institutions	125	50	144	72
Individuals/*hawala*	125	50	56	28
Total	250	100	200	100

As Table 9.2 shows, 72% of the migrant families indicated that they received remittances through banks and money transfer institutions, while only 50% of returnee migrants indicated that they sent remittances through these channels. This variation is due to the fact that the informal channels (*hawala*) often use banks to deliver the money to the recipients. Once the *hawala* person receives the money in the host country, he or she gives an order to the local agent in Ethiopia to effect the payment in birr with full details (name, mobile phone number and address) of the recipient. The agent communicates with the recipient using the telephone number given and asks if the recipient has a bank account or, if not, a convenient bank and branch to which to transfer the money in his or her name. In this way, the recipient ultimately receives the money through the bank and, thus, erroneously assumes that he or she has received the money through a formal channel.

The formal remittance transfer channel

The formal transfer systems are those operated by formal financial institutions and supervised by government agencies. In Ethiopia, all government-owned and private banks, plus other money transfer institutions, are engaged in transferring remittances through formal channels.

The formal transfer system involves transferring money to the recipient through certain banks. The recipient is required to present a valid identification card and the security number of the transfer given by the sender. The bank or money transfer institutions may ask questions such as the identity of the sender and the amount of money sent, to ensure the authenticity of the person claiming the money. The recipient is not required to have an account at the bank from which he or she collects the remittance money, although many banks we interviewed encourage their remittance-receiving clients to open a savings account.

One major advantage of the formal system is its reliability. The senders receive an official receipt and can easily track the payment. Consequently, the chance of losing one's money in the process is almost zero. Moreover, unlike the informal ones, the formal transfer system is entirely lawful. Besides its benefits to the individuals concerned, it brings foreign currency to the government.

Despite its reliability and contribution to the national economy, the formal transfer system has limitations that prevent or discourage migrants from using it. First is the requirement to present valid documents such as passport, residence permit or work permit. The many irregular Ethiopian migrants in the Gulf and South Africa are unable to present such documents. Even migrants who go to the Gulf countries through employment agencies often have their passports taken away by their employers as part of the *kefala* (sponsorship) system, which ties the migrant worker to the employer.[16]

In the survey, 40% of returnee migrants identified a lack of access to formal financial institutions as the primary factor that stopped them from using the system. The migrants noted that they tried to get around this by using various methods, mainly by sending money through another migrant who had valid documents. Also, those who worked for individual households would use their employers to send the money in their name.

The second disadvantage of the formal transfer system as identified by interviewees (26.8%) was the lower exchange rate compared with that in the informal market. In Ethiopia, foreign currency exchange rates are centrally controlled and uniform in all banks; and the banks almost always give a lower rate than the informal system does. The difference between the formal and informal market exchange rates can make a significant difference to the amount of money families receive in birr.

The third challenge, identified by 14% of returnee migrants, was the perceived complexity of the money transfer process of the banking institutions. A large number of Ethiopian migrants have a low education level and little knowledge of the formal transfer system—a challenge exacerbated by limited knowledge of local languages in the destination countries.

The fourth disadvantage, identified by 7% of returnee migrants, was the lack of access to banks by the receiving families. Despite the recent expansion of the banking network in Ethiopia, bank services are not always accessible to the rural population. Many people from rural areas need to travel to big towns to access the service. The relatively high transaction cost and the time taken for the process and for money to be transferred are the last two disadvantages given by 5% and 4% of the returnee migrants, respectively.

The informal remittance transfer channels

The most widely used system to send remittances home is the informal remittance transfer channel. Unlike the formal system, informal transfer systems operate outside conventional banking and financial channels and outside the policies of the origin or receiving countries. Their operation is motivated by the shared economic interest of the senders, the receivers and the transfer agents, and is characterised by speed, lower transaction costs, and easy accessibility. Accordingly, Ethiopian migrants in the Gulf and South Africa widely use informal remittance transfer mechanisms.

Key informants identified two types of informal system. First, there is the transfer of money in person and, second, the use of the *hawala* institutions. According to key informants, transfer of money in person takes place when one happens to find someone travelling back to Ethiopia. On the positive side, it usually does not cost anything and the receiving person receives the cash in hard currency, which he or she can exchange at any time and at better rates on the parallel market in Ethiopia. However, on the negative side, in-person transfer is dependent on the trustworthiness of the person entrusted with the task.

The second and most widely used informal remittance channel is the *hawala* system. Here, an informal agent in the sending country receives the money in the destination country and the associate in Ethiopia pays the recipient in Ethiopian birr. The *hawala* system, according to the key informants, is highly preferred for three reasons. First, it provides a better exchange rate than the formal channel. Second, it is fast and efficient. It was reported that families receive their remittance money from the Gulf and South Africa within two days. Third, it is very simple and does not require any documentation either to send or receive.

According to experts in financial institutions and government offices, the expansion of banking and the mobile telephone network in Ethiopia has led to the expansion and sophistication of the *hawala* system. Previously, the *hawala* dealer in Ethiopia would call the recipient on a landline telephone number given by the sender. There was no way to ensure that the person who picked up the phone was the intended recipient. Because of that, the agent had the additional task of ensuring the authenticity of the recipient before effecting payment and so required the physical presence of the recipient with an identity card. With the expansion of the mobile telephone network, telephone numbers have become identity numbers. Equally, the introduction and expansion of networked banking systems have helped facilitate the transfer of money to recipient families. The local agent of a *hawala* operator simply transfers the money into the bank account of the recipient. The task of authenticating the identity of the recipient is, therefore, transferred to the banks.

Use of remittances at household level

As the results of the qualitative and quantitative data gathered for this study show, there is a large inflow of remittance money in the study *woredas*. A large proportion of the migrants, shown in Figure 9.4 below, decided to migrate in order to support their families. So, it is no surprise that most migrants send money back to their families in Ethiopia.

The knowledge that the majority of the migrants send money to their families was shared by many of the key informants. For instance,

Figure 9.4: Reason for migration

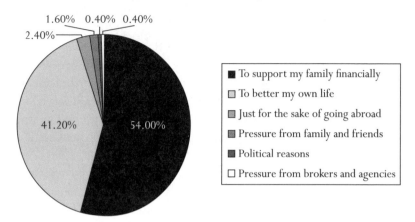

an informant from Kombolcha, Amhara Region, said that a large number of households in his locality receive remittance money from family members who work in Saudi Arabia or other Gulf States.[17] As Table 9.1 shows, 96% of the returnee migrant respondents said that they used to send money to their families.

With remittance money becoming such an important part of household income, it is important to consider how recipient families use the money. Families use remittance money in different ways, depending on the amount they receive and their economic position.[18] In many cases, remittance money is first used to settle the debts incurred by the cost of migration.[19] As Table 9.3 shows, 20% of the returnee migrants said they raised the money for their migration through loans and, hence, debt repayment is an important issue for many households.[20] In addition, remittances are used to regain property such as land that was given as collateral when households secured loans to finance the migration of family members.

As well as repaying debt, remittance money increases family resources to meet daily necessities, covering health and educational expenses, and purchasing household goods. As Table 9.4 indicates, 53.5% of the remittance-receiving families used the money mainly to cover household expenses, including food, clothing, educational costs, and health care.[21]

Table 9.3: Sources of money to finance the migration of family members

Source of money to finance migration	Responses	
	Frequency	Percentage
Loans	49	19.6
My own savings	30	12.0
Family member contributions	171	68.4
Total	250	100

Table 9.4: Expenditure of remittance money by recipient families

Purposes remittance money is used for	Responses	
	Frequency	Percentage
Household expenses such as health, schooling and clothing	107	53.5
House-building	30	15.0
Purchase of farm inputs such as fertiliser, seed, and oxen	15	7.5
House renovation	14	7.0
Purchase of furniture and other household items	9	4.5
Savings	7	3.5
House rental	7	3.5
Starting a new business	3	1.5
Debt repayment	3	1.5
Purchase of a shop	3	1.5
Condominium payment	2	1.0
Total	200	100

The reason why much of the remittance is spent on consumption is that many of the migrant families are poor (see Figure 9.5) and could not make savings from the remittance money they received.[22] Moreover, the amount of remittance migrants sent to families was small (owing to low salaries in the destination countries), and not enough to make savings for long-term investment and asset-building (see Box 1).

Figure 9.5: Distribution of migrants' families by source of income (as a percentage)

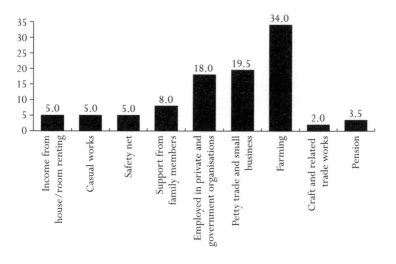

Box 1: Use of remittance money by households[23]

I went to Saudi Arabia intending to change my family's life, mainly through asset-building. In the end, however, I realised that it was impossible to do. The problem is multi-faceted. First, my salary was too small. However hard one works, it is almost impossible to keep and store up life-changing money within a given period. From that little salary, one spends for oneself and to support family. With this, the money is gone. Secondly, the high inflation and cost of living in Ethiopia makes saving and using the remittance money for asset-building difficult. Even if one saves some money, say 100,000 birr ($3,700), he or she can do little with it. Opening a kiosk needs more capital, let alone buying a house. People say, 'in the good old times, by working for a few years in Saudi Arabia, they were able to make a big difference'. This is now impossible. For that reason, many returnee migrants are frustrated and exposed to different kinds of illness, including mental problems.

The use of remittance money for consumption can create ill feelings among migrant workers and their families while they are abroad and after they have returned. For instance, one focus group discussion participant in Harbu said, 'I used to earn 800 Saudi riyals a month and sent a lot of it to my family through the banks every three months. However, when I came back home after three years, there was no change to the family—even the colour of our house was the same as I left it.'[24]

As this study found, only close to 26% of the migrants' families used remittance money for asset-building and savings. Many migrant families become dependent on remittance transfers for daily expenses and there is a widely held feeling that families put pressure on migrant workers to continue working abroad and keep sending money. When migrant workers return home, they face economic difficulties in many cases; some could not even raise the seed money required to get a loan or support from government employment schemes through Micro and Small Enterprises (MSEs). Supporting this, an informant at the Wereilu TVET College said that in the majority of cases in his locality, many of the returnees could not even raise the 20% capital required to secure loans from the Amhara Credit and Savings Institution (ACSI), which plays an important role in the region in job creation for the unemployed youth.[25]

However, when families of migrants use a larger portion of remittances for consumption purposes, this can help the revival of local economies and enable families to send children to school and to finance health care (see, for example, Boxes 2 and 3).

Box 2: Use of remittance money for supporting children's education[26]

My two sisters are working as migrant workers in Saudi Arabia. Our parents are farmers. Even if the income of the family was hand-to-mouth, it was enough to pay for basic expenses. The reason my sisters migrated was to improve their own livelihoods. The family covered the cost of the travel. Their monthly income is about 700 Saudi riyal. The money they send is used to cover the expenses of their children.

In addition to using remittance money to meet the costs of basic consumption, many households, particularly those in the urban areas, used the money for house renovation and to buy household goods—furniture and electronic goods such as television sets, satellite TV receivers and refrigerators.

A small proportion of households were able to make savings and engage in asset-building activities financed by remittance money. Indeed, close to 26% of the migrant families reported using remittance money for productive purposes in different forms. As Table 9.4 shows, the majority of households were engaged in different kinds of asset-building and saving activities, including payment for government low-cost (condominium) housing (1.5%), starting a small business (1.4%), purchasing a shop (1.4%), purchasing oxen for farming and farm inputs (7.5%), and building houses (15%). Of those who said they make savings and engage in asset-building activities, 3.5% had savings in banks.

Box 3: Use of remittance money for health care[27]

Fifteen years ago, I decided to migrate to cover my mother's medical costs. I divorced from my husband to travel to Saudi Arabia. I did not know how much money my family spent to cover the cost of my migration. My sister covered all the travel expenses when she was working in Saudi Arabia. When I was working in Saudi Arabia, my monthly salary was 500 Saudi riyal. I used to send all the money I could to my mother. The remittance money was used mainly to cover the medical costs of my mother, who was ill at that time.

The use of remittance money for asset-building has positive implications for many households. To give a few examples, households that were in a sharecropping arrangement owing to lack of oxen were able to free themselves by buying oxen with remittance money.[28] In some cases, as noted by an informant in the ACSI, Wereilu branch, some families of migrant workers were able to transform their subsistence farming into commercial farming by engaging in such activities as animal fattening.[29]

When we look at the major means of asset-building in the urban and rural areas, we see some differences. In the urban areas, the main means of asset-building is through the procurement of vehicles for business in the transport sector. The vehicles include three-legged *bajaj* taxis, small taxis and minibus taxis. A key informant in Kirkos sub-city of Addis Ababa noted the example of siblings who remained in the country; they were made to train and become drivers to support the household with their earnings. In the rural areas, the most important and most common means of asset-building by using migrant remittances was the construction of houses.[30] In many cases, rental houses were built in nearby urban and peri-urban areas to generate a sustainable income for the migrant household and create an asset for the reintegration of the migrant worker upon his or her return. There are, however, problems associated with this strategy. First, the construction of a house in an urban or peri-urban area without securing a house construction permit from local or municipal authorities may result in the house's demolition—a waste of hard-earned savings.[31] Second, even if the use of remittances for house construction is a good strategy, in many cases there has been conflict over ownership when the migrant worker returns to the locality, as the house is not registered in his or her name.[32] This is not limited to houses; it also happens with other property, such as vehicles. A high prevalence of familial disputes over savings and assets procured with remittance money was reported in localities where there are a large number of migrants (see also chapter 11).[33] The narrative presented in Box 4 exemplifies these incidents.

Box 4: Familial dispute over remittance money[34]

Jemila[35] worked for twenty years in Saudi Arabia. She was sending money to her uncle with the agreement that he will keep the money safe for her. She came back two years ago (2016) when she fell very ill. When she approached her uncle for her money, he refused to give her the money, which he supposedly was keeping for her. She went to the local authorities and made her case. When her uncle was asked, he denied receiving the money she claimed. She went to court but finally dropped the case—because

---

she could not stand in the court against her uncle. Later on, he only agreed to give her a small amount of the money that she transferred to him. He argued that whatever money she sent to him, he spent on his children's education.

Even if the inflow of remittance money to families and communities is seen positively, the money can have adverse repercussions on families and communities. First, according to informants, some families have become dependent on remittance transfers.[36] Second, some family members, largely husbands and younger siblings (usually brothers), have been accused of using the remittance to obtain recreational substances, such as *khat*, alcohol and tobacco, and in some cases *shisha*.[37] Third, some families of migrants spend remittance money extravagantly on the purchase of ornaments, or on the celebration of religious festivals and social events like wedding and memorials for the dead.[38] Although such activities have important social functions, migrant families who receive remittances tend to spend more than families that do not, and so are less likely to use remittances for savings and asset-building activities.[39] Box 5 presents a narrative of such a case in point.

Box 5: Recipient families' expenditure of remittance money[40]

Kalu *woreda*[41] is highly affected by the migration of young people to the Arab countries. In the past few years, a large number of young people including civil servants and graduates of higher learning institutions have migrated to work in the Gulf countries. Without exaggeration, almost every household has at least one member serving as a migrant worker abroad; and most migrants remit money to their family back home. Due to the inflow of remittance money to the locality, lifestyles of the local people have been changing. Some families also engaged in extravagant and unproductive expenditure of the remittance money. In some cases, households organise a traditional prayer ceremony called '*wadaja*', which requires expenditure of a large sum of money. For this ceremony, a large number of people including relatives and friends are served food and drinks. The way families spend remittance money has negative repercussion on migrant workers. When the migrant workers return home, they will learn that the families have spent all the money they sent them. They could not find any support for their reintegration. They have two choices—one is migrating again and continue working abroad, the other is re-entering the poverty they tried to escape by migrating.

Even if there is a realisation among local officials that a large amount of money comes to their localities through remittances, according to informants, no concerted effort is made by local governments and non-governmental organisations to encourage remittance recipients to use the money (or at least some portion of it) for savings and asset-building.[42] Instead, the government and donors have developed programmes which aim to rehabilitate returnees from the Gulf countries.[43]

Conclusion

The magnitude of international migration from Ethiopia has substantially increased in recent decades owing to various political, social and economic factors. Since the 1990s, the Gulf countries and South Africa have emerged as major destinations for a significant portion of Ethiopian labour migrants. Labour migration to the Gulf countries includes both documented and undocumented migrants, while the majority of migrants in South Africa work in small businesses without securing permits. The Ethiopian diaspora and migrant workers remit money for a variety of reasons, ranging from assistance to their families to investment. Indeed, in recent years, remittance flows to Ethiopia have become important sources of foreign currency. In this regard, the NBE reported that the amount of remittances flowing to Ethiopia increased from $3.04 billion in 2013/14 to $3.99 billion in 2015/16.[44] There is limited understanding of the factors that influence migrants to use formal or informal channels of remittance transfer and how remittances influence the socio-economic well-being of households. Based on these premises, the study examined the various channels through which Ethiopian labour migrants in the two destinations send remittances to their families, and how remittances are utilised at the household level.

The study indicated, first, that while almost all of the sample returnee migrants (97%) used to send money to their families back home, 92% of families of migrants acknowledged receiving remittance money through different channels. The widespread practice among migrant workers of sending remittances can be explained by the primary motive for their migration—the desire to improve their and their families' livelihood.

Second, the study showed that remittances are sent by formal and informal channels and sometimes both, each having its own advantages and drawbacks. In the survey, while half of the sample returnee migrants said they had used informal channels to send money, only 28% of the sample families of migrants claimed that they had received remittances through such channels. The high proportion of families claiming to receive remittance money through banks does not explain the growth of the formal transfer system. It shows rather the increasing use of the expanding bank and mobile network by informal operators.

Third, the formal transfer system is considered reliable and contributes to the national economy by bringing much sought-after foreign currency to the country through the banking system. Despite this, the use of the formal transfer system is hampered by some serious limitations. The need for money senders to present valid personal identification documents at the formal money transfer institutions, the lower exchange rates it provides in comparison with the informal market, the 'complexity' of the system, and the high cost of the transaction are all major challenges of the formal system.

On the other hand, the informal system of transferring money is trust-based, operates outside the conventional banking and financial channels, and is motivated by the shared economic interests of sender, receiver and transfer agent. Low transaction costs, speedy transfer and easy accessibility of the remittance are the main reasons why migrants prefer the informal transfer system.

The study also found that the expansion of core banking systems and mobile phones has greatly contributed to the expansion of the informal system. The expansion of banks does not necessarily correlate with the increase of formal remittance transfers. Indeed, agents who collect hard currencies abroad use the banks to deliver remittance money to the recipient families through their counterparts in Ethiopia. This shows the interface that obtains between the formal and informal systems of transferring money.

The study also examined the use of remittance money at the household level. The money is used for different purposes, including debt settlement, consumption and asset-building endeavours. Much remittance money is used for consumption, such as paying for necessities, education and health care. A small number of recipient families used remittance money for (productive) asset-building purposes. In rural areas, the main means of asset-building is the construction of houses in newly emerging towns and nearby peri-urban and urban areas for rent, while in the urban areas (where the price of a plot of land is very high) families use remittance money to start small businesses.

Even if the inflow of remittances has certain positive implications for families and communities, how it is used can have adverse repercussions. The fact that migrant families use large portions of the money for consumption can make them increasingly dependent on remittances. This is largely because of the small sums of money involved and the poor economic situation of the recipient families. However, the use of remittances predominantly for consumption undermines young people's aspirations to bring themselves and their families out of poverty through migration.

10

HETEROGENEITY IN OUTCOMES OF MIGRATION

THE CASE OF IRREGULAR MIGRATION TO SAUDI ARABIA IN HARRESAW, EASTERN TIGRAY

Kiros Birhanu

Introduction

In Ethiopia, the economic impacts and the hardships associated with international migration have been well documented, especially by the Ethiopian government, so much so that they have entered the public narrative. Less has been written about the impact of migration on social life and how ideas evolve in the sending communities. This chapter focuses on both the economic dimension and the more subtle social and cultural dimensions of the impacts of the mostly irregular migration to Saudi Arabia from Harresaw (eastern Tigray). Using empirical data, I show that these impacts are highly heterogeneous, even within this small rural community. The data from Harresaw also shows that the economic returns from irregular migration to Saudi Arabia have significantly deteriorated in the few years preceding 2018, and this has been accompanied by more acute social and family disruptions. However, migration continues to be a major driver of change, arguably exerting more influence on the community's future than government development efforts thus far.

As will be seen in this chapter, the case of Harresaw provides a textbook example of how 'contextuality' underpins the heterogeneity of migration outcomes.[1] Drawing on De Haas's theoretical perspective on migration and development, this case also warns against the 'naivety of recent views celebrating migration as self-help development "from below"'. While agency matters, attention also ought to focus on 'structural constraints and the vital role of states in shaping favourable conditions for positive development impacts of migration to occur'.[2] In Harresaw, where complex structural challenges such as climate change[3] and high rural youth unemployment (see chapter 1 by Alemu) are acutely felt at the local level, outmigration is a logical response by agents trying to overcome these challenges. I therefore join Alemu in suggesting that there is a case for the Ethiopian government to more decidedly orient its own response, policies and actions in such a way that, especially for communities like Harresaw, migration abroad can truly support local development.

This chapter is based on extensive fieldwork in Harresaw, a small remote drought-prone community located in eastern Tigray, with data collected at several points in time in the last three decades. The focus is on data collected in early 2018, contrasting it where relevant with data from 2012. Earlier data provides a historical perspective. The data was collected as part of the Ethiopia WIDE research (see Introduction), focusing on all aspects of the community's life and how they have changed over time. The broad perspective of the WIDE research has limitations with regard to the depth of migration-specific data. However, the changes associated with migration and their effects can be put in the context of other drivers of change, including government interventions—this is indispensable to substantiate the argument outlined above.

In the sections below I first briefly review the literature discussing effects of outmigration, including those beyond the economic sphere. The next section contextualises the empirical data that I use, briefly presenting Harresaw and a historical overview of irregular migration to Saudi from the community. The next sections discuss some of the multiple effects of this migration in the community. The final section draws on these to conclude.

Migration as a strategy with multi-faceted, context-contingent effects

Empirical work suggests that migration is often a deliberate individual or household decision, intended to 'overcome development constraints in the place of origin'[4] and 'to diversify, secure, and, potentially, durably improve their livelihoods' through enabling investments.[5] Whether or not these goals are achieved is contingent on complex interactions between the agents involved in the migration process and the structural factors influencing it at micro-, meso- and macro-levels. The 'contextuality' of these agent–structure interactions explains the heterogeneity in actual migration outcomes.[6] The recognition that migration outcomes are heterogeneous resonates with the suggestion of the editors of this volume that 'assemblage thinking' is a useful tool to analyse migration as a complex social and political reality.

The available literature shows that irregular migration is increasing, despite the horror stories and deportations. According to International Organization for Migration, over 100,000 Ethiopians have returned from Saudi Arabia since March 2017. Migration from Ethiopia has been on the rise since 2010, particularly using the eastern migratory route through Djibouti, Somaliland and Yemen to Saudi Arabia. In 2016, there was a 26% increase in the number of migrants arriving in Yemen, making a record of 117,107 migrants. Of these, 83% were estimated to be Ethiopian.[7]

The literature also highlights that irregular migration to the Middle East is often accompanied by adverse experiences. As Fasil noted, people deported from Saudi Arabia often faced imprisonment or sexual harassment, returning without money and with psychosocial problems.[8] Deportation also leads to family dissatisfaction when expectations of remittances from the migrant are not met.[9] It is common for girls and women to face sexual violence from brokers during their journey, and harsh conditions at their destination. Studies of female migrants indicate that, even though there are some positive experiences, these are the exception, with most women experiencing excessively long working hours, and delayed or partial payment, and many experiencing physical and sexual abuse. The abuse ranges from severe limits on food to acid and chemical attacks; other incidents included repeated beatings, and being thrown down stairs and off balconies, causing serious and permanent injury. Returnee migrants are likely to suffer from physical and psychological health issues owing to abusive working conditions and brutal attacks from traffickers.[10]

Besides these potential negative experiences and effects, irregular migration has a range of mixed economic, social and cultural effects on the sending households and community, whether migration ends up in success or failure. Economically, there can be positive impacts when migrants are employed in destination countries. Remittances are among the most important features of migration that impact on the lives of migrants and their families. Asnake and Zerihun (in chapter 9) indicate that in Ethiopian households with migrants abroad, remittances are used to pay debts and provide increased family resources to pay for daily necessities, health and educational expenses, and household goods. This is in line with Lipton's general observation that more than 90% of remittances are spent on such 'everyday consumption'.[11] However, if we take a 'broader, capabilities-focused perspective on human development', then such expenses should be seen as 'potentially developmental as long as they enhance people's wellbeing and capabilities'.[12]

McDowell and De Haan also indicate that migration, especially by younger men, may create a labour gap which negatively impacts on the economic and livelihood practices of households.[13] However, as the new economics of labour migration theory stresses, depending on the local context and, in particular, the local labour market, such migration may also be an effective household 'risk-spreading' strategy if it allows higher overall income returns, immediate or future, from this household labour allocation.[14]

In non-economic terms, the migration of women potentially brings significant social change in relations between spouses and in gender norms and values. There is no space in this chapter to fully engage with the expanding literature on female migration and women's 'empowerment'. To cite only two studies, these show that migration may make women dissatisfied with rural life and with the compliance with prevailing gender norms expected of them after they come back, especially when men want to maintain their dominant status within the household.[15] This potentially can have disruptive social effects. However, recent empirical work on Ethiopian (female) migrant domestic workers also suggests that, 'despite the extractive dynamic of their migration trajectories, there is nevertheless the possibility of transformative potential that can be realised upon their return' within a contemporary Ethiopian context 'that has become more explicitly supportive of women's rights'.[16]

Similar remarks can be made about the potential social change effects of the migration of young people as a social group. Young people observing the success of migrants and their families and facing limited access to production assets may be encouraged to think of migration as the 'new normal'—the surest way to transition from youthhood to adulthood, as is socially expected of them (see the Introduction). Migration may be perceived as offering, and indeed in some instances may actually offer, a quicker, surer path to independence than education.[17] This may thus lead to a 'culture of migration'.[18]

In the sections below I draw on these discussions to explore some of the effects of irregular migration to Saudi from Harresaw.

Historicity and evolution of irregular migration in Harresaw

In Harresaw, over half of the households are female-headed, as a consequence of the irregular migration of predominantly men, and there are hundreds of landless, mainly young households. Available land has been reallocated but it is vastly insufficient; generally, land and related interactions are a source of tension and conflict. Moving away for work to sustain oneself and one's household has been a longstanding feature of life in Harresaw. Migration to Saudi Arabia has existed in the community for decades, alongside other migration flows, in patterns that have evolved over time. Historically, people have migrated seasonally, or for longer periods, to destinations within Ethiopia such as neighbouring Afar Region, towns in Tigray, and the sesame farms in western Tigray. Before the Ethiopian–Eritrean war of 1998–2000 and the subsequent closure of the border, Eritrea was, for decades, a popular destination for people from Harresaw, who worked on the large irrigated farms or in the capital, Asmara, where people picked up skills such as masonry and carpentry. In the decades following the war, migration to Saudi Arabia, mostly irregular, came gradually to replace migration to Eritrea.

Irregular migration to Saudi Arabia started in 1985, according to one of the men who first migrated, via neighbouring Afar. However, the sharp rise in the number of migrants happened in more recent years. During the mid-1980s famine, a few people from Harresaw migrated to Saudi Arabia using the trade and information links that existed between that town and Afar. The number rose, slowly at first, and then more quickly during and after a severe drought in 1992/93. There was a further steep increase in response to a debt crisis linked to another devastating drought in 2007/08. In those years, migration to Saudi became a means to repay loans for the many households who had been put under pressure by the government to acquire livestock, which died in large numbers from the drought. At that time, it was considered an achievement to be able to repay one's debt. This was also the time when women started migrating to Saudi.

Quite quickly the number of migrants shot up, and people also began to stay away longer and to accumulate capital beyond what was needed for debt repayment. So, in 2012, 400 to 500 people were said to be going every year, and migration to Saudi was morphing from a coping to an investment strategy. Seeing the gains made by earlier migrants that went beyond debt repayment, more ambitious aspirations emerged, and people started to migrate to improve their living conditions as well as to cope with landlessness, low farming productivity, lack of work opportunities, and, generally, the insufficient reach of development interventions in the area.

The context in 2018 was markedly different from that in 2012, with structural changes at local, national and international levels. Locally, structural problems had worsened. A prolonged spell of poor rain between 2013 and 2018 forced people who had started producing crops and vegetables with irrigation to quit, with knock-on effects, such as considerably reduced demands for local daily labour and generally lower household incomes in the community. At the same time, as chapter 1 highlights more broadly, in the community the government rural youth job creation programme was woefully inadequate in providing alternatives to migration for the growing number of landless young people and households.[19]

The national and international context of migration to Saudi Arabia had also radically changed (see chapter1). In response to horror stories of migrants being abused and the decision taken by the Saudi authorities to expel all irregular migrants in late 2013, the Ethiopian government prohibited legal migration in 2013 and intensified its anti-trafficking measures in 2015. These measures contributed to a decline in the number of migrants to Saudi Arabia from Harresaw and other parts of Tigray, especially in the first few months after the ban. However, in 2018 many in Harresaw continued to try their luck. Almost all of those doing so migrated irregularly, in spite of the reopening of legal avenues from 2016. Yet the war and lawlessness in Yemen made the journey far riskier, the decline of the Saudi economy meant lower salaries, and the regular Saudi deportations of irregular migrants cut short migrants' stay. Large numbers of migrants were deported in late 2013 and early 2014—after which crackdowns and deportations continued, with another large wave in 2017, and continuously thereafter on a smaller scale.

These structural changes made migration to Saudi Arabia a much riskier undertaking. There was regular news of mostly young people dying on the way. There was also less chance of success and fewer success stories. And when success was obtained, it was smaller than in the past—only a small number of migrants achieved the level of economic success which many aspired to and which past migrants had achieved.

Having set out the context, in the following sections I discuss a number of the mixed effects of irregular migration to Saudi in Harresaw. It is important to note that, especially in the economic and cultural spheres, migration to Saudi was just one of the contributory factors to the changes that took place. Important too were the effects of the closer links of the community with towns and cities and of the much expanded communications media, especially on youth practices.[20]

Changes in community labour dynamics

One of the major societal impacts of irregular migration on sending communities has to do with changes in labour dynamics. Irregular migration in Harresaw created labour gaps at family and community levels, as migrants' labour contributions disappeared with them. At the household level, this was worse if the migrant died. If he or she was physically or mentally injured, the migrant's return became an additional burden on an already impoverished household.

The household-level labour gap was reduced to some extent when migrants could send remittances, because replacement labour could then be paid for. But it did not solve the problem, as explained by LB, a woman whose husband was at the time of the interview repeatedly migrating. Her land is ploughed by one of her brothers. He ploughs it once, but the land needs ploughing two or three times. Therefore, LB does not produce as much as she could from her land. She is also the one dealing with the life of her household, for instance, looking after her child at school. She is left alone to make household decisions.

The labour gap was also mentioned as an issue in relation to collective community works and government-organised community public works. The labour shortage is seen at weddings, burials and commemorations of deaths. In the past, when somebody died, young people took the body to the burial grounds, but with the absence of youth labour, older men now perform the task. The shortage of manpower to carry pregnant women to the health centre, located outside the community, was mentioned as an issue by a health extension worker. Community leaders also stated that many development team members[21] migrate to Saudi each year, hampering the implementation of government-organised public works such as soil and water conservation. This affected both productive safety-net public works[22] and the 'free community labour' activities.

Other economic changes

At individual and household levels, economic changes from outmigration to Saudi spanned a wide range, from strongly negative outcomes when migration was financed by debt and the migrant died or was unable to reach or find work at the destination, to better outcomes when migrants were able to send remittances or save for themselves. Some of the factors influencing these outcomes included: (1) the economic background of migrants, especially whether they funded their migration through borrowing or with support from their parents' savings or assets; (2) whether they reached their destination; (3) whether they got a job once they arrived in Saudi Arabia or not, and how well paid the job was; (4) how long they managed to stay in the country before being deported; and (5) in what condition they managed to return. As seen earlier, migrants were more likely to face challenges with regard to all of these factors in 2018, which explains the decline in economic returns already mentioned.

The success of migrants depended not only on their journey and the job opportunities at the destination but also on the situation they faced on return, with regard to investment in the community or the *woreda* town. Coming back from Saudi Arabia with large savings did not automatically translate into success: there were cases of returnee migrants with relatively large sums of money who did not easily find good investment opportunities. The *woreda* officials said that they wanted to focus on those returnees to advise them what to do, rather than on the deportees or those who voluntarily agreed to be repatriated and returned with less money. But even with that advice, constraints on investment arose from the underdeveloped local context in the *woreda* as a whole, even in the *woreda* centre Atsbi. The case of EL, a man from Harresaw who migrated to Saudi Arabia several times and who in 2018 was living in Atsbi, illustrates this point. After a first migration experience, he opened a shop in Atsbi but did not make a good return. He sold everything, closed his shop and migrated again. He came back with money and built a house, which he was partly renting. However, he had no other occupation and wanted to migrate again as his savings were declining. He explained:

> These days, unlike when I was running my shop before my last migration, Atsbi's market is saturated. Everyone is opening a shop, or a pub, or starting metalwork, but Atsbi is a small town and the market is small. So, if I started something I might go bankrupt. For the same reason I don't want to take a loan from the bank; in addition, the interest rate is very high.

One of the community-wide effects of irregular migration to Saudi Arabia has been the growth of the small but expanding non-farm sector in Harresaw centre. This was achieved by a number of returnees opening shops, leisure places or other mainly service businesses. These businesses led to the intensification of links with towns through the migrants or migrants' families who had trade links with those towns for their local businesses or invested there. This also expanded the range of goods and services available to other community members. These trends, in turn, fuelled a number of other effects discussed below.

Changes in local consumption patterns

Migration to Saudi Arabia brought significant changes in local consumption patterns in the community. Remittances impacted on the social and cultural lives of receiving families through their consumption. Migrants' families were better able to afford the basics of food, shelter and clothing and to cover health and education costs. Remittances made possible better living standards, repayment of loans, and some shift in economic activity. Some people, mainly before the start of the Saudi Arabia crackdown on irregular migrants, were able to buy electronic goods including TVs, smartphones and models of rechargeable lamps not found in local markets. These items were mostly sent from Saudi Arabia. A few migrants were able to build important assets like houses and business in the locality and in Atsbi.

The migrants and their families were able to spend a lot on wedding ceremonies (giving gold as the bride price or dowry and inviting many people, including some from outside the *tabia*), mourning ceremonies and commemorations of the dead. However, migration to Saudi was also a way for some young men to save enough to be able to start a small business on their return and establish an independent livelihood, which they saw as indispensable for starting out on married life.

Migrants' families are most likely to be the first to acquire new fashions and new models of mobile phones in the community. Irregular migration to Saudi also brought wider community-level effects. One of the most visible changes attributed to migration involved young people's clothing—although, as noted above, Harresaw's closer links to towns and cities also contributed to these trends. It was common to see young men and women wearing new types of expensive clothes and competing among themselves. This was said to be the result of returnees from Saudi Arabia wearing better clothes; others tried to copy them and considered migrating because they were impressed by the fashions. The clothes of the returnees were not common in the community and the new trends, especially baggy jeans worn without a belt, were disliked by adults. Young women wearing trousers when they returned from Saudi or from towns were also frowned upon. However, unlike young men, who continued to do as they pleased, young women explained that they changed back to wearing clothes acceptable to the community—keeping other clothes like jeans for trips to towns. In 2018, people also said that some migrants had returned with savings in the previous year but were spending their money on gambling and alcohol.

These more consumerist trends were far more visible in 2018 than in 2012. When asked why they didn't use their savings for something more productive, young returnees noted that what they had saved was not enough to start anything worthwhile—suggesting that the rise in consumerist trends was linked to the reduced chances of success for migrants. For some other members of the community, these 'consumerist' attitudes were seen as laziness and a source of worry.

Aspirations and worries

The exposure of rural youth to the relative wealth and success of migrants, combined with changing tastes and material aspirations due to the growing connectedness of the community, made the rural way of life less appealing and discouraged local people from working in traditional sectors—which in any case offered limited possibilities.[23] This encouraged more outmigration. Young people aspired to migrate to Saudi Arabia, and some parents aspired to have their children migrate. Other factors compounding this included widespread and growing landlessness, especially among younger generations, the regular drought and low farming productivity in the area, and the absence of government interventions that would be effective in improving people's lives in the community.

There has been a significant shift in what young people and many community members aspire to. Previously, many aspired to attain a certain level of education and obtain a job in this way. However, in 2018, the aspirations of many young people had shifted away from education-related jobs towards migration as a way to be able to establish their own businesses. The hope invested in education was dashed when youngsters observed that many of their slightly older peers, who had completed Grade 10, remained unemployed in the community. At the same time, visible examples of people succeeding in migration without much education was said to be one of the reasons for students to drop out and engage in irregular migration. In 2012, most of those interested in migrating were less educated young people; but by early 2018, educated youth, including teachers, development agents and other government employees, also aspired to migrate and did so in significant numbers. Whilst there were exceptions, with a few youth aspiring to study further and enter professional jobs, there was a sense that, in general, young people in Harresaw had become less interested in education, and their only wish was to migrate.

People said that the youth wanted to get enough money to move to towns and lead their lives there. This was reflected in the aspirations of the majority of the young men and women interviewed in 2018, who considered migration to Arab countries as the only way to get enough money to move to the towns in a short period of time. The relatively positive attitude that people from Harresaw had developed towards migration was, in turn, a further incentive for young people to consider migrating and for parents to consider it for their children.

On the other hand, some interviewees vividly highlighted the uncertainty, worries and real harms that migration also brought. The widespread aspiration of young people to migrate was a concern for parents as well as for the young people themselves, while simultaneously they were worried about unemployment if they stayed put. And so, as explained by LB, who had a repeatedly migrating husband:

> in their mind, there is only Saudi. One day you can see this guy rearing chicken or something and the day after, he has gone. They hear 'Saudi' in their ears all the time … now, nobody knows how many are going, how many are returning, how many are dying and where. People from Harresaw are disappearing and nobody knows for sure where and how many. Recently, my sister's husband died in Saudi when he was pushed off a building he was working in. They could not pay to repatriate the body and he had to be buried there. And to an extent, they were lucky because they knew he had died.

Another example was the head of a middle-income household in Harresaw, with a daughter who had migrated to Saudi a year before and a son to Afar three months before. None of his children had been involved in government youth interventions. His main worries for them and their future were unemployment and migration. He explained that he was deeply concerned that his younger children might also want to migrate to Saudi and Afar as their siblings had done. Harresaw is replete with such family stories and experiences.

Family and social tensions

In 2018, the strong desire of many young people to migrate had become a concern for many households and for the community as a whole, because of the multiple burdens it placed on a family to send a child away. If all children went, parents had nobody around to help them; also, young people wanting to migrate often tended to do nothing productive until they were able to realise their aspirations, and so they were already of no help. To cover migration expenses, the would-be migrants requested money from their parents and parents were placed in financial difficulty when they sold livestock or rented out their farming land to help their children. This led to conflicts within households, either because parents were reluctant to help a child migrate or, when migrants found a way to fund their own migration and went without their parents' consent, they put them in financial difficulty if they were not successful. No one was immune: even a former *kebele* leader, a social court leader at the time of interview, had been in conflict with one of his sons who had migrated without his consent, only to be stopped before crossing into Saudi Arabia, leaving his father with a debt. Some respondents felt this had led to a trend of general deterioration in intergenerational relationships in the community.

It was observed that young people no longer obeyed their parents, let alone listened to other elders in the community. There seemed to be considerable heterogeneity and ambiguity in the positions of parents towards migration to Saudi. Many respondents argued that parents wanted their children to migrate. Others indicated that parents' interest in getting their children to migrate had declined over the previous few years owing to the frequent cases of death and imprisonment. Interviews with parents whose children were away or wanting to migrate often reflected considerable anxiety, while simultaneously they showed signs of resignation, as there were so few other opportunities for those who stayed. Those who did not migrate or did not have any migrant household members were similarly ambiguous. For instance, a priest of St Rufael Church said, when talking about young people obsessed with migration, 'We don't support migration, but we understand their frustration so we cannot criticise them harshly. What do we have to tell them?' He then criticised youth programmes for being insufficient in coverage and ineffective (asking, for instance, what youth should eat during the years it takes for a eucalyptus to grow), and the government for not doing enough to give young people skills that they could use and pass on to others.

A *woreda* education supervisor of the Harresaw schools highlighted the huge loss for the community that could ensue from irregular migration when he recalled the news of deaths caused by irregular migration, which included clever students from the area: 'Among them, there were our clever students whom we were proud of, and trusting that they would join universities with good points and be successful in education. When we heard the news, we cried and felt deep sorrow but we could not help it except cursing illegal migration.' People, especially parents and spouses of migrants, who have information about the high risks of the journey to Saudi and the life there, live in stress. They worry a lot about the future of their children or spouses and what might happen to them while trying to cross into Saudi illegally. This was expressed as follows by a group of men from Harresaw, some of whom had migrated themselves or had children or spouses trying to migrate:

> those who have a migrant away, son or daughter, don't have a stable life; their life is full of stress about what happens to the migrant; they worry if he or she doesn't call, that they may have died. Those who have their children with them are much luckier. Those with their children away are like blind people, they don't see what is happening to their child. Moreover, they miss the help that this young man or woman could have given to the household.[24]

Mixed gendered impacts

The experience of migration among men and women has an impact on gender roles and responsibilities. Gender roles shift when husbands stay away or when women migrate themselves. As mentioned above, in Harresaw migration to Saudi Arabia was initially a male undertaking, but women also started to migrate during and after the 2007/08 drought. In 2018 all the young women interviewed knew other women of their age who were or had been in Saudi, some of them saying they knew twenty or thirty; others had migrated themselves. There were also a few instances of young couples in which both spouses migrated.

Migration to Saudi Arabia enabled young women to establish an independent livelihood. This can be seen as positive, as empowerment in many ways. It was certainly in stark contrast to the past when marriage was a prerequisite for a woman wanting to establish an independent household—which, for most women, was nothing else than a transition from being under the authority of a father to that of a husband. In contrast, some women migrant returnees were able to acquire important resources like houses, and to establish their own businesses. Some respondents even thought that young women who migrated to Saudi were more successful than the young men.

Some young women with migration experience were critical of the lives of women in the community. For instance, a young returnee showed the researcher photos of herself in Saudi wearing modern clothes and a modern hairstyle. She complained that she had to avoid such styles now because they were taboo in the community; this she considered a form of backwardness. Highlighting other aspects, such as women's role in the household, and their reproductive role, she added:

> Previously, it was not common for young women to migrate to Saudi like young men. It is since 2000 EC [2007/08] that it became very common. Young women used to marry farmers here and they were leading a bad life, having children and serving their husbands as slaves. However, the situation currently has changed. Young women are migrating to Saudi and improving their livelihoods independently. I became aware of the hardship and sufferings of life for young women here after I saw so many things in Saudi. For instance, women here suffer too much during labour. Women in Saudi give birth without any pain because there is a medicine to eliminate the pain. I was very surprised when I saw this and felt pity for young women in my community who suffer too much during labour.

Migration to Saudi has also led to shifts in intra-household decision-making patterns. Women with husbands in Saudi Arabia made decisions on matters which would otherwise have been handled by husbands. However, for some of them, this was a mixed blessing, as they faced difficulties managing these matters. AB, whose husband was in Saudi Arabia, explained that her husband's migration did not bring much change for her. The money he sent was used to repay the government loan which had financed his migration and for household expenses. Also, her husband did not send money regularly because of the shortage of jobs in Saudi. Generally, she thought that households where the husband was present were better off, because they could plan together and support each other. AB said that when the husband was away, everything was difficult, including raising the children; children were more difficult to control in the absence of their father and it was the job of the father, more than that of the mother, to control them. Her own father died in Saudi, and so she wanted her husband to be with her.

LB, whom I quoted above, mentioned the sadness which comes when a husband and father is regularly away. She said that in her neighbourhood, out of fifty households only four have an absent husband. The others live by doing local daily labour or by migrating to Afar. Compared with wages in Saudi, she said, what they earned was nothing, it was living from hand-to-mouth. But she did not believe she was the lucky one. For her, the other women were the lucky ones to have their husbands around, or if he migrated to Afar he could return whenever they decided and become involved with the children. In her case, her children didn't even know their father, as he'd been away all the time. Others might think she had a lot of money, but that was not the case, as most of the money he made would be used to finance his next trip. Moreover, she added, money was not the only thing that keeps a family alive.

There are cases of family disruption when both parents are migrants—a trend that was also on the rise in 2018. An influential woman, who since the death of her husband has been head of the household, talked of 'young women who migrate and leave children with their grandparents', who struggle to raise them. For instance, she was raising her migrant daughter's children, and stressed that this was a 'heavy burden for the grandparents, who struggle to ensure the children's food, schooling, health care and other needs'. She added that this was becoming common and there were probably more than thirty such cases in the community.

Other incidents of family disruption arose because of tensions between spouses when one of them was a migrant (more often the husband), sometimes leading to divorce. There were also cases of successful male migrants who had initiated divorce and were getting married to another wife when they came back.

Migration to Saudi also impacted on the process of young people forming couples. In 2018 some respondents mentioned that migration to Saudi Arabia increased marriageability for both male and female migrants. They were sought as marriage partners because of the prospect that they would return with money and could afford assets such as land and houses. When asked what kind of man they would like to marry, many young women expressed a preference for a businessman, and said that migrants were, therefore, good prospects as they could acquire the capital needed to establish a business. Others suggested that migration was enabling young people to fulfil their desire to get married. For the majority, getting married and establishing an independent household was difficult. Young men struggled to afford the costs of the wedding and of the dowry, let alone to establish an independent livelihood. In contrast, some of those returning from Saudi Arabia with money were able to organise the wedding feast, pay the dowry, establish their household and, for some, acquire some assets or start a small business. Yet others stressed that young returnees found it difficult to interact with counterparts who had never migrated, because of the large experiential gap between them. This was said to be particularly true for young women with migration experience.

Irregular migration and the Orthodox Church

People from Harresaw are predominantly Orthodox Christians. The Orthodox Church in Harresaw is an important and influential institution, and priests are usually respected figures. However, the Church was not immune to the effects of irregular migration in the community. In turn, this was said to be a major factor in what people described as a decline in religious practices.

One consequence of migration was that churches were left with fewer serving ministers, because many deacons and some priests had migrated to Saudi. This was already mentioned as a possible problem by community members in 2012. In 2018, it had become a fact and was said to have led to people spending less time engaged in religious activities than in the past. Some people thought that the observance of religious rules and norms was becoming weaker, less strict. People were not as committed about fasting and church attendance. The number of religious students going for education outside the community had dropped as well. The fact that deacons and even priests were also migrating to Saudi added to the momentum of migration in general. In addition, people disliked the fact that deacons and priests had to adopt a Muslim lifestyle in Saudi, and then provide religious services again back home as if nothing had happened upon their return. Community members had less trust in these religious figures, and they reduced their involvement in religious activities as a result.

Somewhat paradoxically, even though it was well known that some priests migrated, the Church, as an influential institution in the community, was expected by the government to convey official messages about the negative sides of irregular migration. Church leaders did so but refrained from fully condemning the migrants or stigmatising their actions. As a priest from St Rufael Church stated, 'We also have responsibilities as members of the community, and when our government is asking us to educate the youth, for instance against migration, we do so. But the Church will not formally condemn them.'

Conclusion

As the chapter shows, irregular migration to Saudi has become an intrinsic part of the community's life in Harresaw. This is not because people are happy about migration but because they can see no better way to secure their livelihood or, for the more ambitious, because they try to 'durably improve it'.[25] In particular, migration to Saudi is a local response to widespread youth unemployment and climate change that is undermining farming prospects. As some of the literature makes clear, the data also shows that while the intention of irregular migration to Saudi in Harresaw is economic improvement, the impact of migration goes beyond economic gains or losses. There are subtle as well as visible social, cultural and spiritual impacts that are affecting migrants, their families and the community, both negatively and positively.

In the chapter I also show that, as De Haas highlights, both the economic and non-economic outcomes of migration are heterogeneous.[26] This is so in several ways. First, outcomes differ from one individual and household within the community to another, worsening the situation of some (for instance, the woman who couldn't even bring back her husband's body) and improving it (as was intended) for others (for instance, the returnees who were able to build a house or open a shop or another business), although this was not always lasting. Outcomes are also heterogeneous across the different dimensions affected by migration. Effects can be positive in one dimension but migration can bring undesired impacts in other dimensions—for example, remittances help pay for schooling and food, but losing a husband's labour or a father's guidance is a significant loss. Migration outcomes are also heterogenous in that they relate not only to the migrant and those directly involved in her or his migration experience, such as parents, grandparents, spouses and children, but also to the community as a whole (for instance, the effects on young people's marriages). Moreover, outcomes are heterogenous in that various people may have different perspectives about whether, on balance, migration effects are positive or negative or, indeed, different views about whether an effect is positive or negative, such as the greater decision-making role which women with migrant spouses have to assume.

Finally, in this chapter I also show that in Harresaw, while individual or household-specific circumstances do matter in determining the outcomes of irregular migration to Saudi, there also has been an underlying general trend of deteriorating outcomes, clearly visible from the 2012 and 2018 data. It is also clear that the main reasons for this trend have been structural changes at the national and international level, making this migration riskier and less profitable. This has compounded the negative effects of structural changes at the local level (such as drought curtailing irrigation opportunities, or ever-rising youth unemployment). Arguably, these structural changes have strongly constrained, instead of promoting, migrants' agency; yet many in the communities have continued to try to migrate, seeing no other option.

11

THE MORAL ECONOMY OF IRREGULAR MIGRATION AND REMITTANCE DISTRIBUTION IN SOUTH WOLLO

Teferi Abate Adem

Introduction

This chapter is primarily concerned with culturally expected developmental cycles of households and related kin- and neighbourhood-based moral-economic entitlements that are relevant for understanding the local drivers of informal labour migration.[1] Ethnographic data on these previously overlooked micro-level processual and contextual issues was collected while revisiting a rural community in South Wollo, first in the summer of 2016, and again in October 2018 and August 2019. During each visit, I noted that the everyday conversation of farmers was dominated by widely shared anxiety about the well-being of yet another group of young men and women who had left home for work in Saudi Arabia as irregular (undocumented) immigrants.

While drinking coffee together or interacting as small groups in other social situations, neighbours would tell each other their news about these prospective labour migrants, collectively referred to as 'children on the road', typically beginning with the most recent update on their whereabouts. On good days, sending families received telephone calls, confirming the 'safe arrival' of migrants at a named transit point. On bad days, the news dealt with worrisome accounts of someone on the journey reportedly captured by ransom-seeking bandits or greedy smugglers. On other days, when there was no news at all, concerned villagers prayed to Allah and invoked the mediation of religious authorities and spiritual forces believed to safeguard these at-risk migrants at all times and in all places.

I take these deeply felt fears and concerns as points of entry to explore possible links between the decisions of prospective irregular labour migrants and the range of adaptive responses by which South Wollo's drought-prone smallholder households cope with changing demographic, economic and environmental conditions. I hope to achieve this objective by examining the kind of culturally expected entitlements and related moral-economic resources that both prospective migrants and their parents seek to access and effectively benefit from when undergoing the following three, analytically separable decision nodes. These nodes are (1) the initial decision to depart, (2) financing informal migration and (3) the micro-politics of remittance distribution. The goal is to capture the decision-making agency of both individual immigrants and sending households by following the sources and directions of help—broadly defined to include both financial support and other facilitating services—across successive phases of the migration process.

My analysis of these complex drivers of rural labour outmigration underscores the relevance of the economic decision-making model that the anthropologist Dan Bauer proposed for culturally similar Tigrayan households in the early 1970s. As I show below, the model's applicability to current household decisions reveals the continued commitments of both sending families and young migrants to long-standing Amhara–Tigray perceptions of the household (*'beteseb'*) as a residential and transient unit, primarily based on envisioned reciprocal benefits, as opposed to enduring, and presumably non-negotiable, primordial obligations.

THE MORAL ECONOMY OF IRREGULAR MIGRATION

Parameters of household decision-making in traditional Amhara–Tigray society

The household remains the basic unit of residence and economic organisation in northern Ethiopia—home of the culturally related Amhara and Tigray peoples. However, as noted by many observers, the dominant 'north Ethiopian household' is not culturally expected to be sociologically enduring across generations.[2] In comparison with the 'family' in pre-modern Western Europe, for example, the Ethiopian household is conceived of as a transient unit that begins with marriage, expands over the ensuing years by increasing its size and asset ownership, gradually shrinks, and eventually ceases to exist with the death of its founding head. This perception is sharply reflected in the commonly used vernacular term for household, '*beteseb*', which translates as 'people of the house'. In both Amharic and Tigrinya languages, the emphasis in the very meaning of the term is on 'common residence' or, more precisely, 'being persons of the house', as opposed to enduring kinship-based ties.[3]

This perceived primacy of temporal residence over lasting kinship ties can be ethnographically captured, among other domains and structural features, in the greater autonomy highland Ethiopian households enjoy in decision-making.[4] Led by a single head, commonly the 'man of the house' but sometimes a widow or single woman, the household is responsible for making a range of day-to-day as well as season-to-season economic decisions.[5] In making these decisions, a successful household head is expected to consider not just his or her own immediate individual self-interest but also the well-being of all the other household members. If not treated fairly, adult household members are generally expected to improve their lot either by influencing the decisions of the household head or by leaving the household altogether for better opportunities elsewhere.[6]

The migration decision stories I present from South Wollo underscore the centrality of the above-described managerial duty of adjusting the household size to meet changing resource conditions in determining the economic viability of households. In this way, the stories suggest a direct correlation between the likelihood of departing as a prospective informal labour migrant and the developmental cycle of

223

sending households. I will elaborate this presumed link by using the flow chart that Dan Bauer proposed for capturing the multiple decision paths of Tigrayan households in the early 1970s (see Figure 11.1).

As Bauer correctly noted, farming household heads need periodically to adjust their household size to meet changing resource conditions. In an economically viable ideal household, one potential imbalance triggering such action was the lack of a sufficient number of able-bodied people to complete a range of culturally defined gender- and age-specific tasks. During Bauer's fieldwork in Tigray, one of the commonest strategies for resolving this imbalance was hiring the children of less-fortunate relatives or neighbours to work as ploughmen, shepherds or maids. If this option was not feasible for some reason, well-off household heads recruited new household members by drawing on a range of cultural mechanisms such as fostering or occasionally

Figure 11.1: A pathway analysis of household decision-making[7]

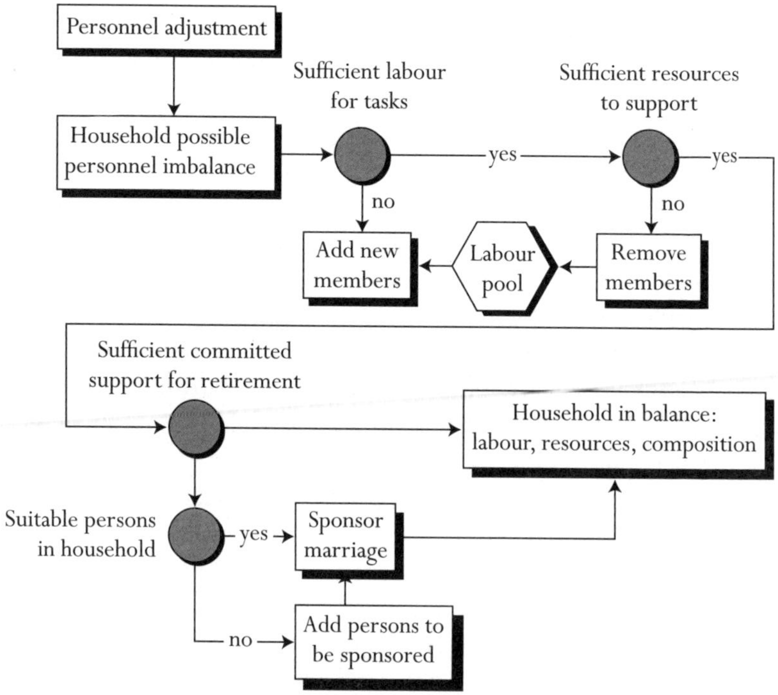

adopting the children of asset-poor relatives in exchange for periodic material support or a promise of access to a share of land.[8]

A second node of potential imbalance occurs when labour-sufficient households face a lack of sufficient food or productive assets (most notably land, oxen and cash). If not correctly resolved, this imbalance may reduce these households' ability to derive maximum benefits from the agricultural labour of each household member. Fortunately, rural communities in Tigray and other parts of highland Ethiopia have a range of informal mechanisms for addressing this imbalance.[9] Household heads with sufficient male power and some land could, for example, arrange with a neighbour who owned a pair of oxen but lacked a ploughman, to use the oxen in exchange for labour service, a share of the harvest, fixed rent, or any combination of these mechanisms.[10] Similarly, poor landowners who face looming droughts could rent out their land to their better-off neighbours and use part of the money to cover the transport cost for migrating in search of wage work elsewhere.[11] The remaining money from this transaction is often used for consumption and other expenses of the households they leave behind.[12]

The third node of potential imbalance, especially relevant for elderly household heads, is related to the availability of suitable persons who can be trusted to provide decent care during their retirement. In the event of there being no dependable person, ageing household heads can recruit a new person, preferably a grandson or a similarly close relative, in exchange for sponsoring his marriage and, depending on their wealth and generosity, providing the new couple with assets to start building their own household.[13]

My main contention throughout this chapter is that the local drivers of informal labour migration can be plausibly contextualised within similar imbalances facing sending households and individual migrants. More specifically, I argue that most of the young household members documented in this study decided to become informal labour migrants as part of a broad strategy of addressing the needs of otherwise able-bodied adult household members which could not be effectively met with available household resources. In this regard, reference to informal labour migration as a possible option typically crops up in the private conversation of household members when the prospective migrant comes of a culturally expected marriage age. In the absence of other routes for transitioning to adulthood by marrying a suitable spouse, building an independent household and acquiring productive assets, many young men and women are likely to continue leaving South Wollo for work as informal labour migrants.

Framing migration decisions as household strategies

As I have mentioned, the broad thesis I examine in this chapter is that the irregular migration of rural youth in South Wollo, whether to the Middle East or other destinations like Djibouti and Sudan, should be traced to household dynamics. I specifically argue that migration decisions ought to be regarded as one of the many strategies that the heads of smallholder household units and their adult members pragmatically consider as a way of improving their common economic well-being.

In advancing this argument, however, I also recognise that irregular transnational migration is qualitatively different from the regular household economic decisions depicted in Figure 11.1. First, irregular transnational migration requires more money and promises more far-reaching benefits than any other single economic decision in the culturally expected developmental cycle of households. Second, the decision to depart as a prospective irregular migrant entails deeply felt moral-economic dilemmas and risks for both the individual migrant and the households they leave behind. As I show below, most prospective irregular migrants know that they cannot possibly acquire sufficient money to finance the cost of their migration by themselves. Instead, they have to collect additional money from others by drawing on delicate kinship-based ties and affective considerations. If these requests are declined, the inability to pay in time for smugglers (or in some cases ransom-seeking bandits) could lead to the death of the prospective migrant, while also irreversibly destroying social relationships back in the sending communities.

By the same cultural logic, the migration of young household members is often viewed by concerned relatives and fellow villagers as a sign of regrettable failure on the part of household heads who were supposed to help their young members successfully transition to adulthood. As a result, heads of sending households often become objects of gossip and public criticism. Public disapproval tends to be severe and even confrontational, especially when the prospective informal migrants happen to be unmarried young girls. There is a widely shared concern that girls on the road will be more prone to abuse and violence. Furthermore, there is an affective concern that in the course of their long sojourn in the Middle East, migrant girls will lose their desirability as wives. This includes their ability to have babies and their willingness to re-adapt to the boredom of rural life upon return.

Data collection and research questions

The chapter draws on several short visits to a rural village in the highlands of South Wollo, most recently in August 2019 and, prior to that, in March and October 2018. This village, which I call 'Lay Amba' for the sake of anonymity, consists of the homesteads of 56 closely related farmers. I chose this village for a practical reason. I know most of the residents intimately as they are also my close relatives. Building on this connection has enabled me to collect rich ethnographic data on otherwise 'hard-to-observe' domains of rural life, including the promises and perils of informal migration both at the household and individual levels. I employed two main data collection strategies.

The first strategy consisted of impromptu conversations on informal youth outmigration while visiting households and in other encounters. Some of the informative conversations on this subject were with relatives and family friends—including many from neighbouring villages—who came to visit me. Additional and often less subject-focused conversations occurred when I joined neighbours and extended family members as they gathered to drink coffee together or sat in a habitual common space to spend their leisure time. These conversations generated important observations highlighting migration-related concerns, specific messages, and key expressions that farmers shared among themselves in their vernacular discourse on the subject.

The second data collection strategy was conducting theme-focused, unstructured interviews with two groups of carefully selected informants. The first group of interviewees was heads of households with one or more members who had lived (or were still living) as undocumented immigrant workers in Saudi Arabia or one of the oil-rich Gulf countries. The second group was returnee young people who had previously worked in these countries as irregular (undocumented) migrants. These probing interviews allowed me to generate detailed migration-related qualitative data for a total of eight sending households and five returnee migrants (only one of whom was female). In doing so, I also learned of the stories of 14 pioneer migrants, some of them outside Lay Amba, who played a significant role in the migration decision of my interviewees.

All the returnee migrants lived in their own relatively newer houses located in a commercially desirable roadside settlement that also functioned as the area's 'town'. By contrast, all of the sending household heads lived in Lay Amba in older homesteads that were thinly scattered on the middle contours of low-rising ridges. In respect of their livelihood strategies, returnee migrants took advantage of the all-weather road that passes through the 'town' to juggle three types of commercial pursuit: retailing consumer goods, running tea or drinking houses, and dealing with livestock or crops. When I asked if they would call themselves '*negade*', literally 'trader'—the generic local term for these kinds of off-farm activities—all of the returnee migrants disagreed. Instead, returnees thought of themselves as engaged in '*yetim yemayaders sira*', literally work that doesn't bring about any improvement. By contrast, the sending households were headed by farmers, all of them male, primarily subsisting on the cultivation of cereals and pulses, augmented by the rearing of livestock and some remittances from migrant household members.

The interviews uniformly focused on three main themes related to the migration experiences of informants. The first concerned the time and specific context in which the idea of irregular migration first cropped up, and was possibly discussed, in the lives of interviewees. The second theme explored how the migration cost of the individual migrant household member under discussion was financed. The final theme was whether the interviewee received remittances expected from a migrant family member under discussion. A follow-up theme involved whether the remittance received was distributed in ways that benefited some household members more than others. Taken together, informants' responses to these unstructured interviews and probing follow-ups provided rich qualitative data for examining the drivers of informal labour migration at the levels of both individual migrants and sending households. I further argue that exploring these issues requires a nuanced understanding of the range of economic as well as moral and emotional dilemmas that each of these actors encounters at different phases of the migration process.

As I show below, there are three important decision stages, or strategic nodes, relevant for this study. First is the initial conversation, or arguably its absence, about whether a certain household member should be allowed to migrate or not. Then comes a decisive moment related to financing the costs of migration. The third decision stage involves intra-household negotiations over the distribution of expected remittances and, in some cases, negative financial outcomes such as unpaid debts and additional loans. To capture the range of perspectives and preferences involved at each decision node, I draw on a nuanced analysis of key expressions and meanings I came across while reading transcripts of the interview responses and discussion notes.

How irregular migration is considered in intimate household spaces

As I mentioned above, one of the themes I explored through interviewees sought to describe retrospectively when and under what specific household conditions and individual life-cycle events they first discussed the promises and perils of irregular migration among household members. Their responses greatly support my broad claim that migration decisions should be regarded as one of many strategies that the heads of smallholder household units and their adult members pragmatically consider as a way of improving their common economic well-being. In five of the eight sending households interviewed, the idea of resorting to irregular migration as an option cropped up for the first time when male household members were preparing for the mandatory Ethiopian General Secondary Education Certificate Examination (EGSECE) at the end of Grade 10. According to Ethiopia's current education policy, which has been in place since the early 2000s, students whose performance is low in the Grade 10 national exam are effectively excluded from joining both college preparatory and vocational programmes. In the absence of other public-funded educational opportunities, many unsuccessful students in Lay Amba pressed parents, as well as other household members, to let them depart as pro-spective irregular migrants.

The intimately personal conversations of household members about this risky consideration can be illustrated by taking the story of a pio-neer returnee whom I call, for the sake of anonymity, OG.

OG is the oldest son of a farmer with a total of nine household mem-bers (six sons, one daughter, and two ageing parents). OG described himself as being an average student in all his grades. However, in the Grade 10 exam, which he took when he was 19 years old, OG scored badly in most of the subjects. One July morning in 2009, OG's grand-mother took the initiative to explore a plan for him with his father and other family members. OG's father proposed a marriage plan and outlined the many promises of having his eldest son as a next-door neighbour. Both of OG's grandparents enthusiastically supported the proposal and started to count the names of potentially suitable spouses. OG showed no objection for a while. One Thursday, while selling onions at a market, however, he heard a rumour that led him to con-sider irregular migration. OG was told that a group of six boys, includ-ing a cousin of his from the same village who happened to be a few years older than him, had found an Isuzu truck driver who had agreed to pick them up from somewhere in Djibouti for a safe ride to the shores of the Red Sea. 'All the young men had to do', OG was told, 'was find their way to the said destination in Djibouti.'

OG followed up this rumour by contacting the said cousin immediately. Things moved fast thereafter. The nephew welcomed OG's company and even offered to facilitate contact with pioneer migrants in Saudi Arabia who would help with transportation and other costs. With this promise in mind, OG disclosed his intention, first to his father and then to the grandparents. The response from both was an absolute no. To persuade OG to change his mind, the father offered to sell his prized mule and give him the money to buy whatever his heart desired. On their part, OG's grandparents offered to designate him as heir on their land title certificate. Refusing all these offers, OG joined the group of prospective migrants and left the village on the morning of 9 October 2009. His father recalls how sad he felt that morning. On her part, the grandmother would not yield from her utter dismay at OG's decision by refusing to give him her much-sought blessings and farewell wishes.

At first glance, OG's decision in the conversation appears to contra-dict the wishes of his father and grandparents. However, there was an anthropologically interesting twist to this story towards the end of my interview when I stood up to say goodbye to all family members in the room. I used this opportunity to ask OG's mother, whom I had not talked to until this point, to explain why her son left home without even some food to eat on the road. The mother replied, displaying a sense of certainty and conviction in her sound and eyes, as follows:

> What my husband has been telling you this entire time is not true. OG left in the presence of many neighbours and relatives who came to wish him farewell. My husband refused to consent to OG's decision only out of a sense of shame. He was trying to save himself from being an object of village gossip and backbiting for letting his elder son take a dangerous route when he could otherwise send him by plane.

I want to underscore this twist because it suggests that OG's father may have privately agreed to his son's decision to depart. However, in the more visible public spaces where this decision was expected to evoke shaming and disrespect by concerned villagers and relatives, OG's father had to display uncompromising disagreement. As I show below, blaming prospective illegal migrants who are already well on their way for leaving without the blessing of their parents is an important strategy for financing migration expenses. The blame reinforced the image of OG's father as a sorrowful parent and increased his ability to mobilise culturally expected entitlements in times of emergency from kinship ties with pioneer migrants still living in the Middle East.

In a majority of other cases, however, the departure decision of prospective migrants was approved by parents and justified by concerned relatives. One such example involves another young man whom I call HT.

> Unlike OG, HT attended a college preparatory programme in the district capital. But then he failed in most subjects at the Ethiopian University entrance examination. Uncertain about what to do next, HT heard about private colleges in Dessie that might admit him for training in employable fields like an elementary school teacher or registered nurse. However, HT also learned that the college cost was too expensive for his family to afford. In the absence of any supporter, HT wanted to try his luck by departing with friends as prospective informal migrants. His parents agreed to the decision. When I interviewed him in October 2018, HT recalled the prayer ritual his mother organised to wish him Allah's protection from all things evil.

I want to underscore HT's status as a high school graduate, which appears to be the most important reason for explaining why his parents agreed to his otherwise risky decision to depart as an informal labour migrant. Unlike OG, who was forced to drop out of school at the end of Grade 10, HT had already invested two more years to complete high school. During these years, HT left home for the district capital where shared a rented house with other students. In the eyes of most farmers, this experience often discourages students like HT from transitioning to adult farmers by marrying a suitable wife, establishing an independent household, and acquiring sufficient land, livestock and other productive assets. Instead, most high school graduates appear more likely to succeed by pursuing a town-based, non-agricultural livelihood. From what I surmise, it is this perception of a better alternative in non-agricultural pursuits that encouraged FT's parents to consider informal labour migration as a plausible strategy for enabling him to acquire much-needed initial capital.

Financing irregular migration to Saudi Arabia

All the irregular migrants in this study travelled to Saudi Arabia with the help of paid smugglers. From what I heard, the preferred route from South Wollo consisted of several segments. First, prospective migrants travelled on their own to a designated transit point somewhere in the Afar Region of Ethiopia. On arrival, the migrants met smugglers who would load them on a rented Isuzu truck. With up to seventy prospective immigrants, the truck zigzagged along rarely travelled desert paths to transfer them to a transit point close to the border of either Djibouti or Somalia. The prospective migrants continued travelling by another truck, in some cases trekking on foot, to a transit point along the Red Sea coast where small boats awaited them. After crossing the Red Sea, migrants found themselves in a hostage-like situation in Yemen. Smugglers wouldn't allow them to proceed to the next destination until each migrant paid for the transportation and security services received thus far. After paying the required money, migrants travelled by vehicle to a final point within Saudi Arabia where they often faced threats of abuse unless the smugglers received additional payment.

Given the rapidly devaluating Ethiopian birr, the financial cost of this trip for farmers has reportedly increased from about 40,000 birr per person (about US$3,460 at the time) in 2009[14] to 92,000 birr per person (about $$3,150) in 2019.[15] This is a lot of money to amass for young people with no land or other productive assets to sell. Interestingly, prospective migrants find innovative financing strategies to make their journey less expensive than the cost of airplane flights of regular *hajj* and *umrah* pilgrims. After all, if not to minimise financial barriers (and arguably bureaucratic red tape), what is the point of venturing across an illegal border crossing, as opposed to a regular aeroplane flight during the pilgrimage season?

As mentioned above, smugglers at designated transit points do not allow migrants to proceed to the next destination unless the payment agreed upon for the previous segment is fully paid. From the stories I gathered, the travel cost to the Red Sea remained relatively inexpensive. In 2019, for example, the total cost was estimated at less than 3,000 birr. Most prospective migrants have enough money to pay for this when they leave home, including OG, who had saved about 7,000 birr by selling onions he had planted on a leased plot. In the event that migrants found this too expensive to pay by themselves, smugglers helped them by suggesting a less expensive route to the Red Sea, including trekking on foot through some sections of the desert.

The lion's share of the payment was made when migrants faced abuse, including threats of gradual and painful death at the hands of greedy smugglers and ransom-seeking bandits later in the last two transit points; first in Yemen and finally in Saudi Arabia. All the successful migrants from Lay Amba resolved this problem by acquiring help from earlier migrants in Saudi Arabia and the Gulf countries. Not surprisingly, a majority of the pioneer migrants in the stories offered their help to prospective migrants only after intense negotiations with their parents back home. In all cases, their parents offered to intercede only after judging the cultural weight of the expected request in the context of their socially expected entitlements and relationship with the parents of prospective immigrants.[16]

I next want to highlight the central role of culturally expected kinship-based entitlements and affective considerations in raising financial support for migrants who are already well on the road. I illustrate the role of these factors by continuing with OG's story:

After arriving in Yemen, OG called a nephew in Jeddah to ask for a loan. OG chose this particular nephew, whom I call KY, because of a promise of help shown to him in a previous conversation. When called from an unidentified number in Yemen, however, KY declined to answer the phone. In the absence of other numbers to call, OG asked the help of smugglers to allow him to call his father back in Lay Amba. After receiving this call, OG's father discussed the situation with his cousin (KY's father). Understanding the cultural and affective consequences of declining this request, KY's father sent a word urging him to help OG no matter what. Over the next three days, KY and his sister, Z, collected enough money to allow OG to continue to the final payment point inside Saudi Arabia. In doing so, KY also negotiated that OG should pay the next instalment by finding the name and contact address of other long-staying migrant relatives. To this end, KY offered to find the telephone numbers of certain relatives on OG's mother's side. That plan worked perfectly. KY's search located the named relative living in the same town (Jeddah). To the delight of everyone, that relative paid the remaining expense and also offered to host OG in his apartment until he started earning sufficient income on his own to live on.

Not all financing attempts were successful. I want to end this section by summarising the unfortunate and sad case of a young prospective migrant, TS, who was reportedly shot by armed men while his relatives were still collecting money to pay for his release:

TS's parents had died when he was young. As a consequence, TS was raised and cared for by his older, and only, brother in a village not far from Lay Amba. Before his departure in September 2018, TS had received the consent of his older brother. To this end, the brother had also offered to request relatives and friends in Saudi Arabia for the loan to pay for TS's release both in Yemen and Saudi Arabia. Unfortunately, however, TS arrived in Yemen in bad shape, surviving a near-death experience by drowning while travelling on a crowded small boat across the Red Sea. Because of this ordeal, TS reportedly lost his will to survive. He incited frequent fights with smugglers, aggravating them to mistreat him more than other migrants. One unfortunate evening, TS was shot and killed by an armed camp guard while ostensibly trying to escape. He died a sudden death, while his migrant relatives in Saudi were busy trying to pool sufficient money to secure his release in time. Shortly after that, a local contact of the smugglers broke the sad news to TS's brother on the phone. A commemorative burial service which was well attended took place a week later.

THE MORAL ECONOMY OF IRREGULAR MIGRATION

The politics of remittance distribution among sending household members

As the survey results compiled by Asnake and Zerihun in chapter 9 show, Ethiopian labour migrants, including undocumented young men and women living in Saudi Arabia and the Gulf countries, generously remitted money to their loved ones left behind. In small-scale communities like Lay Amba, where social relations are intensely face-to-face and personal, information on the flow of migration remittances tended to be publicly available. Receiving households had very little or no space to hide whether, and to some extent how much, their 'children from abroad' remitted. This is because receiving household heads or other beneficiaries would soon be observed by fellow villagers while engaged in economic transactions that they could not otherwise be expected to afford.

For example, a parent who had just received a good sum of money would be seen purchasing livestock or other productive assets on the next market day. By then, friends and neighbours had come to know that the money was remitted by a particular migrant. If the information was not disclosed as yet, people commonly asked about the sources of such money. According to my observation, there are no qualms about asking such questions and talking about remittance-related information. In this respect, beneficiary parents often expressed their gratitude by disclosing that they had received money from a migrant household member. Similarly, those neighbours who were in the know used the opportunity to commend these households for their good fortune and success in having members who thought well enough of their families back home to remit money to them.

At the same time, some concerned residents of Lay Amba shared stories of particular households where increased remittances reportedly caused growing conflicts over its distribution among members. From what I surmise, much of the conflict centred on disagreements as to whether certain household members, relatives or friends benefited more than others. Not surprisingly, this concern was reinforced by longstanding kinship-based duties and entitlements that customarily reinforced inequality in intra-household relations, often along the lines of gender, generation and age. In the context of remittance distribution, this cultural expectation encouraged unequal distribution in ways that favoured fathers over mothers, brothers over sisters, senior siblings over juniors, and extended family members over biologically unrelated friends.

Potential conflicts arose when young migrants sought to use remittances to assert their will within the household. In Lay Amba, this happened to the parents of a migrant young man whom I call HM. The short version of this story goes as follows:

> HM earned a lot of money from selling fresh meat to fellow Ethiopians in the Jeddah area on holidays while regularly working as a shepherd. Over the first three years, this young man reportedly remitted more money to his mother than he did to his father.[17] After tolerating this for some time, the father brought the case to the village elders, cursing HM for disobeying his paternal authority and scolding the mother for reinforcing this behaviour by wasting the money she received exclusively on herself, such as purchasing used clothes or making unreasonably large contributions to religious institutions. The elders sought to reconcile the couple, by reminding them to reflect on the long good years they had lived together but leaving the contradiction unresolved. As I learned during my last visit, HM's parents lived separately but without officially divorcing. HM's mother has moved out to a brandnew and nice-looking house she built with remittance money. The father has tolerated this as the house is officially called 'HM's [future] house'. The father still hopes that HM will take care of him when he comes back to live as his next-door neighbour.[18]

These migration-induced cleavages, along gender and generational lines, suggest that some household members may actually benefit more from remittances than others. However, I understand that the ethnographic vignettes I have drawn on in this chapter do not make for broad generalisations.

Conclusion

Drawing on ethnographic data collected from a South Wollo rural community I called 'Lay Amba', this chapter has discussed the decision-making agency of both individual labour migrants and the households, neighbours and relatives they left behind. Exploring this link required contextualising informal labour migration as one of many strategies that household heads and their adult family members pragmatically consider in response to the culturally expected developmental cycles and changing resource conditions of their household units. The specific conditions of the case-study migrants and sending households described in this chapter support the continued relevance of the ethnographically informed economic decision flow chart (see Figure 11.1) that the anthropologist Dan Bauer suggested in the 1970s.[19]

At the same time, the chapter has underscored the qualitatively unique nature of illegal labour migration decisions as distinct from any other single medium- or long-term household economic decision. Beyond commonly anticipated economic promises and perils, illegal transnational labour migration creates deeply felt moral dilemmas and adverse emotional risks for both the individual migrants and the households and close relatives they leave behind.

The discussion of the critical role of affective kinship-based ties and culturally expected entitlements in facilitating informal labour migration has a significant policy implication. It suggests that the conventional policy focus on the economic promises and perils of illegal migration has to be expanded to include less visible, but equally consequential, effects that occur in the intimately private spaces of households, neighbourhoods and kinship-based groups. One example of these understudied issues is the micro-politics of remittance distribution at the household and individual levels. As the story of HM's family demonstrates, increased remittances to financially starving households can transform the bargaining powers of household members in ways that tend to exacerbate conflictual relations in terms of gender, generation and age. In the context of kinship and related affective considerations, the chapter also shows that a pioneer migrant's inability to help prospective migrants when they needed it most can destroy, possibly beyond repair, carefully maintained and longstanding social relationships and collectively enforced norms and shared values.

CONCLUSION

Fana Gebresenbet and *Asnake Kefale*

This short conclusion seeks to weave the findings of the preceding chapters together and highlight major insights. We contend in this book that the study of migration should be carried out in the particular historical and social context of the origin communities. Doing this helps one to discern the historical and conjectural 'birth' of outward migration to a particular destination country at a particular moment in time. Afterwards, the phenomenon of migration will have its own life, in some cases evolving towards an entrenched practice (or tradition) in sending communities. The empirical cases examined in almost all of the chapters of this volume were derived from 'migration hotspot' or core sending areas in Ethiopia, and they represent the reality in such contexts.

This volume depicts a nuanced view of migration from Ethiopia and its impacts by using rich empirical insights. In this way, a methodical and deliberate gaze is placed on the thinking, values and practices of human agents at the grass-roots levels, primarily on the youth (as migrants, potential migrants, returnees and deportees) and on sending families and communities.

As we have noted, Ethiopia's rate of international migration is lower than the sub-Saharan Africa average. There has, however, been a significant spike in outward migration in the past two decades. Along with the spike, many of the contributions in this volume (see chapters 4, 5, 7, 8 and 10) show that through repeated cycles of successful or unsuccessful migration, and the flow of ideas, imaginations and remittances, international migration has been reified as a viable alternative for creating a future by the youth and communities. Here, we outline some of the major insights that were derived from the contributions in this volume.

Migration assemblage and the agency of actors

One major insight from this volume concerns the assemblage and reassemblage of migration processes. This process is by and large a response to structural factors that provide opportunities and challenges to migration both in origin and in destination countries. For example, Ethiopian migration to Saudi Arabia (and the Gulf more broadly) has been shaped by the following major structural factors: land scarcity and drought and related socio-economic pressures since the 1980s in northern Ethiopia, the distribution of oil rents to Saudi households, and lax labour policies to enable the importation of female domestic labour,[1] the 2011 Arab Spring and the scapegoating of labour migrants for Saudi's social and economic woes, and the development of policies of 'Saudisation' of the labour force, which resulted in the adoption of stricter laws that restrict the employment of foreign workers.[2] As a result, more than 160,000 Ethiopians in late 2013 and early 2014 were forcibly deported from Saudi Arabia. As a consequence, the Government of Ethiopia (GoE) banned labour migration in 2013 and introduced laws that put heavier penalties on so-called traffickers and brokers. The other factor that influenced irregular migration to Saudi Arabia was the war in Yemen. Even if one assumes that conflicts adversely affect irregular migration, the war in Yemen did not lead to a decline in the number of irregular migrants passing through Yemen to Saudi; instead, after a slight decline at the onset of the conflict, there was an increase in following years.[3]

Similarly, Ethiopian migration to South Africa has been shaped by a range of interrelated factors, including the end of apartheid and the adoption of liberal asylum policies at the beginning of the 1990s, the relaxation of entry requirements to South Africa during its hosting of the FIFA World Cup in 2010, the increasing difficulties for irregular migrants to South Africa to secure official permits to stay in the country since the beginning of 2000s, the tendency of South Africans to blame refugees and migrants (particularly from other African countries) for the country's socio-economic ills, and the rise of xenophobia. On the Ethiopian side, migration to South Africa was mediated by such factors as youth unemployment in Ethiopia, aspirations to migrate to South Africa, and political persecution.

As this volume has shown, the migration process was constantly assembled and reassembled by human agents, primarily migrants and brokers, in the light of structural (macro-) factors like the ones outlined above. That is why we have deliberately focused on the agency of migrants, sending families, and brokers. We did not, however, completely disregard structural factors. What we observed in many of the empirical chapters (see, for example, chapters 2, 5 and 9) is how agents constantly interact with structural factors to take advantage of, circumvent and resist them, and thereby not only make migration possible but also ensure the 'informal' transfer of remittances.

The interaction between structure and agency is also present in meso-level explanatory variables like social networks consequent to the development of a sizeable migrant population. Decades of migration and the presence of a relatively large group of migrants from certain localities in destination countries have created dense threads linking the origin and destination locations (see chapter 8). The ubiquitous availability and use of smartphones and ICTs in more recent years has further consolidated the social networks linking sending and destination countries.

Thus, international migration should be viewed as a complex phenomenon which is undergoing a constant process of assembling, disassembling and reassembling. While structural macro- and meso-level factors related to social networks are important, the agency of the youth, brokers and members of the local community is even more so. The nature of international migration from a certain locality to the most-desired destination evolves over time, manifesting changes in the particular routes followed, the risks, range of actors and expenses involved, and the financial returns of migration.

Aspiration, morality, and agency in migration

Aspiration is a necessary condition for migration, but it needs to be supported by the requisite capabilities for its realisation.[4] In areas where international migration has become normative, previous experiences of migration and its socio-economic impacts inform societal imaginations and communal archives. These will be heavily relied upon in the youth's future-making projects (see chapters 4 and 5). Selective remembering and archiving of past migration experiences determine the imagination of the 'good life' by the youth.[5] As a result, aspirations for migration constitute only a subset of the general aspirations for a decent future and but one strategy towards achieving this.

Life aspirations are not, however, exclusively focused on economic and material modernity. There is the 'higher-order' normative intention of 'helping the family' and improving the household's 'status' in engaging in migration too (see chapters 5 and 7). These 'higher-order' aspirations are inherently linked to established norms of siblings helping each other and offspring supporting struggling families and providing old-age care to parents. Another type of 'higher-order' aspiration is to successfully transition from youthhood to adulthood by meeting expected social requirements (see chapter 4).

Mulugeta (chapter 7) asserts that the normative expectations of both parents or relatives and a potential migrant are solidified by poverty: parents are expected to somehow finance the migration of a son or daughter and the migrant is required to remit money back to the family—and these are smoothed and facilitated by kinship and social ties. In this way, the 'higher-order' normative expectations are 'learned'[6] but will be met by the financial returns a migrant expects to make through work in the destination country. Moreover, such aspirations have transformative potential beyond the immediate economic interpretations.[7]

Aspirations change and evolve under the influence of structural factors. This is best illustrated in the case of Harresaw, Tigray, where migration to Saudi Arabia commenced as a coping strategy in the second half of the 1980s but evolved into an investment strategy by the early 2010s. However, by the end of the 2010s, irregular migration was less attractive, following restrictive laws in Saudi Arabia from late

2013. As a result, irregular migration to Saudi Arabia then regressed into becoming a coping strategy (see chapter 10).

Contradicting the official position of state authorities, which criminalises actors and practices that facilitate irregular migration (see chapters 2, 8 and 11), migration facilitation has moral dimensions in the sending communities. First, brokers are part of the social milieu and are governed by social sanctions. They are, especially when located in sending communities, not only in the business of making money. They have a social standing to protect by providing a safe and reliable service. Second, the migration expenses are covered by sending families and relatives. In some cases, familial and social relations are (ab)used to generate the required sum, usually from those already in the destination country. Thus, the 'migration industry' concept has a serious deficieny when it comes to understanding these dynamics. Third, there is also a culturally expected entitlement—layered by generational, gender and kinship links—to the remittances a migrant sends, whether within the family, to relatives or to friends. Moreover, tensions and conflicts occur within families when entitlements to remittances appear to be infringed upon (see chapter 11). Fourth, social institutions are exported to the destination countries and become repurposed to meet socio-economic demands. This can even lead to perverting the institutions, and changing them into enabling platforms for the exploitation of new arrival migrants, including brides (see chapter 8).

This discussion shows that international migration should not be viewed in material or economic dimensions only. Social norms of cooperation within a family or community and communal morality explain how migration is financed, how proceeds from migration are distributed, and how risks are reduced. Thus, it would be grossly wrong to attempt to understand migration decision-making dynamics without the proper socio-cultural context.

Subjective understanding of risks and agency

Perhaps the starkest expression of the agency of key local actors is to be found in how risk is assessed and considered in deciding to migrate or not. Government and NGO campaigns against irregular migration more often than not take the position that migrants are unaware of the risks involved in irregular migration or are tricked by brokers. What is apparent from the empirical chapters of this book is the reasonable level of awareness among potential migrants about the risks. But the presence of the risks and awareness of them do not stop potential migrants from migrating. This implies a conscious cost-benefit analysis on the side of potential migrants and their families. Following Müller-Mahn, Everts and Stephan, we argue that the perception of risk and reaction to the geography of risk involve a perspectival, subjective process.[8] Thus, the perceived risk informing the actions of experts and state agents is not the only relevant one. The subjective evaluation and comparison of risks that the youth undertake matter more for an understanding of their thinking and decision-making, than what others (including government authorities) would take as an objective risk assessment.

If potential migrants and their families make the conscious decision to migrate in the face of expected risks, we should also examine the risks or challenges they experience in their villages or towns. At the most basic, the risk to be avoided will be economic—emanating from land scarcity or youth landlessness and unemployment. Teferi (in chapter 11) conceptualises the decision to migrate as part of a household's strategy to reallocate human resources and in due course diversify risks and increase the household's welfare. Fana (in chapter 4) makes the case that the greatest risk that the youth are 'running away' from (by migrating) is the serious difficulty of meeting the requirements for the transition into adulthood. This risk is conceptualised as getting 'stuck' in the temporal field[9] of youthhood indefinitely.

Human agency involves taking lessons from past iterations, assessing the desirability of potential alternatives, and conducting practical evaluations of these alternatives.[10] One could expect that the selective remembering of successes and collective amnesia when it comes to risks form an integral part of the archives and imaginations accumulated locally. It is from this same archive that future potential migrants draw lessons to construct alternatives. Such selectivity in remembering and forgetting is, however, not unique to migrants and disadvantaged groups, but is an inherent part of the project of utilising the past to meet contemporary socio-economic and political demands.

Moreover, potential migrants and brokers take deliberate actions to reduce, circumvent or avoid the risks involved in the (irregular) migration process. These actions range from the careful selection of a 'good' broker by sending families (see chapter 2) and the intentional choice of a certain time for migration (e.g., the Ramadan fasting season for migration to the Middle East, when the border police are expected to be less strict), to the instrumental utilisation of rituals to cope with the dangers associated with migration and living in a foreign culture (see chapter 6). Religion is also invoked—be it in the form of neighbour-hood prayers prior to and during migration, holding special religious artefacts such as *tsebel* (holy water), *emnet* (holy soil) and religious books, and practising religious acts during the actual migration, as well as institutional support (see chapters 2, 6 and 8).

Female irregular migrants face the additional risk of sexual violence, including rape, en route as well as in destination countries. This is also well recognised by migrants and sending families. The chosen actions range from arranging for a wedding before a girl migrates to make sure that she loses her virginity under wedlock in a socially accepted man-ner, to taking a long-term contraceptive (see chapter 6).[11] Here, again, we see the subjective evaluation of risk and choice of safeguards: rather than avoiding the risk altogether, the attempt here is to control girls' sexuality and avoid unwanted pregnancy.

Regulating irregular migration: explaining policy failures

Without a doubt, international migration has emerged as one of the most important, complex and controversial global policy issues of our times. This rise in importance of international migration could best be illustrated by the inclusion of the International Organization for Migration (IOM) within the UN family and the signing of the Global Compacts on Migration (GCM) and Refugees (GCRF) by the UN member states in the second half of 2010s. These policy developments come on the back of building momentum for such global responses in previous years, and the need to share the burden of hosting large num-bers of refugees.

But since the beginning of the twenty-first century, there has been a rise of right-wing populism in the West, which among other things has scapegoated migrants for various socio-economic woes. Similarly, South Africa was hard hit by xenophobia. Saudi Arabia, which has also emphasised the adverse impact of labour migration on the unemployment of Saudi citizens, adopted the policy of 'Saudisation' of its labour force. In response to these changes, there has been a concerted effort in origin countries like Ethiopia to keep potential migrants in their home countries through initiatives aimed at promoting job creation, provision of skills training, and start-up capital too.[12] In Ethiopia, the policy of stemming irregular migration was complemented by banning labour migration in 2013 and its criminalisation (strictly implemented from 2015) by the authorities.

The socio-economic and political impact of Covid will likely affect migrants after the pandemic ebbs. Saudi Arabia has not stopped deporting illegal migrants during the pandemic period, while the reduced income in Saudi households led to a reduction in incomes of domestic workers. The strains on economies, more importantly on the lower sections of society, will likely entrench the Saudisation of the labour force in Saudi Arabia and lead to a continuation and intensification of the trend of migrant-unfriendly policies in South Africa and Europe.

These interventions have, however, failed to bring the desired policy objectives (see chapter 1). 'Regulatory failure' in migration-related policies is not uncommon.[13] Among other things, the lack of holistic development policies which cover all aspects of the calculus is one major consideration in understanding policy failures. However, this will not help us understand why we have reverse outcomes. For example, the ban on regular labour migration in Ethiopia only made all potential migrants opt to migrate irregularly—it did not reduce the number of labour migrants. The criminalisation of brokerage services did not significantly impact on the brokers, as they developed new but riskier and more expensive routes. Neither did the government succeed in controlling brokers through punitive measures (see chapters 1 and 2).

What is apparent here is the seeping of the private (the familial, personal, and traditional-cultural) into the public sphere. This has significantly detracted from the effectiveness of policies. For example, as chapter 2 shows, the GoE was not able to apprehend a large number of brokers mainly because of the lack of cooperation from society. The services of brokers, although illegal and deemed criminal by the government, are regarded as a licit and important service by the local community. This view is even held by government officials entrusted with the responsibility of hunting down brokers. The rationale guiding their actions is best captured by the following quote from chapter 2: 'Say what the government wants and do what is good for your family.' In this way, social values, interests and norms restrain officials from acting on information they themselves have; some officials even engage in the same 'criminal act' they are entrusted to fight.

The chapters included in this volume also repeatedly raise the point that brokers (and the migration assemblage as a whole) provide the means by which the youth can secure a decent future. In chapter 2 we have seen that brokers at local level are called 'door openers' (they open up opportunities and futures), while, as chapter 7 shows, remittances are replacing government aid and support to communities in Kambata. Consequently, attempts to stamp out brokers and disrupt the whole migration assemblage without providing alternatives is set to fail from the very outset.

The (negative) influence of social norms and values on public norms and the effectiveness of government actions is well known. The African studies and development studies literature is replete with such cultural-traditional explanations of governance and development failures in Africa as a manifestation of, among other things, neo-patrimonialism.[14] While social norms are powerful and impactful, the failure of migration regulation policies in Ethiopia shows that the public sphere does not come with a strong norm, and the boundary it sets is porous enough to admit influences from grass-roots and private actors. We do not want to imply that this supports the argument of the weakness of the African state, for the failure of migration policies is also the norm, rather than the exception, in Europe and the US.[15] Rather, we strongly suggest that future research should focus on the 'real governance' of migration in Africa, by paying particular attention to the interaction and imbrications of social and private norms.[16]

Migration, social change, and 'everyday globalisation'

An increase in global migration is often viewed as one major expression of globalisation. Evidence offered for this includes the sheer size of the migrant population, the volume of remittance flows, and regional and global policy measures to regulate migration.[17] This book has high-lighted expressions of globalisation in mundane, routinised everyday life, what we call 'everyday globalisation'. This often falls outside the radar of most studies of globalisation, as the focus is usually on macro- and systemic processes. In this volume, we focus more on cultural markers of integration and interaction across world regions tied together by migrants.

Globalisation by its very nature promotes the transformation of the old order and existing social relations, and produces emergent fluid, heterogeneous social relations. This is evident in Ethiopian rural communities, which have become a key source of outward irregular migration. These communities, which are poorly integrated with the national political and economic centre, are losing their cultural-traditional norms, values and practices owing to the influences of returnee migrants and the conduct of migrants who work and reside in foreign countries (see chapters 8 and 11). In other words, while the old is dying or being eroded, the new, the modern, has not yet become entrenched.

The migration experience is bringing several social changes to send-ing communities, expressed through increased consumption, engage-ment in trade activities, and urbanisation. A more fundamental change has to do with changes in social norms and expectations. It is now increasingly clear that individuals or households are no longer satisfied with accumulating social capital within the home area and Ethiopia alone, but look abroad. Having a child or close relative abroad is emerging as an important sign of status and measure of self-worth at local level.

Local society is not complete by itself any longer. Migration, or the role of prior migrants, determines a crucial part of socio-economic life in the sending communities. Take the example of making a successful transition into adulthood. For many youth, migration is a crucial com-ponent of the transition to adulthood (see chapter 4). Accordingly, the destination countries are not simply 'far-off lands', but critical arenas in the mind-map which the youth develop in strategising as to how to make the transition to adulthood.

Moreover, the migration experience is changing considerations in the marriage marketplace too. Expected gender roles are showing some reversal: returnee women are preferred for the money they are supposed to have saved up (see chapters 6 and 10), while wives with a migrant husband are now burdened with additional roles. As a result, marriages are becoming tense and unstable. To some informants in Harresaw, it is much better to have a husband seasonally migrating to Afar (within Ethiopia) and thus being able to share more of the burden of raising children, than migrating to the Gulf (see chapter 10).

The social changes brought about by migration—which is a deeply gendered experience—are reflected and experienced differently by men and women. For example, in addition to changes in the marriage marketplace and the reversal of roles and expectations mentioned above, Yordanos (in chapter 10) highlights the fact that Ethiopian men in South Africa have ample free time to socialise, while women and wives are burdened with household chores and business management. Such role reversal is distinctly visible in married couples and work relations. This experience of Ethiopian migrants in South Africa also tells a story of exploitation of women and wives, often after a man or future husband sponsors her migration expenses. This contradicts the dominant view in the literature in which migration is understood as empowering women, in Ethiopia too.[18] The reality is, however, that women make the decision to migrate and proceed to migrate under a patriarchal socio-cultural system; after reaching their destination, they often work under the same conditions, and the money they remit is primarily controlled by men (see chapter 11). Therefore, the findings of this book would caution against the dominant narrative of 'migration as emancipation or empowerment' for female migrants.

Even if there is empowerment, it is ephemeral, as is shown by the example of women coming home with baggy jeans but dropping them quickly in Harresaw (see chapters 5 and 10). Female migrants are quicker to fall back on established patriarchal norms and hierarchies, abandoning freedoms learned in the destination country.

Conversely, culture itself enables and facilitates the migration process and its outcomes—be it through locally rooted brokers or the provision of trust, the backbone in informal remittance transfers—as migration is culturally and socially entrenched in imaginations and aspirations. Culture and social relations simultaneously enable migration and are influenced by it. There are similar impacts in destination countries, which often get blown out of proportion by social and political elites to divert attention from public socio-economic concerns. One example could be Saudi's labour law (*Nitaqat*), which was signed in April 2013, more as part of preventive reforms to preclude the spread of the Arab Spring to Saudi Arabia. The discourse behind this law blamed migrants for Saudi's socio-economic ills. It also gave the authorities a freer hand to track, imprison, maltreat and deport irregular migrants.

As these insights from this volume show, the story of migration told from the vantage point of the migrant and sending communities is less economic and more social. Accordingly, the volume recognises the agency of migrants and sending communities, rather than over-emphasising the importance of macro-level drivers of migration. In a nutshell, such an approach helps shed light on the unique nuances that are intrinsic to the migration process. Moreover, it is apparent that one of the key problems of migration policies has been the over-emphasis in policy discourses on structural factors and the irregularity of migration. Policies meant to stem irregular migration have ended up strengthening it. It is, therefore, imperative for researchers and policy-makers to give proper attention to the multiple agents who play crucial roles in the migration processes, to glocal aspirations, and to local traditions and norms.

NOTES

INTRODUCTION: MULTIPLE TRANSITIONS AND IRREGULAR
MIGRATION IN ETHIOPIA

1. For a similar critique, see Bakewell 2010; De Haas 2007; 2014.
2. Giddens 1990.
3. Stones 2005.
4. Ibid.: 5.
5. World Bank 2011.
6. Asnake and Zerihun 2015; see also chapters 7, 8 and 10.
7. RMMS 2016b.
8. RSA, Department of Home Affairs 2016.
9. See MGSoG 2017; RMMS 2016b.
10. Bloch and Chimienti 2011.
11. EUTF 2015.
12. Linz and Stepan 1998.
13. Baumle 2009: 1.
14. Emch et al. 2017: 131.
15. Ibid.
16. Ibid.
17. Ibid.
18. CSA 2013a.
19. Ibid.
20. Alemayhu and Yihunie 2014.
21. CSA 2013b.
22. Kelly and Martinez 2018.
23. Zelinsky 1971.
24. Wood and Hine 2013.
25. Aryeetey et al. 2014.
26. GoE, MoYSC 2004.

27. Wood and Hine 2013.
28. Wyn and White 2014: 9.
29. Honwana 2012.
30. Tyyskä 2014: 4.
31. Honwana 2013: 29.
32. Ibid.
33. Asnake and Zerihun 2015.
34. Ibid.
35. Ibid.
36. Ibid.: 25.
37. Aalen 2006.
38. Turton 2006.
39. Abbink 2006; Asnake 2013.
40. See Tesfaye 2007.
41. Dorosh et al. 2012.
42. NBE 2013.
43. Trines 2018.
44. GoE, MoE 2018: 29.
45. Addis Zemen 2019.
46. Blunch and Laderchi 2015; Schewel and Fransen 2018.
47. Pankhurst et al. 2018.
48. Juárez et al. 2013.
49. Cohen 2006; see also Yordanos and Zack 2020.
50. See Skeldon 2012; 2018; Schewel and Asmamaw 2019.
51. Abrahamsen 2016.
52. Ibid.: 255.
53. Acuto and Curtis 2014; Deleuze and Guattari 1980.
54. Abrahamsen 2017: 255.
55. See Abrahamsen 2016.
56. Xiang and Lindquist 2014.
57. Beauchemin 2018.
58. For a strong critique of limitations imposed by methodological nationalism in migration research, see Wimmer and Schiller 2003.
59. Li 2007: 264.
60. Giddens 1990; see also Bakewell 2010.
61. Poelma 2019.
62. De Haas 2014; see also chapter 3.
63. Latour 2005; Sassen 2006.
64. De Haas 2014.
65. Acuto and Curtis 2014.
66. See WIDE (NA), 'WIDE story', available at: https://ethiopiawide.net/history/ (accessed 5 March 2021).

1. INTERROGATING THE INTER-LINKAGE BETWEEN ETHIOPIAN MIGRATION POLICIES AND IRREGULAR MIGRATION

1. Solimano 2010: 4.
2. IOM 2017a: 15.
3. Castles et al. 2014.
4. IOM 2017a: 13.
5. Bourbeau 2011: 1.
6. Carling and Hernández-Carretero 2011: 46.
7. Carling and Hernández-Carretero 2011: 52.
8. Mallett et al. 2017: 8.
9. Alpes and Sørensen 2015; Czaika and De Haas 2013; Czaika and Hobolth 2016; Koser and Kuschminder 2016.
10. Browne 2015: 2. In this chapter, as Fernandez (2017) observed, irregular migration refers to both an illegal entry (by crossing the physical boundary of a state) and the condition created even after a legal entry (by overstaying a short visit visa, exiting an employment contract to escape abuse, sponsorship-linked 'free visa', and pregnancy and birth of a child). These all could create illegality and irregular migration status.
11. Flahaux and De Haas 2016: 11.
12. ENA 2019a; 2019b; *New Arab* 2019.
13. The Amharic term '*sidet*' is narrow and refers to forced migration which either happens because of persecution or high levels of poverty (e.g., food insecurity).
14. The Amharic term '*felset*' is broad and implies permanent or temporary change of residency. It includes the decision of people to go and reside within the country or abroad to improve their livelihoods.
15. IOM 2017b: 8.
16. Solomon 2016: 134; Schewel and Asmamaw 2019.
17. Schewel and Asmamaw 2019: 11.
18. Solomon 2016: 134.
19. IOM 2017a: 46.
20. Fransen and Kuschminder 2009: 17; MGSoG 2017: 3.
21. Marchand et al. 2017.
22. Asnake and Zerihun 2015: 5–6; De Regt 2007: 5; IOM 2017b: 5.
23. RMMS 2016.
24. MGSoG 2017: 3.
25. RMMS 2016b: 1.
26. IOM 2015: 1.
27. Abel et al. 2018; Adamnesh et al. 2016.
28. See *Addis Fortune* 2017.
29. Adamnesh et al. 2016; Fikremariam 2016.

30. GoE, MoUDH 2012: 11, 16–20.
31. GoE, MoUDH 2012: 3, 21.
32. Abel et al. 2018.
33. Asnake and Zerihun 2015.
34. Daniel 2016: 58.
35. Girum and Eden 2014: 2; Eyob 2017.
36. Eyob 2017.
37. Girum and Eden 2014.
38. Ibid.
39. Ethiopian Youth Revolving Fund Establishment Proclamation No. 995/2017.
40. Robel 2017.
41. Asnake and Zerihun 2015; Emebet 2001.
42. De Regt 2007: 12–13.
43. De Regt 2007; Emebet 2001.
44. Emebet 2001: 6.
45. See Article 6(1) of Proclamation 2009.
46. See Article 7(2b) of Proclamation 2009.
47. For up to 500 workers $30,000, for 501–1,000 workers $40,000, and for above 1,001 workers $50,000 or its equivalent in Ethiopian birr.
48. ILO 2011: ix.
49. Jones et al. 2014c: 39.
50. De Regt and Medareshaw 2016; Fernandez 2013, 2017; Human Rights Watch 2018; Jones et al. 2014c.
51. Abraham 2014; Human Rights Watch 2015.
52. Alemayehu and Demisew 2014.
53. IOM 2019. See also De Regt and Medareshaw 2016: 229.
54. Shaban 2017.
55. *Daily Star* 2008.
56. *Arab News* 2018.
57. *Woreda*, district, is the second-lowest administrative unit, while *kebele* is the lowest.
58. Asnake and Zerihun 2015: 47.
59. Mehari 2017: 40.
60. Al Jazeera 2013; Prevention and Suppression of Trafficking in Persons and Smuggling of Migrants Proclamation no. 909/2015.
61. Crisp 2000: 6.
62. Markussen 2018.
63. EU 2015: 6.
64. Markussen 2018: 9.
65. EU 2015: 1–4; Markussen 2018: 9.
66. EU 2015: 4.
67. This phrase is coined as a reference to the forced displacement of mas-

sive numbers of refugees from Syria and their arrival at the borders and on the shores of Europe. As a result, this period has played a vital role in (re)shaping European migration policy and caused Europe to be trapped in a border security (political) versus humanitarianism (moral) dilemma.

68. Alemu and Carver 2019.
69. Osman 2018.
70. *Addis Fortune* 2018; ENA 2019b.
71. *Ethiopian Herald* 2019.
72. Castles 2004, cited in Fernandez 2013: 817.
73. Emebet 2001: 17.
74. ILO 2011: 34.
75. Asnake and Zerihun 2015: 46.
76. Fernandez 2013; ILO 2011.
77. Fernandez 2013.
78. ILO 2011: 35.
79. ILO 2011.
80. *Addis Fortune* 2018.
81. Bezabeh 2017.
82. FBC 2020.
83. RMMS 2017.
84. Ibid.: 16.
85. Human Rights Watch 2015; RMMS 2017.
86. Fernandez 2013.
87. Ibid.: 821.
88. Conducted in Gondar in February 2017.
89. ILO 2017: 4, 45–9.
90. *Addis Fortune* 2018.
91. ENA 2019b.
92. *Addis Standard* 2018.
93. Jones et al. 2014c.
94. Asnake and Zerihun 2015; Kuschminder 2014.
95. GTPs are national development plans that have been adopted with the aim of transforming and bringing development to the country. So far two GTPs have been introduced, GTP I (2010–15) and II (2015–20).
96. Adamnesh et al. 2016.

2. 'SAY WHAT THE GOVERNMENT WANTS AND DO WHAT IS GOOD FOR YOUR FAMILY': FACILITATION OF IRREGULAR MIGRATION IN ETHIOPIA

1. Hernández-Léon 2008; Salt and Stein 1997.
2. Hernández-Léon 2008: 154.

3. Herman 2006: 217; Sanchez 2015.
4. Guday and Kiya 2013; Abebaw 2012; Grabska 2016; Zeyneba 2016; Kiya 2019.
5. Achilli 2018; Ayalew 2019.
6. Andersson 2014; Achilli 2018.
7. Cf. Alpes 2013; 2017.
8. Deleuze and Guattari 1980.
9. Sanchez 2017.
10. Achilli 2018; Sanchez 2017; Zhang et al. 2018.
11. Alpes 2017; Sanchez 2017.
12. Documents of the Migration Directorate in the Ministry of Labour and Social Affairs.
13. Asnake and Zerihun 2015: 22.
14. Asnake and Zerihun 2015.
15. Cf. Makoye 2016.
16. De Regt and Medareshaw 2016.
17. Of course, in recent years, the Ethiopian government's efforts were also backed up by the EU's externalisation of border controls (Gaibazzi et al. 2017: 5–10), which is noticeable in the north-western route that leads to Europe.
18. SAHAN 2016.
19. Sisay 2019: 36–7.
20. Discussion with the staff of the Hadya Zone Attorney General office in July 2019, Hosaena, Hadya Zone.
21. Cf. Fekadu et al. 2019.
22. De Regt and Medareshaw 2016; Girmachew 2018; Ayalew 2018.
23. Botti and Phillips 2019.
24. Discussion with immigration official in July 2018 and April 2019, Addis Ababa.
25. Cf. Horwood 2009.
26. Discussion with immigration official in July 2018 and April 2019, Addis Ababa.
27. Achilli 2016: 102.
28. Fekadu et al. 2019.
29. Discussion with immigration official in April 2019, Addis Ababa.
30. Cf. De Regt and Medareshaw 2016.
31. Cf. Fekadu et al. 2019; Yordanos 2018.
32. Ayalew et al. 2018.
33. Cf. Sanchez 2017; Achilli 2018; Belloni 2016; Alpes 2013.
34. Belloni 2016.
35. Cf. De Regt and Medareshaw 2016; Asnake and Zerihun 2015; Fekadu et al. 2019.

36. Belloni 2016.
37. IOM 2019a.
38. Botti and Phillips 2019; UN 2015.
39. IOM 2018a; IOM 2018b.
40. Ayalew et al. 2018; Fekadu et al. 2019.
41. Ayalew et al. 2018.
42. Fekadu et al. 2019.
43. We are aware of the ethical issues involved here. As a public figure, 'the chief administrator' is easily identifiable. But, since the person had passed away, using this example for our analysis does not at least affect the person.
44. *Kebele* is the smallest territorial administrative unit in Ethiopia.
45. Interview with Adane in Gimbichu, Soro district.
46. The urban Hadya consider the expansion of Hosaena city, the several recently opened commercial banks in Hosaena and small towns to have benefited from foreign currency through *hawala* money transfers. The similar-coloured buses that travel around Hadya Zone, purchased by the migrants, are symbols of modern-day Hadya migration.
47. Hagan and Ebaugh 2003.
48. Interview with an official of the Ministry of Labour and Social Affairs, July 2019, in Addis Ababa; interview with Hadya Zone Police Department, May 2018, in Hosaena.
49. Carling 2002; cf. Alpes 2017.
50. Zhang et al. 2018: 6.
51. Zhang et al. 2018: 9.

3. THE DRIVERS OF YOUTH MIGRATION IN ADDIS ABABA

1. Mehari 2016.
2. MGSoG 2017.
3. Mehari 2016.
4. Asnake and Zerihun 2015.
5. MGSoG 2017.
6. Mehari 2016.
7. Todaro 1969; Harris and Todaro 1970 in Manning 2004; Asnake and Zerihun 2015.
8. Emirbayer and Mische 1998.
9. The lowest tier of local government in Addis Ababa.
10. De Haas 2011.
11. Todaro 1969; Harris and Todaro 1970 in Manning 2004.
12. De Haas 2011: 8.
13. Harris and Todaro 1970 in Manning 2004.

14. De Haas 2011.
15. Collins 1994; Wallerstein 1974.
16. Carling 2014.
17. CSA 2016.
18. Tegegne et al. 2015.
19. Ibid.
20. KII with Addis Ababa Bureau of Labour and Social Affairs, 10 January 2017; FGD with returnees, Kirkos sub-city, 16 January 2017.
21. Mehari 2016.
22. Castles 2004.
23. Dekker and Engbersen 2012.
24. FGD with returnees, Addis Ketema sub-city, 11 January 2017.
25. In-depth interview with mother of potential migrant, Arada sub-city, 15 January 2017.
26. Kandel and Massey 2002: 982.
27. Individual interview with returnee, Arada sub-city, 15 January 2017.
28. FGD with returnees, Addis Ketema, 24 October 2018.
29. Crawford 1973 in Zanker 2008.
30. De Jong and Fawcett 1981.
31. KII with *woreda* Labour and Social Affairs, 12 January 2017; FDG with potential migrants, Arada sub-city, 24 January 2017; in-depth interview with returnee, Addis Ketema sub-city, 25 October 2018.
32. Tegegne et al. 2015: 93.
33. Balaz and Williams 2014.
34. De Haas 2011.
35. Bakewell et al. 2011.
36. Emirbayer and Mische 1998: 970.
37. Emirbayer and Mische 1998.
38. Bakewell et al. 2001.
39. Individual interview with returnee, Addis Ketema, 25 October 2018.
40. FGD with returnees, Kirkos sub-city, 16 January 2017.

4. HOPELESSNESS AND FUTURE-MAKING THROUGH IRREGULAR MIGRATION IN TIGRAY, ETHIOPIA

1. Mains 2007; 2012; Mains et al. 2013.
2. On similar developments in Jimma, see Mains 2007.
3. Surprisingly, aspiration for education does not appear to change expectations for marriage at an earlier age (Herman et al. 2011). See also Mains 2012.
4. Skjerdal 2011.
5. Li 2017: 2.

6. For a comparable case, see Sommers 2012.
7. It could also be argued that the breakup of governance structures promotes informal and illegal activities including cross-border migration. See *Lancet Infectious Diseases* 2017.
8. UNHCR 2017.
9. IOM 2019b.
10. For example, in early September 2019, the Council of Ministers approved a draft proclamation, still awaiting ratification by the House of People's Representatives, which establishes a National Council against the practice of human trafficking led by the Prime Minister and includes the death penalty as one punishment for human traffickers. See Yohannes 2019.
11. De Regt and Medareshaw 2016; IOM 2019b.
12. Asnake and Zerihun 2015: 23.
13. Asnake and Zerihun 2015: 28.
14. See Asnake and Zerihun 2015.
15. For details on this, see Fana and Beyene 2017.
16. Interview with Assefa Tegegn, Senior Expert, Regional BoLSA, 9 January 2017.
17. De Haas 2009; Bakewell et al. 2011.
18. Cohen 2004; Timmerman et al. 2014.
19. De Haas 2009; Bakewell et al. 2011.
20. While the recorded figures show that there are 2.65 male irregular migrants for every female from the region, informants in Atsbi Wenberta and Raya Alamata give a rough approximation of two men for every female migrant from their *woreda*.
21. Interview with Haftom G. Michael and Haftewoini Lilay, Labour and Social Affairs Office, Abi Adi, 16 January 2017.
22. Horwood 2016.
23. Ibid.
24. FGD with returnees, Atsbi Endasellassie, 22 January 2017.
25. Serneels 2007.
26. Broussard and Tsegay 2012; Beshir 2014; Gezahegn 2015.
27. CSA 2012: 4.
28. World Bank 2016a.
29. CSA 2012: 6.
30. CSA 2012; Gezahegn 2015.
31. See also Mains 2007; 2012.
32. Similarly, this different temporal experience of long periods of unemployment by men and women could be part of the explanation for the higher number of men migrating irregularly than women.
33. Eyob 2017.
34. Honwana 2012.

35. FGD with young men, Waja Timuga, 14 January 2017.
36. FGD with young men, Atsbi Endasellassie, 23 January 2017.
37. Interview with experts at BoLSA of Raya Alamata, 12 January 2017, and Atsbi Wenberta *woreda*, 23 January 2017.
38. Interview with expert at Atsbi Wenberta *woreda*'s BoLSA, 23 January 2017.
39. FGD with women returnees, Waja Timuga, 15 January 2017.
40. FGD participant, a divorcee and returnee, in Atsbi Endasellassie, 26 January 2017.
41. FGD participant, a housewife from a poor household, in Waja Timuga, 14 January 2017.
42. World Bank 2016a.
43. Eyob 2017: 46.
44. Interview with MSE Development Bureau experts at regional level, 11 January 2017, as well as Raya Amalata, 13 January 2017, Abi Adi, 17 January 2017, and Atsbi Wenberta *woreda*, 24 January 2017.
45. Interview with experts at BoLSA, 23 January 2017, and MSE Development Bureau, 24 January 2017, of Atsbi Wenberta *woreda*.
46. Interview with expert at DECSI, 23 January 2017, and MSE Development Bureau, 24 January 2017, of Atsbi Wenberta *woreda*.
47. Interview with experts at the region's MSE Development Bureau, 11 January 2017, and BoLSA, 9 January 2017, experts at Atsbi Wenberta *woreda*'s BoLSA, 23 January 2017, and MSEDB, 24 January 2017, as well as Raya Alamata *woreda*'s BoLSA, 12 January 2017, and MSEDB, 24 January 2017.
48. Interview with experts at the region's MSE Development Bureau, 11 January 2017, and BoLSA, 9 January 2017, experts at Atsbi Wenberta *woreda*'s BoLSA, 23 January 2017, and MSEDB, 24 January 2017, as well as Raya Alamata *woreda*'s BoLSA, 12 January 2017, and MSEDB, 24 January 2017.
49. Interview with experts at the region's MSE Development Bureau, 11 January 2017, and BoLSA, 9 January 2017, experts at Atsbi Wenberta *woreda*'s BoLSA, 23 January 2017, and MSEDB, 24 January 2017, as well as Raya Alamata *woreda*'s BoLSA, 12 January 2017, and MSEDB, 24 January 2017.
50. Interview with MSEDB experts at regional level, 11 January 2017, as well as Raya Amalata, 13 January 2017), Abi Adi, 17 January 2017, and Atsbi Wenberta *woreda*, 24 January 2017.
51. See Sommers 2012.
52. FGD with young men, Abi Adi, 16 January 2017.
53. FGD with women, Waja Timuga, 15 January 2017.
54. Mains 2007; 2012; Mains et al. 2013.
55. FGD with young men, Atsbi Endasellassie, 26 January 2017.

56. FGD with young men, Atsbi Endasellassie, 26 January 2017.
57. FGD with young men, Abi Adi, 16 January 2017.
58. FGD with young men, Waja Timuga, 14 January 2017.
59. Ibid.
60. FGD with young men, Atsbi Endasellassie, 23 January 2017.
61. De Haas 2009; Bakewell et al. 2011; Cohen 2004; Timmerman et al. 2014.
62. Sommers 2012.
63. Dobler 2020; Grabska 2020; Serawit 2020; Wyss 2019.
64. David Harvey (1990) uses this term to refer to capitalism's geographical expansion and restructuring to (at least temporarily) resolve its internal contradictions and crises.
65. De Haas 2011; 2014.
66. Appadurai 2013: 285–300.
67. In this chapter, I don't pay much attention to anticipation. See Appadurai 2013: 286.
68. Appadurai 2013: 288.
69. Interview with experts at BoLSA, 23 January 2017, and Planning and Finance Bureau, 23 January 2017, of Atsbi Wenberta *woreda*.
70. Interview with experts from Urban Development, Trade and Industry Bureau, 12 January 2017, and BoLSA, 12 January 2017, of Raya Alamata *woreda*.
71. See FBC 2019.
72. Interview with Assefa Tegegn, 9 January 2017, and Nigisti W. Rufael, 4 January 2017, at BoLSA, Mekelle; and FGD with young men, Waja Timuga, 14 January 2017.
73. Interview with Assefa Tegegn, 9 January 2017, and Nigisti W. Rufael, 4 January 2017, at BoLSA, Mekelle; and FGD with young men, Waja Timuga, 14 January 2017.
74. Mains 2012.
75. Appadurai 2013: 292.
76. Ibid.
77. De Haas 2011; 2014.
78. Sen 1999.
79. De Haas 2011; 2014.
80. De Haas 2011: 18.

5. MIGRATION ASPIRATIONS AND 'GLOCAL IDEAS OF THE GOOD LIFE' IN TWO RURAL COMMUNITIES IN SOUTHERN AND NORTH-EASTERN ETHIOPIA: A COMPARATIVE PERSPECTIVE

1. Geertz 1973.
2. Carling and Schewel 2018: 959.

3. Collins 2017: 2.
4. Boccagni 2017: 2.
5. Carling and Collins 2018: 911.
6. Appadurai 2004: 67.
7. Robertson 2012: 196.
8. The Productive Safety Net Programme (PSNP) provides cash transfers six months of the year in chronically food-insecure areas to households identified as neediest by their community, in return for labour, except for households without able-bodied adults.
9. Dom 2012a.
10. Bevan and Pankhurst 1996a.
11. Dom 2019a; 2019b.
12. Tibebe 1999.
13. Bevan and Pankhurst 1996b.
14. Dom 2012b.
15. Frankowska 2019a.
16. In the remainder of the chapter, migration-focused interviews and focus group discussions in Harresaw and Aze Debo are dated. Interviews and focus group discussions on broader or other issues, in which migration appeared, were all conducted between 20 January and 28 March 2018.
17. Appadurai 2004: 68.
18. Carling and Collins 2018: 916.
19. Father of two migrants to South Africa, Aze Debo, 19 March 2018.
20. Father of two sons who migrated to South Africa and a daughter returnee from Sudan, Aze Debo, 17 March 2018.
21. Member of *kebele* cabinet, Aze Debo, 14 March 2018.
22. Young man, 19, from a rich household, supporting grandparents' farming, Aze Debo, 17 March 2018.
23. Father and mother of two sons who migrated to South Africa, Aze Debo, 17 March 2018.
24. Father of two sons who migrated to South Africa and a daughter returnee from Sudan, Aze Debo, 16 March 2018.
25. Three young women returnees from Sudan, Aze Debo, 18 March 2018.
26. Collins 2018.
27. Young woman returnee from Kuwait talking about young men's migration to South Africa, Aze Debo, 19 March 2018.
28. Young man, 25, from a poor family, returnee from Sudan and aspiring to migrate to South Africa, Aze Debo, 18 March 2018.
29. Grade 12 young man, returnee after detention en route to South Africa, Aze Debo, 14 March 2018.
30. Focus group discussion with young men on young people's life in the community, Aze Debo.

31. Young man, married, who does not want to migrate, Aze Debo, 21 March 2018; see also Carling and Collins 2018.
32. Wife of primary school head teacher, cabinet member for education, Aze Debo, 13 March 2018.
33. Young man, returnee from South Africa, married, Aze Debo, 14 March 2018.
34. Young woman returnee from Sudan, talking about young men's migration to South Africa, Aze Debo, 15 March 2018.
35. Focus group discussion with young men about young people's life in the community, Aze Debo.
36. Father of two sons who migrated to South Africa and one daughter returnee from Sudan, 16 March 2018.
37. Pankhurst and Dom 2019.
38. Carling and Collins 2018: 916.
39. Ray 2006.
40. Father of two migrant sons to South Africa, talking about his eldest son, Aze Debo, 19 March 2018.
41. Returnee from South Africa, talking about another migrant, Aze Debo, 20 March 2018.
42. Would-be migrant from rich family, 19, Aze Debo, 17 March 2018.
43. *Kebele* Youth League chair, Aze Debo, 13 March 2018.
44. Young male returnee after detention en route, 14 March 2018.
45. Father of a son who migrated to South Africa, Aze Debo, 16 March 2018.
46. Many different people in Harresaw mentioned the lack of hope because of no other option, as a strong migration push factor.
47. One young man, 30, married, three children, landless, uneducated, returnee from Saudi, in an impromptu group discussion with young men, several of them returnees or deportees (FGD 1), Harresaw, 4 March 2018.
48. Young woman selling local alcoholic drink in parents' house, aspiring to migrate, Harresaw, 1 March 2018.
49. Young man interviewed on young people's life in the community, Harresaw.
50. One man in a focus group discussion (FGD 2) with adult men, Harresaw, 3 March 2018.
51. Young woman, married, interviewed as a small crop trader, Harresaw.
52. Carling and Collins 2018.
53. Adult man in FGD 2, Harresaw, 3 March 2018.
54. Returnee from Saudi living in *woreda* centre, Atsbi, 4 March 2018.
55. Young man, married, 24, ex-shoeshiner, now successful businessman, never migrated and not interested in doing so, Harresaw, 1 March 2018.
56. Women's Affair's *tabia* cabinet representative, Harresaw, 1 March 2018.

pp. [108–120] NOTES

57. Focus group discussion (FGD 2) with adult men, Harresaw, 3 March 2018.
58. Chief priest of one of Harresaw's churches, 55, Harresaw, 2 March 2018.
59. Impromptu group discussion with young men, several of them returnees or deportees (FGD 1), Harresaw, 4 March 2018.
60. Young woman whose husband repeatedly migrates (she passed Grade 10 but could not continue, is working at the *tabia* social court, has two children), Harresaw.
61. Rose and Baird 2013.
62. Pankhurst 2019.
63. Favara 2017; Rose and Baird 2013.
64. Head teacher of primary school, Aze Debo, 13 March 2018.
65. Boccagni 2017.
66. Focus group discussion on gender and social effects of migration, men of various ages including one returnee and two fathers of migrants or returnees, Harresaw, 14 March 2018.
67. Adult woman interviewed on three main issues in the community, Harresaw.
68. Chief priest of one of Harresaw's churches, 55, Harresaw, 2 March 2018.
69. Hirschman 1972.
70. Returnee from South Africa, Aze Debo, 14 March 2018.
71. Returnee (twice) from Saudi, married, two children, Harresaw, 5 March 2018.
72. Young man, landless, married, two children, returnee from Saudi, Harresaw, 1 March 2018.
73. Appadurai 2004; Ray 2006.
74. Appadurai 2004; Boccagni 2017; Carling and Collins 2018.
75. Robertson 2012.
76. Appadurai 2004: 67.
77. Fernandez 2020: 3.
78. Collins 2017: 4.
79. Di Nunzio 2019: 25.

6. RITUALS OF MIGRATION: SOCIALLY ENTRENCHED PRACTICES AMONG FEMALE MIGRANTS FROM AMHARA NATIONAL REGIONAL STATE

1. Personal names of informants used in this chapter are pseudonyms.
2. *Emnet* is incense ash or soil used among followers of the Ethiopian Orthodox Church for healing purposes. The ash comes from the incense burned during sermons while the soil can be collected from any holy ground, in most cases from the church compound.

3. Pedersen and Rytter 2018: 2604.
4. CSA 2013a.
5. RMMS 2014.
6. Girmachew 2018; Jones et al. 2014c.
7. Grabska 2016; Hailemichael 2014; Shewit 2013; Abbink 1994; Kaplan 1993.
8. Kaplan and Rosen 1994.
9. RMMS 2016c.
10. RMMS 2014.
11. Federal Democratic Republic of Ethiopia Anti-trafficking Council 2015.
12. RMMS 2014.
13. Kosec et al. 2018: 933.
14. GIZ 2018.
15. RMMS 2014.
16. RMMS 2016c; Horwood 2015; RMMS 2014; Guday and Kiya 2013.
17. Olivier 2017.
18. Jones et al. 2014c.
19. Gete et al. 2008: 26.
20. Asnake and Zerihun 2015.
21. Fernandez 2010.
22. Girmachew 2018; Grabska 2016; Jones et al. 2014c; RMMS 2014.
23. Aguilar 2018: 93.
24. Grimes 2000: 261.
25. Van Hear 2010.
26. Monsutti 2007.
27. Duntley 2005.
28. Eisenburch, in Bhugra and Becker 2005: 19.
29. Bhugra and Becker 2005.
30. Bell 1992: 169.
31. Hondagneu-Sotelo and Cranford 2006; Jolly and Reeves 2005; Piper 2005; Carling 2005.
32. Piper 2005: 9.
33. Guday and Kiya 2013: 129.
34. RMMS 2014: 21.
35. Aguilar 2018.
36. 'Rituals: Definition, Types & Challenges', *Study.com*, 26 August 2016, study.com/academy/lesson/rituals-definition-types-challenges.html
37. Van Gennep 1960.
38. Pedersen and Rytter 2018: 2606.
39. Turner 1967.
40. Jones et al. 2014c.
41. The religious practice of *wadaja* is a communal prayer and blessing where

the relationship with the supernatural is bridged. The religious practice puts the accent on a wide range of concerns like wealth, health, peace and security, marriage, productivity and others.

42. Kiya 2013.
43. Pedersen and Rytter 2018.

7. IRREGULAR MIGRATION AMONG A KAMBATA COMMUNITY IN ETHIOPIA: VIEWS FROM BELOW AND THEIR IMPLICATIONS

1. Earlier versions of this chapter were presented at the 20th International Conference of Ethiopian Studies (Mekelle, Ethiopia) and an International Conference on Irregular Migration (Nairobi, Kenya). I hereby acknowledge that the paper benefited from comments at these conferences. I am sincerely indebted to the individuals who provided the data for this research.
2. Porumbescu 2015.
3. Frankowska 2019b.
4. Ibid.
5. e.g., Crowley et al. 2016; Ellis 2015; Kurekova 2009.
6. Bakewell 2010: 2.
7. Crowley et al. 2016; UNECA 2017.
8. Bloch and Chimienti 2011: 10.
9. Porumbescu 2015.
10. Crowley et al. 2016.
11. Dom 2019c; Mulugeta and Bayissa 2020.
12. Beshir 2014; Jerusalem 2016; Tariku 2018.
13. Girmachew 2019.
14. Flahaux and De Haas 2016: 1.
15. UNECA 2017.
16. Fernandez 2020.
17. Cvajner and Sciortino 2010.
18. Porumbescu 2015; chapter 8 in this volume.
19. Asnake and Zerihun 2015.
20. e.g., ILO (2011) cited in Marchand et al. 2016.
21. Asnake and Zerihun 2015.
22. In south Ethiopia the feast is the most important annual event and takes place for more than seven days; families, including migrants, have to gather, exchange different gifts and make different rituals. In such a case, remittances seem not only to provide the money for this event, which may require longer preparations for some households, but also to show that those who are out of country and cannot be physically present in their homeland are represented or remembered.

23. Frankowska 2019b.
24. e.g., Gurieva and Dzhioev 2015.
25. e.g., Crowley et al. 2016.
26. UNECA 2017.
27. Leerkes 2016.
28. Ibid.
29. e.g., Zedner (2013) cited in Leerkes 2016.
30. e.g., Cornelius (2001) cited in Leerkes 2016.
31. See also Asnake and Zerihun 2015.

8. GENDER RELATIONS IN A TRANSNATIONAL SPACE: ETHIO-PIAN IRREGULAR MIGRANTS IN SOUTH AFRICA

1. Curran and Saguy 2001; Curran and Rivero 2003.
2. Curran et al. 2005.
3. Curran and Saguy 2001; Curran and Rivero 2003.
4. The UK's Department for International Development (DFID) funds the MOOP research programme consortium. It focuses on the relationship between migration and poverty—especially migration within countries and regions—across Asia and Africa. For details, see www.migrating-outofpoverty.org.
5. Wehmhoerner 2015.
6. Teller and Assefa 2011.
7. Yordanos 2015.
8. Teshome 2010.
9. Yordanos 2015.
10. Yordanos 2016; Yordanos and Zack 2019.
11. Yordanos 2015.
12. Yordanos and Zack 2019.
13. Zack and Yordanos 2016.
14. Teshome et al. 2013; Yordanos 2016.
15. Yordanos 2016.
16. Ibid.
17. Teshome 2010; Yordanos 2015.
18. Zack and Yordanos 2019.
19. Salih 2001.
20. Pessar and Mahler 2003.
21. Jaji 2016.
22. Yordanos and Zack 2019; Yordanos 2016.
23. Yordanos and Zack 2019.
24. All names in this chapter are pseudonyms.
25. Hagan 1998.

26. Amel 2012.
27. Madianou and Miller 2011.
28. Yordanos 2016.
29. *Idir* in Amharic could be translated as a burial association. It is formed by people in the same locality in order to support one another when households lose family members, or to hold a significant social occasion like a wedding.
30. Zack and Yordanos 2016.
31. Amel 2012.
32. Yordanos 2015.
33. Amel 2012; Zack and Yordanos 2016.
34. Yordanos 2015.
35. Amel 2012.
36. Waite and Lewis 2017.
37. Zack 2017.
38. SERI 2017.
39. Rogerson 2015.
40. Yordanos et al. 2019.
41. Landau and Pampalone 2018.
42. Yordanos and Zack 2019.
43. Curran and Saguy 2001.
44. Lindley 2007.
45. This came in a post-interview informal discussion. I used this term to capture his rather lengthy explanation of how some women use men's weak sides to manipulate them—mainly their emotions. Other men who thought some wives were emotionally blackmailing them shared the same feeling.
46. Yordanos and Zack 2019.

9. REMITTANCES AND HOUSEHOLD SOCIO-ECONOMIC WELL-BEING: THE CASE OF ETHIOPIAN LABOUR MIGRANTS IN THE GULF COUNTRIES AND SOUTH AFRICA

1. This chapter is adapted from a longer report published by the authors: *Migration, Remittances and Household Socio-economic Wellbeing: The Case of Ethiopian Labour Migrants to the Republic of South Africa and the Middle East.* Addis Ababa: Forum for Social Studies, 2018.
2. NBE 2016.
3. *Woreda* is an Amharic term for district.
4. Kombolcha is an urban *woreda*. At the same time, it serves as the capital of the Kalu *woreda*.
5. Asnake and Zerihun 2015; FSS 2017.
6. *Kebele* is the lower level of administrative unit under the *woreda*, or district.

7.   World Bank 2011.

8.   Ghosal 2015: 177.

9.   NBE 2015/16.

10. NBE 2016/17.

11. Isaacs 2017.

12. Ibid.: 6.

13. The term *hawala* is an Arabic word that has come to refer to the formal transfer of money through formal banking and postal services. However, in this study, the term *hawala* is used in its original meaning to refer to the semi-organised informal money transfer system.

14. Isaacs 2017: 13.

15. Kapur 2003: 12.

16. Asnake and Zerihun 2015.

17. Interview with a local official, Kombolcha City, Amhara Region, 3 March 2018.

18. Interview with a member of a recipient family, Shashemene, 11 March 2018.

19. FDG with experts of Halaba Special *woreda*, Women and Children's Affairs Office, Halaba, 23 February 2018.

20. The returnee survey showed that the migrants pay on average 17,200 birr ($625.50) for the migration, while the response from the migrant families shows an average expense of 20,075 birr ($730).

21. Interview with an official in the Addis Ababa City Administration Bureau of Labour and Social Affairs, 19 February 2018.

22. Interview with official of the Kombolcha City Women, Children and Social Affairs Office, Kombolcha, Amhara Region, 3 March 2018; interview with official of the Tigray Regional Bureau of Social Affairs, Mekelle, 20 March 2018.

23. Interview with a returnee migrant from Saudi Arabia, Halaba Special *woreda*, SNNPR, 26 February 2018.

24. FGD with returnees in Kallu/Harbu, 13 March 2018.

25. Interview with official of the Wereilu TVET College, Wereilu, 20 March 2018.

26. FGD with migrant's family, Wereilu, 20 March 2018.

27. FGD with returnees in Kallu/Harbu, 11 March 2018.

28. Interview with an elder in Kombolcha City, Amhara Region, 16 March 2018.

29. Interview with official of the Amhara Credit and Savings Institution (ACSI), Wereilu branch general manager, 20 March 2018.

30. Interview with returnee migrant from South Africa, Halaba Special *woreda*, SNNPR, 26 February 2018; interview with an official of the Kombolcha Agricultural College, Amhara Region, 15 March 2018.

31. Interview with returnee migrant from South Africa, Halaba Special

woreda, SNNPR, 26 February 2018; interview with an official of the Kombolcha Agricultural College, Amhara Region, 15 March 2018.

32. Interview with an officer of the Wereilu branch of the Commercial Bank of Ethiopia, 19 April 2018.
33. Interview with an official of the Kirkos sub-city, *woreda* 10 Labour and Social Affairs Office, 20 February 2018.
34. FGD with returnees in Kallu/Harbu, 11 March 2018.
35. Original name has been changed.
36. Interview with an expert of the Kombolcha City Women, Children and Social Affairs Office, Kombolcha, Amhara Region, 15 March 2018.
37. Water pipe tobacco. Interview with an expert of the Kombolcha City Women, Children and Social Affairs Office, Kombolcha, Amhara Region, 15 March 2018.
38. Interview with an expert of the Kalu *woreda* administration, Kombolcha, 14 March 2018.
39. Ibid.
40. Ibid.
41. Kalu is a *woreda* neighbouring on Kombolcha. Its capital is located in Kombolcha.
42. Interview with an expert of the Kalu *woreda* administration, Kombolcha, 14 March 2018.
43. Ibid.
44. NBE 2016.

10. HETEROGENEITY IN OUTCOMES OF MIGRATION: THE CASE OF IRREGULAR MIGRATION TO SAUDI ARABIA IN HARRE-SAW, EASTERN TIGRAY

1. De Haas 2010.
2. Ibid.: 227.
3. Dom 2020.
4. De Haas 2010.
5. McDowell and De Haan 1997; Bebbington 1999; Ellis 2000, cited in De Haas 2010.
6. De Haas 2010.
7. IOM 2018c.
8. Fassil 2017.
9. Grabska et al. 2019.
10. Mulugeta et al. 2016; Jones et al. 2014c.
11. Lipton, cited in De Haas 2010.
12. De Haas 2010, drawing on Sen 1999.
13. McDowell and De Haan 1997.

14. De Haas 2010.
15. Schewel 2018.
16. Fernandez 2020.
17. Schewel 2018.
18. Massey et al. 2016; Heering et al. 2004, cited in De Haas 2010.
19. Dom 2019a; chapter 5 in this volume.
20. Pankhurst 2019.
21. Development team is an informal government structure which facilitates the implementation of government interventions.
22. The productive safety net is a food security programme which ultimately aims to improve the livelihood of communities by filling food gaps and building assets. The programme provides food rations or cash to food-insecure households; among them, able-bodied people are supposed to carry out work allocated to them.
23. Pankhurst 2019.
24. A male FGD participant.
25. De Haas 2010.
26. Ibid.

11. THE MORAL ECONOMY OF IRREGULAR MIGRATION AND REMITTANCE DISTRIBUTION IN SOUTH WOLLO

1. A previous version of this chapter was presented at the Workshop on Migration and Displacement: Roots of Vulnerability, Roads to Solution, held at Hilton Addis Ababa, 21–22 March 2019, under the auspices of UK Research and Innovation (UKRI), in collaboration with the International Committee of the Red Cross (ICRC) and the Organization for Social Science Research in Eastern and Southern Africa (OSSREA). I thank the organisers, Professor Laura Hammond (GCRF Challenge Leader—Conflict and Displacement, UK Research and Innovation) and Dr Truphena Mukuna (executive director of OSSREA), for the opportunity to present my findings, while also learning from the feedback and excellent works of other participants. This final version has benefited from both editorial comments and discussion with fellow authors at the Book Workshop held on 25–26 July at the Institute for Peace and Security Studies (IPSS), Addis Ababa University. Finally, I thank the returnee migrants and household heads I interviewed, who shared their unique perspectives on irregular migration.
2. Hoben 1973.
3. Hoben 1963; Levine 1965; Bauer 1985.
4. Weissleder 1965.
5. McCann 1987; Pankhurst 1992.

6. Weissleder 1965.
7. Adapted from Baker 1985: 103.
8. Bruce 1976.
9. Dessalegn 1991; Castro 2012.
10. Dessalegn 2009; McCann 1987; Teferi 1998.
11. Morrissey 2013.
12. Gray and Mueller 2012; Sharp et al. 2003.
13. Bauer 1985.
14. For a quick (but arguably an unofficial) exchange history of birr, see https://www1.oanda.com/currency/converter/.
15. According to a media release by the Ethiopian Islamic Affairs Supreme Council (EIASC), the comparable cost for travelling to Saudi Arabia by plane as a *hajj* pilgrim was 93,000–98,800 birr per person (https://allafrica.com/stories/201808010298.html). The reported cost of irregular migration from South Wollo is much higher than comparable data for Tigray (see chapter 4) and Addis Ababa (see chapter 3). This is mainly because the expense of regular labour migrants is limited to fees for a passport and medical check-up (and, in recent times, training). The higher cost of irregular labour migration may also have to do with the unpredictability of the ways smugglers at different transit points determine their 'service' costs. Unfortunately, I lack any information on this aspect of the migration process other than what informants tell me.
16. The anthropologist Milena Belloni (2016) observes a similar pattern in the ways Eritrean undocumented refugees in Libya claimed kinship-based cultural entitlements while en route to Europe.
17. For transferring the money, HM relied on the trust of personal friends and other informal providers in ways that Asnake and Zerihun describe in chapter 9.
18. Drawing on ethnographic research in South Wollo's Worebabo district, Saleh Seid Adem provides strikingly similar vignettes, linking increased remittances from female labour migrants to a substantial decline in the intra-household bargaining powers of fathers (Saleh 2019).
19. Bauer 1985.

CONCLUSION

1. Asnake and Zerihun 2015.
2. See Looney 2004.
3. Wilson-Smith 2019.
4. De Haas 2014.
5. Appadurai 2013; see chapter 5 of this volume.
6. As in the case of all social norms. See De Herdt and Olivier de Sardan 2015.

7. See Carling and Collins 2018; Collins 2017.
8. Müller-Mahn et al. 2018.
9. This could be contrasted with the use of 'stuck' in the migration litera-ture in reference to migrants stranded in transit countries for long peri-ods of time with precarious legal status and high insecurity (Dobler 2020; Grabska 2020; Serawit 2020; Wyss 2019).
10. See Emirbayer and Mische 1998; also chapter 3 this volume.
11. Jones et al. 2014a; 2014b.
12. See EUTF 2015.
13. Castles 2004.
14. For a superb critique of this view, see Mkandawire 2015.
15. Castles 2004; Ambrosetti and Paparusso 2015; Sayegh 2019.
16. For a general discussion, see De Herdt and Olivier de Sardan 2015.
17. See Ray 2007.
18. Fernandez 2020; Schewel 2018.

REFERENCES

Aalen, L. (2006) 'Ethnic federalism and self-determination for nationalities in a semi-authoritarian state: The case of Ethiopia', *International Journal on Minority and Group Rights*, 13 (2–3), pp. 243–61.

Abbink, J. (1994) 'The irrevocable past: History and image of the Beta Esra'el', *Cahiers d'Études Africaines*, 136 (XXXIV-4), pp. 693–700.

——— (2006) 'Ethnicity and conflict generation in Ethiopia: Some problems and prospects of ethno-regional federalism', *Journal of Contemporary African Studies*, 24 (3), pp. 389–413.

Abebaw, M. (2012) 'Trafficked to the Gulf States: The experiences of Ethiopian returnee women', *Journal of Community Practice*, 20 (1–2), pp. 112–33.

Abel T. et al. (2018) 'Youth unemployment and entrepreneurship in Ethiopia: Evidence from Dire Dawa and Addis Ababa', *CBMS Network Updates*, XVI (1), pp. 1–3.

Abraham, T. (2014) *Assessment of the Socio-economic Situation and Needs of Ethiopian Returnees from KSA* (Addis Ababa: IOM).

Abrahamsen, R. (2016) 'Africa and international relations: Assembling Africa, studying the world', *African Affairs*, 116 (462), pp. 125–39.

——— (2017) 'Assemblages', in X. Guillaume and P. Bilgin (eds.), *Routledge Handbook of International Political Sociology* (London: Routledge), pp. 253–61.

Achilli, L. (2016) 'Irregular migration to the EU and human smuggling in the Mediterranean: The nexus between organized crime and irregular migration', in IEMed (ed.), *IEMed Mediterranean Yearbook 2016: Mobility and Refugee Crisis in the Mediterranean* (Barcelona: IEMed).

——— (2018) 'The "good" smuggler: The ethics and morals of human smuggling among Syrians', *Annals of the American Academy of Political and Social Science*, 676 (1), pp. 77–96.

REFERENCES

Acuto, M. and Curtis, S. (2014) 'Assemblage thinking and international relations', in M. Acuto and S. Curtis (eds.), *Reassembling International Theory* (London: Palgrave Pivot), pp. 1–15.

Adamnesh A., Oucho, L. and Zeitlyn, B. (2016) 'Policy Brief: Rural–urban migration and poverty in Ethiopia', Migrating Out of Poverty Research Programme Consortium, available at: http://www.migratingoutofpoverty.org/files/file.php?name=gp002-ethiopia-policy-brief-sep14.pdf&site=354 (accessed 24 March 2020).

Addis Fortune (2017) 'Parliament approves youth fund', vol. XVII, no. 876, 13 February 2017.

Addis Standard (2018) 'Ethiopia overseas employment in new push to send professionals, graduates to Gulf States', 30 October 2018, available at: http://addisstandard.com/news-ethiopia-overseas-employment-in-new-push-to-send-professionals-graduates-to-gulf-states/ (accessed 24 March 2020).

Addis Zemen (2019) 'Editorial', *Amharic Daily*, 7 July 2019, available at: https://www.press.et/Ama/?p=13668.

Adimassu, Y. G. (2015) *Federalism vis-à-vis the Right to Freedom of Movement and Residence: Critical Analysis of the Law and the Practice in Ethiopian Perspective* (Hamburg: Anchor Academic Publishing).

Aguilar, F. V. (2018) 'Ritual passage and the reconstruction of selfhood in international labor migration', *Journal of Social Issues in Southeast Asia*, 33 (S), pp. 87–130.

Al Jazeera (2013) 'Ethiopians banned from moving abroad for work', 25 October 2013.

Alemayhu Bekele and Yihunie Lakew (2014) 'Projecting Ethiopian demographics from 2012–2050 using the spectrum suite of models: Policy brief, USAID and Health Policy Project', available at: https://www.healthpolicyproject.com/pubs/724_PROJECTINGETHIOPIAN.pdf (accessed 22 March 2020).

Alemayehu Seifeselassie and Demisew Bizuwerk (2014) *Post-arrival Humanitarian Assistance to Ethiopians Returning from the Kingdom of Saudi Arabia: An Account of IOM's Operation in Assisting over 160,000 Ethiopian Returnees* (Addis Ababa: IOM).

Alemu Asfaw Nigusie and Carver, F. (2019) 'The comprehensive refugee response framework: Progress in Ethiopia', Working Paper, Humanitarian Policy Group and Overseas Development Institute.

Alpes, M. J. (2013) 'Migration brokerage, illegality, and the state in Anglophone Cameroon', DIIS Working Paper No. 07, Copenhagen.

——— (2017) 'Why aspiring migrants trust migration brokers: The moral economy of departure in Anglophone Cameroon', *Africa*, 87 (2), pp. 304–21.

REFERENCES

Alpes, M. J. and Sørensen, N. N. (2015) 'Migration risk campaigns are based on wrong assumptions', Danish Institute for International Studies Policy Brief, May.

Ambrosetti, E. and Paparusso, A. (2015) 'Immigration policies in the EU: Failure or success? Evidences from Italy', in D. Strangio and G. Sancetta (eds.), *Italy in a European Context* (London: Palgrave Macmillan).

Amel, B. (2012) 'The Ethiopian clubs: The development of social institutions and identities amongst Ethiopians in Johannesburg', Master's thesis, Faculty of Humanities, School of Arts, University of the Witwatersrand, South Africa.

Andersson, R. (2014) *Illegality, Inc.: Clandestine Migration and the Business of Bordering Europe.* (Oakland, CA: University of California Press).

Appadurai, A. (2004) 'The capacity to aspire: Culture and the terms of recognition', in R. Vijayendra and M. Walton (eds.), *Culture and Public Action* (Stanford, CA: Stanford University Press), pp. 59–84.

————(2013) *The Future as Cultural Fact: Essays on the Global Condition* (London: Verso).

Arab News (2018) 'Ethiopia lifts ban on domestic workers moving overseas', 1 February.

Aryeetey, Ernest, Baah-Boateng, William, Ackah, Charles Godfred, Lehrer, Kim and Mbiti, Isaac (2014) 'Ghana', in Hiroyuki Hino and Gustav Ranis (eds.), *Youth and Employment in Sub-Saharan Africa: Working but Poor* (New York: Routledge).

Asnake Kefale (2013) *Federalism and Ethnic Conflict in Ethiopia: A Comparative Regional Study* (London: Routledge).

Asnake Kefale and Zerihun Mohammed (2015) *Ethiopian Labour Migration to the Gulf and South Africa* (Addis Ababa: Forum for Social Studies).

Ayalew, T. (2018) 'Refugee protections from below: Smuggling in the Eritrea–Ethiopia context', *Annals of the American Academy of Political and Social Science*, 676 (1) pp. 57–76.

Ayalew, T., Adugna, F. and Deshingkar, P. (2018) 'Social embeddedness of human smuggling in East Africa: Brokering Ethiopian migration to Sudan', *African Human Mobility Review*, 4 (3), pp. 1333–58.

Ayalew, T. (2019) 'Precarious mobility: Infrastructures of Eritrean migration through the Sudan and the Sahara Desert', *African Human Mobility Review*, 5 (1), pp. 1482–509.

Bakewell, O. (2010) 'Some reflections on structure and agency in migration theory', *Journal of Ethnic and Migration Studies*, 36 (10), pp. 1689–708.

Bakewell, O., De Haas, H. and Kubal, A. (2011) 'Migration systems, pioneers and the role of agency', Working Paper no. 48, International Migration Institute.

Balaz, V., Williams, A. M. and Fifekova, Elena (2014) 'Migration decision making as complex choice: Eliciting decision weights under conditions of imperfect and complex information through experimental methods', *Population, Space and Place*, 22 (1), pp. 36–53.

Bauer, D. F. (1985) *Household and Society in Ethiopia*, 2nd edn (East Lansing, MI: Michigan State University).

Baumle, A. K. (2009) 'Introduction: A discipline in transition', in A. K. Baumle (ed.), *Demography in Transition: Emerging Trends in Population Studies* (Cambridge: Cambridge Scholars Publishing), pp. 1–11.

Beauchemin, C. (2018) 'Introduction', in C. Beauchemin (ed.), *Migration between Africa and Europe* (Cham: Springer), pp. 1–8.

Bebbington, Anthony (1999) 'Capitals and capabilities: A framework for analyzing peasant viability, rural livelihoods and poverty', *World Development*, 27 (12), pp. 2021–44.

Bell, C. (1992) *Ritual Theory, Ritual Practice* (Oxford: Oxford University Press).

Belloni, M. (2016) '"My uncle cannot say no if I reach Libya": Unpacking the social dynamics of border-crossing among Eritreans heading to Europe', *Human Geography*, 9 (2), pp. 47–56.

Addis Fortune (2018) 'Regulations guard the door for potential Middle Eastern workers', vol. 19, no. 972, 15 December 2018.

Beshir B. D. (2014) 'Unemployment experience of youth in Addis Ababa', Master's thesis, International Institute of Social Sciences, the Hague.

Bevan, P. and Pankhurst, A. (1996a) *Ethiopia Village Studies: Harresaw, Atsbi Woreda, Tigray* (Addis Ababa and Oxford: Addis Ababa University and the Centre for the Study of African Economies).

——— (1996b) *Ethiopia Village Studies: Aze Debo's, Kembata* (Addis Ababa and Oxford: Addis Ababa University and the Centre for the Study of African Economies).

Bezabeh, S. A. (2017) 'UN/masking narratives: An alternative account of Horn of Africa migration', Policy Report no. 04/03, United Nations University Institute on Globalization, Culture and Mobility, Barcelona (UNU-GCM).

Bhugra, D. and Becker, Matthew A. (2005) 'Migration, cultural bereavement and cultural identity', *World Psychiatry*, 4 (1), pp. 18–24.

Bloch, A. and Chimienti, M. (2011) 'Irregular migration in a globalizing world', *Ethnic and Racial Studies*, 34 (8), pp. 1271–85.

Bloch, A. and Milena, C. (2011) 'Irregular migration in a globalizing world', *Ethnic and Racial Studies*, 34 (8), pp. 1271–85.

Blunch, Niels-Hugo and Laderchi, Caterina Ruggeri (2015) '"The winner takes it all": Internal migration, education and wages in Ethiopia', *Migration Studies* 3 (3), pp. 417–37.

Boccagni, P. (2017) 'Aspirations and the subjective future of migration:

REFERENCES

Comparing views and desires of the "time ahead" through the narratives of immigrant domestic workers', *Comparative Migration Studies*, 5 (4), available at: https://doi.org/10.1186/s40878–016–0047–6.

Botti, D. and Phillips, M. (2019) 'Record numbers of refugees and migrants arrive in Yemen amidst intensifying and complicated war', available at: https://reliefweb.int/report/yemen/record-numbers-refugees-and-migrants-arrive-yemen-amidst-intensifying-and-complicated (accessed 22 August 201).

Bourbeau, P. (2011) *The Securitization of Migration: A Study of Movement and Order* (London: Routledge).

Broussard, N. and Tsegay G. T. (2012) 'Youth unemployment: Ethiopia country study', International Growth Centre Working Paper, London School of Economics.

Browne, E. (2015) *Impact of Communication Campaigns to Deter Irregular Migration*, Helpdesk Research Report (Birmingham: Governance and Social Development Resource Centre, University of Birmingham).

Bruce, John Winfield (1976) 'Land reform planning and indigenous communal tenures: A case study of the tenure "Chiguraf-Gwoses" in Tigray, Ethiopia', PhD dissertation, University of Wisconsin.

Carling, J. (2002) 'Migration in the age of involuntary immobility: Theoretical reflections and Cape Verdean experiences', *Journal of Ethnic and Migration Studies*, 28 (1), pp. 5–42.

————(2005) *Gender Dimensions of International Migration: Global Migration Perspective* (Geneva: Global Commission on International Migration).

————(2014) 'Scripting remittances: Making sense of money transfers in transnational relationships', *International Migration Review*, 48 (1), pp. S218–62.

Carling, J. and Collins, F. (2018) 'Aspiration, desire and drivers of migration', *Journal of Ethnic and Migration Studies*, 44 (6), pp. 909–26.

Carling, J. and Hernández-Carretero, M. (2011) 'Protecting Europe and protecting migrants? Strategies for managing unauthorised migration from Africa', *British Journal of Politics and International Relations*, 13 (1), pp. 42–58.

Carling, J. and Schewel, K. (2018) 'Revisiting aspiration and ability in international migration', *Journal of Ethnic and Migration Studies*, 44 (6), pp. 945–63.

Carter, B. and Rohwerder, B. (2016) 'Rapid fragility and migration assessment for Ethiopia', available at: http://www.gsdrc.org/wpcontent/uploads/2016/02/Fragility_Migration_Ethiopia.pdf (accessed 20 September 2018).

Castles, S. (2004) 'Why migration policies fail', *Ethnic and Racial Studies*, 27 (2), pp. 205–27.

REFERENCES

Castles, S., De Haas, H. and Miller, M. J. (2014) *The Age of Migration: International Population Movements in the Modern World* (London: Palgrave Macmillan).

Castro, A. (2012) 'Social vulnerability, climate vulnerability, and uncertainty in rural Ethiopia: A study of South Wollo and Oromiya zones of Eastern Amhara Region', in A. Castro et al. (eds.), *Climate Change and Threatened Communities: Vulnerability, Capacity and Action* (Rugby: Practical Action), pp. 29–40.

CBMS Network (2018) 'Youth unemployment and entrepreneurship in Ethiopia: Evidence from Dire Dawa and Addis Ababa', *CBMS Network Updates*, XVI (1), pp. 1–3.

Cohen, D. (2006) *Globalization and its Enemies* (Cambridge, MA: MIT Press).

Cohen, J. H. (2004) *The Culture of Migration in Southern Mexico* (Austin, TX: University of Texas Press).

Collins, F. (2017) 'Desire as a theory for migration studies: Temporality, assemblage and becoming in the narratives of migrants', *Journal of Ethnic and Migration Studies*, 44 (6), pp. 964–80.

Collins, R. (1994) *Four Sociological Traditions* (New York: Oxford University Press).

Crisp, J. (2000) 'Africa's refugees: Patterns, problems, and policy challenges', New Issues in Refugee Research Working Paper no. 28, UNHCR.

Crowley, H., Duvell, F., Sigona, N., McMahon, S. and Jones, K. (2016) 'Unpacking a rapidly changing scenario: Migration flows, routes and trajectories across the Mediterranean', available at: http://www.medmig.info/research-brief-01-unpacking-a-rapidly-changing-scenario/ (accessed 24 March 2020).

Crummey, D. E. (2018) *Farming and Famine: Landscape Vulnerability in Northeast Ethiopia, 1889–1991* (Madison, WI: University of Wisconsin Press).

CSA (Central Statistical Agency) (2012) 'Key findings on the 2012 Urban Employment Unemployment Survey, September 2012', available at: http://adapt.it/adapt-indice-a-z/wp-content/uploads/2015/01/Survey-2012-ethiopia.pdf (accessed 18 July 2019).

CSA (2013a) *Population Projection of Ethiopia for All Regions at Wereda Level from 2014–2017* (Addis Ababa: CSA).

——— (2013b) *Ethiopia Labour Force Survey 2013* (Addis Ababa: CSA).

——— (2016) *Statistical Report on Urban Employment Unemployment Survey* (Addis Ababa: CSA).

Curran, S, Garip, F., Chung, Y. and Mahidol, K. (2005) 'Gendered migrant social capital: Evidence from Thailand', *Social Forces*, 84 (1), pp. 225–55.

Curran S, and Rivero, E. (2003) 'Engendering migration networks: The case of Mexican migration', *Demography*, 40 (2), pp. 289–307.

REFERENCES

Curran, S and Saguy, A. (2001) 'Migration and cultural change: A role for gender and social networks', *Journal of International Women's Studies*, 2 (3), pp. 54–77.

Cvajner, M. and Sciortino, G. (2010) 'Theorizing irregular migration: The control of spatial mobility in differentiated societies', *European Journal of Social Theory*, 13 (3), pp. 389–404.

Czaika, M. and De Haas, H. (2013) 'The effectiveness of immigration policies,' *Population and Development Review*, 39 (3), pp. 487–508.

Czaika, M. and Hobolth, M. (2016) 'Do restrictive asylum and visa policies increase irregular migration into Europe?', *European Union Politics*, 17 (3), pp. 345–65.

Daily Star (2008) 'Ethiopia bans citizens from seeking work in Lebanon', 5 May 2008.

Daniel Gebretsadik (2016) 'The cause of educated youth unemployment and its socioeconomic effect in Addis Ababa', Master's thesis, Department of Geography and Environmental Studies, Addis Ababa University.

Dannecker, P. (2005) 'Transnational migration and the transformation of gender relations: The case of Bangladeshi labour migrants', *Current Sociology*, 53 (4), pp. 655–74.

De Haas, H. (2007) 'Turning the tide? Why development will not stop migration', *Development and Change*, 38 (5), pp. 819–41.

————— (2009) 'Migration system formation and decline: A theoretical inquiry into the self-perpetuating and self-undermining dynamics of migration processes', International Migration Institute Working Paper no. 19, University of Oxford.

————— (2010) 'Migration and development: A theoretical perspective', *International Migration Review*, 44 (1), pp. 227–64.

————— (2011) 'The determinants of international migration: Conceptualising policy, origin and destination effects', International Migration Institute Working Paper no. 32, University of Oxford.

————— (2014) 'Migration theory: Quo vadis?', International Migration Institute Working Paper no. 100, University of Oxford.

De Herdt, Tom and Olivier de Sardan, J.-P. (eds.) (2015) *Real Governance and Practical Norms in Sub-Saharan Africa: The Game of the Rules* (London: Routledge).

De Jong, G. F. and Fawcett, J. T. (1981) 'Motivation for migration: An assessment and a value-expectancy research model', in G. F. de Jong and R. W. Gardner (eds.), *Migration Decision Making: Multidisciplinary Approaches to Microlevel Studies in Developed and Developing Countries* (New York: Pergamon Press), pp. 13–58.

De Regt, M. (2007) 'Ethiopian women in the Middle East: The case of migrant domestic workers in Yemen', Paper for the African Studies Centre

REFERENCES

Seminar, 15 February 2007, available at: https://www.ascleiden.nl/pdf/paper-deregt.pdf (accessed 24 March 2020).

De Regt, M. and Medareshaw Tafesse (2016) 'Deported before experiencing the good sides of migration: Ethiopians returning from Saudi Arabia', *African and Black Diaspora: An International Journal*, 9 (2), pp. 228–42.

Dekker, R. and Engbersen, G. (2012) 'How social media transform migrant networks and facilitate migration', International Migration Institute Working Paper no. 64, University of Oxford.

Deleuze, G., and Guattari, F. (1980) *A Thousand Plateaus: Capitalism and Schizophrenia* (Minneapolis, MN: University of Minnesota Press).

Dessalegn R. (1991) *Famine and Survival Strategies* (Uppsala: Scandinavian Institute of African Studies).

———— (2009) *The Peasant and the State: Studies in Agrarian Change in Ethiopia 1950s–2000s* (Addis Ababa: Addis Ababa University Press).

Di Nunzio, M. (2019) *The Act of Living: Street Life, Marginality, and Development in Urban Ethiopia* (Ithaca, NY: Cornell University Press).

Dobler, G. (2020) 'Waiting: Elements of a conceptual framework', *Critical African Studies*, 12 (1), pp. 10–21.

Dom, C. (2012a) 'Harresaw: Community situation report 2011', Ethiopia WIDE, available at: http://ethiopiawide.net/wp-content/uploads/Harresaw-Community-Report_Web.pdf (accessed 24 March 2020).

————(2012b) 'Aze Debo'a: Community situation report 2011', Ethiopia WIDE, available at: http://ethiopiawide.net/wp-content/uploads/Aze-Deboa-Community-Report_Web.pdf (accessed 24 March 2020).

————(2019a) 'Harresaw: Community report 2018', Ethiopia WIDE, available at: http://ethiopiawide.net/wp-content/uploads/Harresaw_CR_2018.pdf (accessed 24 March 2020).

————(2019b) 'Climate change and migration in rural eastern Tigray: Global and local factors and actors', *International Journal of Ethiopian Studies*, XIII (1), pp. 107–22.

————(2019c) 'Economic experiences of rural young people', in A. Pankhurst and C. Dom (eds.), *Rural Ethiopia in Transition: Selected Discussion Briefs* (Addis Ababa: PDRC).

———— (2020) 'Climate change and migration in rural eastern Tigray: Global and local factors and actors', *International Journal of Ethiopian Studies*, XIII (1), pp. 93–108.

Dorosh, P., Schmidt, E. and Admasu Shiferaw (2012) 'Economic growth without structural transformation: The case of Ethiopia', *Journal of African Development*, 14 (2), pp. 7–40.

Duntley, M. (2005) 'Ritual studies', in G. Thomson (ed.), *Encyclopedia of Religion*, available at: https://www.encyclopedia.com/environment/encyclopedias-almanacs-transcripts-and-maps/ritual-studies (accessed 24 March 2020).

REFERENCES

Ellis, B. (2015) 'The production of irregular migration in Canada', *Canadian Ethnic Studies*, 47 (2), pp. 93–112.

Emch, M., Root, E. D. and Carrel, M. (2017) *Health and Medical Geography*, 4th edn (London: Guilford Press).

Emebet K. (2001) 'Ethiopia: An assessment of the international labour migration situation; The case of female labour migrants', GENPROM Working Paper no. 3, ILO.

Emirbayer, M. and Mische, A. (1998) 'What is agency?', *American Journal of Sociology*, 103 (4), pp. 962–1023.

ENA (Ethiopian News Agency) (2019a) 'PM Abiy repatriates more than 100 Ethiopian inmates from Sudan', 18 August.

ENA (2019b) 'Some 75 Ethiopian domestic workers leave for Saudi Arabia legally', 9 August.

Ethiopian Herald (2019) 'Ethiopia Saudi agree to raise the minimum wage for Ethiopian workers', 10 January.

EU (2015) 'Fact sheet: The European Union's cooperation with Africa on migration', 9 November2015, available at: https://ec.europa.eu/commission/presscorner/detail/en/MEMO_15_6026 (accessed 24 March 2020).

EUTF (2015) 'Stemming Irregular Migration in Northern and Central Ethiopia: SINCE', available at: https://ec.europa.eu/trustfundforafrica/region/horn-africa/ethiopia/stemming-irregular-migration-northern-central-ethiopia_en (accessed 12 March 2020).

Eyob B. Gebremariam (2017) 'The politics of youth employment and policy processes in Ethiopia', *IDS Bulletin*, (48) 3, pp. 33–50.

FBC (Fana Broadcasting Corporation) (2019) 'Tigray regional state expressed condolences over the death of more than 40 Ethiopians as they cross the Red Sea', available at: https://www.facebook.com/fanabroadcasting/posts/2210270922396968.

FBC (2020) 'Community-oriented movement should be at the centre of the fight against human trafficking—Mr Demeke Mekonen', *Fana 90* news programme, 17 January.

Fana G. and Beyene T. (2017) *Socio-economic Assessment for ILO project 'Stemming Irregular Migration in Northern and Central Ethiopia (SINCE)': Research Report for Tigray National Regional State* (Addis Ababa: Forum for Social Studies).

Fassil Demissie (ed.) (2017) *Ethiopians in an Age of Migration: Scattered Lives beyond Borders* (New York: Routledge).

Favara, M. (2017) 'Do dreams come true? Aspirations and educational attainments of Ethiopian boys and girls', *Journal of African Economies*, 26 (5), pp. 561–83.

Federal Democratic Republic of Ethiopia Anti-trafficking Council (2015) *Trafficking in Person Report* (Addis Ababa: Government of Ethiopia).

REFERENCES

Fekadu Adugna Tufa, Deshingkar, P. and Tekalign Ayelew (2019) 'Brokers, migrants and the state: Berri Kefach "door openers" in Ethiopian clandestine migration to South Africa', Migrating Out of Poverty Working Paper no. 56, Brighton, University of Sussex.

Fernandez, B. (2010) 'Cheap and disposable? The impact of the global economic crisis on the migration of Ethiopian women domestic workers to the Gulf', *Gender and Development*, 18 (2), pp. 249–62.

———— (2013) 'Traffickers, brokers, employment agents, and social networks: The regulation of intermediaries in the migration of Ethiopian domestic workers to the Middle East,' *International Migration Review*, 47 (4), pp. 814–43.

———— (2017) 'Irregular migration from Ethiopia to the Gulf States', in P. Fargues and N. M. Shah (eds.), *Skilful Survivals: Irregular Migration to the Gulf* (Jeddah: European University Institute and Gulf Research Center), pp. 243–67.

———— (2020) *Ethiopian Migrant Domestic Workers: Migrant Agency and Social Change* (Cham: Palgrave Macmillan).

Fikremariam Y. H. (2016) 'Migration decisions and experiences: A study of migrants from *Sekela Woreda* (West Gojjam) to Addis Ababa', Master's thesis, Department of Social Anthropology, Addis Ababa University.

Flahaux, M. L. and De Haas, H. (2016) 'African migration: Trends, patterns, drivers', *Comparative Migration Studies*, 4 (1), pp. 1–25.

Frankowska, A. (2019a) 'Aze Debo: Community report 2018', Ethiopia WIDE, available at: http://ethiopiawide.net/wp-content/uploads/Aze-Debo_CR_2018.pdf (accessed 24 March 2020).

Fernandez, B. (2019b) 'Selected aspects of social protection', in A. Pankhurst and C. Dom (eds.), *Rural Ethiopia in Transition: Selected Discussion Briefs* (Addis Ababa: PDRC).

Fransen, S. and Kuschminder, K. (2009) 'Migration in Ethiopia: History, current trends and future prospects', Migration and Development Country Profiles Paper Series, Maastricht Graduate School of Governance.

FSS (Forum for Social Studies) (2017) 'Socio-economic assessment migration and labour market: "Stemming Irregular Migration in Northern and Central Ethiopia (SINCE)": Report for the International Labour Organization (ILO)', available at: http://www.ilo.org/wcmsp5/groups/public/---africa/---ro-addis_ababa/---sro-addis_ababa/documents/publication/wcms_613907.pdf (accessed 15 July 2018).

Gaibazzi, P., Bellagamba, A. and Dünnwald, S. (2017) 'Introduction: An Afro-Europeanist perspective on EurAfrican borders', in P. Gaibazzi, S. Dünnwald and A. Bellagamba (eds.), *Euro-African Borders and Migration Management: Political Cultures, Contested Spaces, and Ordinary Lives* (New York: Palgrave Macmillan), pp. 3–28.

REFERENCES

Geertz, C. (1973) *The Interpretation of Cultures: Selected Essays* (New York: Basic Books).

Gete Zeleke, Woldie Asfaw, Degefa Tolosa, Betre Alemu, and Trutmann, P. (2008) 'Seasonal migration and rural livelihoods in Ethiopia: An empirical study', Working Paper no. 3, Global Mountain Program (GMP), Lima.

Gezahegn A. (2015) 'Youth unemployment in two Ethiopian cities: Nature, challenges and consequences', in P. B. Mihyo and T. E. Mukuna (eds.), *Urban Youth Unemployment in Eastern and Southern Africa: Features, Challenges, Consequences and Cutback Strategies* (Addis Ababa: Organization for Social Science Research in Eastern and Southern Africa), pp. 65–100.

Ghosal, S. (2015) 'Workers' remittances, one of the reliable sources of capital inflows to Ethiopia: Its performance analysis towards shaping the economic growth', *International Journal of Interdisciplinary and Multidisciplinary Studies*, 2 (6), pp. 174–85.

Giddens, A. (1990) 'Structuration theory and sociological analysis', in J. Clark, C. Modgil and S. Modgil (eds.), *Anthony Giddens: Consensus and Controversy* (London: Falmer Press), pp. 297–315.

Girmachew Zewdu (2018) 'Ethiopian female domestic labour migration to the Middle East: Patterns, trends, and drivers', *African and Black Diaspora: An International Journal*, 11 (1), pp. 6–19.

Girmachew Adugna (2019) 'Migration patterns and emigrants' transnational activities: Comparative findings from two migrant origin areas in Ethiopia', *Comparative Migration Studies*, 7 (5), pp. 1–28.

Girum A. and Eden T. (2014) 'Work creation for the rural youth', WIDE Discussion Brief no. 3, June.

GIZ (2018) 'Better migration management: Horn of Africa', Newsletter, March–September 2018, available at: https://www.giz.de/en/downloads/Oktober%202018%20(Englisch).pdf (accessed 24 March 2020).

GoE (Government of Ethiopia) (1998) Private Employment Agency Proclamation No. 104/1998 (Addis Ababa: GoE).

——— — (2009) Employment Exchange Services Proclamation No. 632/2009 (Addis Ababa: GoE).

——— (2015) Prevention and Suppression of Trafficking in Persons and Smuggling of Migrants Proclamation No. 909/2015 (Addis Ababa: GoE).

——— (2016) Ethiopia's Overseas Employment Proclamation No. 923/2016 (Addis Ababa: GoE).

——— (2017) Ethiopian Youth Revolving Fund Establishment Proclamation No. 995/2017 (Addis Ababa: GoE).

———, MoE (Ministry of Education) (2018/2010 EC) Report on the Main Activities of the Higher Education Sector of the Ministry of Education (Amharic) (Addis Ababa: Ministry of Education).

———, Ministry of Finance and Economic Development (2012) *Ethiopia's*

REFERENCES

Progress towards Eradicating Poverty: An Interim Report on Poverty Analysis Study (2010/11) (Addis Ababa: Ministry of Finance and Economic Development).

————, MoLSA (Ministry of Labour and Social Affairs) (2012) *National Social Protection Policy of Ethiopia* (Addis Ababa: GoE).

————, MoUDH (Ministry of Urban Development and Housing) (2012) *Micro and Small Enterprise Development Policy and Strategy* (Addis Ababa: GoE).

————, MoYSC (Ministry of Youth, Sports and Culture) (2004) *Federal Democratic Republic of Ethiopia, FDRE, Ethiopia Youth Policy* (Addis Ababa: Ministry of Youth, Sports and Culture)

Grabska, K. (2016) *Time to Look at Girls: Adolescent Girls' Migration to Sudan* (Geneva: IHEID).

———— (2020) '"Wasting time": Migratory trajectories of adolescence among Eritrean refugee girls in Khartoum', *Critical African Studies*, 12 (1), pp. 22–36.

Grabska, K., De Regt, M. and Del Franco, N. (2019) *Adolescent Girls' Migration in the Global South: Transitions into Adulthood* (Cham: Palgrave Macmillan).

Gray, Clark L. and Mueller, Valerie (2012) 'Natural disasters and population mobility in Bangladesh', *Proceedings of the National Academy of Sciences*, 109 (16), pp. 6000–5.

Grimes, R. (2000) 'Ritual', in W. Braun and R. T. McCutcheon (eds.), *Guide to the Study of Religion* (London: Cassell), pp. 259–70.

Guday E. and Kiya G. (2013) 'The conception of gender in migration to the Middle East: An anthropological study of gendered patterns of migration in North Wollo Zone of Amhara Region, Ethiopia', *Ethiopian Journal of Development Research*, 35 (1), pp. 107–46.

Gurieva, L. and Dzhioev, A. (2015) 'Economic theories of labor migration', *Mediterranean Journal of Social Sciences*, 6 (6), pp. 101–9.

Haas, H. and Van Rooij, A. (2010) 'Migration as emancipation? The impact of internal and international migration on the position of women left behind in rural Morocco', *Oxford Development Studies*, 38 (1), pp. 43–62.

Hagan, J. (1998) 'Social networks, gender and immigrant incorporation: Resources and constraints', *American Sociological Review*, 63 (1), pp. 55–67.

Hagan, J. and Ebaugh, H.R. (2003) 'Calling upon the sacred: Migrants' use of religion in the migration process', *International Migration Review*, 37 (4), pp. 1145–62.

Hailemichael N. (2014) 'Causes and consequences of human trafficking: A case study in Metema town', Master's thesis, Department of Social Anthropology, Addis Ababa University.

Hampshire, K. (2006) 'Flexibility in domestic organization and seasonal migration among the Fulani of northern Burkina Faso', *Africa*, 76, pp. 402–26.

REFERENCES

Harvey, D. (1990) *The Condition of Postmodernity* (Oxford: Blackwell).

Herman, E. (2006) 'Migration as a family business: The role of personal networks in the mobility phase of migration', *International Migration*, 44 (4), pp. 191–230.

Herman, M., Hogan, D., Tefera B., Fasil T. et al. (2011) 'Better-educated youth as a vanguard of social change? Adolescent transitions to later marriage and lower fertility in southwest Ethiopia', in C. Teller and Assefa Hailemariam (eds.), *The Demographic Transition and Development in Africa: The Unique Case of Ethiopia* (Dordrecht: Springer), pp. 89–101.

Hernández-León, R. (2008) *Metropolitan Migrants: The Migration of Urban Mexicans to the United States* (Berkeley, CA: University of California Press).

Hirschman, A. (1972) *Exit, Voice, and Loyalty: Responses to Decline in Firms, Organizations, and States* (Cambridge, MA: Harvard University Press).

Hoben, A. (1963) 'The role of ambilineal descent groups in Gojjam Amhara social organization', PhD dissertation, University of California, Berkeley.

———— (1973) *Land Tenure among the Amhara of Ethiopia: The Dynamics of Cognatic Descent* (Chicago: University of Chicago Press).

Hondagneu-Sotelo, P. and Cranford, Cynthia (2006) 'Gender and migration', in Janet Saltzman Chafetz (ed.), *Handbook of the Sociology of Gender* (Houston: Springer), pp. 105–26.

Honwana, Alcinda (2012) *The Time of Youth: Work, Social Change and Politics in Africa* (Boulder, CO: Lynne Rienner Publishers).

Honwana, Alcinda (2013) 'Changing patterns of intimacy among young people in Africa', in Ulf Engel and Manuel J. Ramos (eds.), *African Dynamics in a Multipolar World* (Leiden: Brill).

Horwood, C. (2009) *In Pursuit of the Southern Dream: Victims of Necessity; Assessment of the Irregular Movement of Men from East Africa and the Horn to South Africa* (Geneva: International Organization for Migration).

———— (2015) 'Irregular migration flows in the Horn of Africa: Challenges and implications for source, transit and destination countries', Occasional Paper Series no. 18, Australian Government Department of Immigration and Border Protection.

———— (with Kate Hooper) (2016) 'Protection on the move: Eritrean refugee flows through the greater Horn of Africa', available at: http://samuelhall.org/wp-content/uploads/2018/02/Local-Integration-Ethiopia-full-report-Jan-2018.pdf (accessed 17 July 2019).

Human Rights Watch (2015) 'Detained, beaten, deported: Saudi abuses against migrants during mass expulsions', available at: https://www.hrw.org/report/2015/05/10/detained-beaten-deported/saudi-abuses-against-migrants-during-mass-expulsions (accessed 24 March 2020).

———— (2018) 'Yemen detained African migrants tortured, raped', available at: https://www.hrw.org/news/2018/04/17/yemen-detained-african-migrants-tortured-raped (accessed 24 March 2020).

REFERENCES

ILO (International Labour Organization) (1997) 'Private Employment Agencies Convention (No. 181/1997)', available at: https://www.ilo.org/dyn/normlex/en/f?p=NORMLEXPUB:12100:0::NO::P12100_INSTRUMENT_ID:312326 (accessed 24 March 2020).

———— (2011) *Trafficking in Persons Overseas for Labour Purposes: The Case of Ethiopian Domestic Workers* (Addis Ababa: ILO Country Office).

———— (2017) *The Ethiopian Overseas Employment Proclamation No. 923/2016: A Comprehensive Analysis* (Addis Ababa: ILO Country Office).

IOM (International Organization for Migration) (2015) *Background Paper: Human Trafficking and Smuggling of Migrants in the Context of Mixed Migration Flows: State of Play in the IGAD Region* (Addis Ababa: ILO Country Office).

———— (2017a) *World Migration Report 2018* (Geneva: ILO)

———— (2017b) *National Labor Migration Management Assessment: Ethiopia* (Addis Ababa: ILO).

———— (2018a) 'IOM facilitates the return of 300 stranded Ethiopian migrants from Tanzania', available at: https://www.iom.int/news/iom-facilitates-return-300-stranded-ethiopian-migrants-tanzania (accessed 23 September 2019).

———— (2018b) 'IOM helps 67 Ethiopian stranded migrants return from Tanzania', available at: https://www.iom.int/news/iom-helps-67-ethiopian-stranded-migrants-return-tanzania (accessed 23 September 2019).

———— (2018c) 'Regional migrant response plan for the Horn of Africa and Yemen (2018–2020)', available at: https://www.iom.int/sites/default/files/country/docs/regional_migrant_response_plan_for_the_h.a_yemen.pdf (accessed 5 February 2020).

———— (2019) 'Return of Ethiopian migrants from the Kingdom of Saudi Arabia', available at: https://reliefweb.int/sites/reliefweb.int/files/resources/KSA%20Factsheet_March%202019_Regional%20Data%20Hub.pdf (accessed 24 March 2020).

Isaacs, L. (2017) *Research Study to Enhance the Volume and Value of Formal Remittances to Ethiopia* (Brussels: International Organization for Migration).

Jaji, R. (2016) 'The patriarchal logic, "encroaching" femininity and migrant Zimbabwean women', in *Kabbo ka Muwala [The Girl's Basket]: Migration and Mobility in Contemporary Art in Southern and Eastern Africa* (Harare: National Gallery of Zimbabwe), pp. 18–31.

Jerusalem Yibeltal Yizengaw (2016) 'Higher education and the labour market in Ethiopia: A tracer study of graduate employment in engineering from Addis Ababa and Bahir Dar universities', PhD dissertation, Centre for Comparative Education and Policy Studies, Addis Ababa University, Addis Ababa.

Jolly, S. and Reeves, Hazel (2005) *Gender and Migration: Overview Report* (Brighton: Institute of Development Studies.

REFERENCES

Jones, N., Bekele Tefera, Stephenson, J., Gupta, T. and Pereznieto, P. (2014a) 'Early marriage in Ethiopia: The role of gendered social norms in shaping adolescent girls' futures', available at: https://www.odi.org/sites/odi.org.uk/files/odi-assets/publications-opinion-files/9483.pdf.

————— with Guday Emirie, Bethelihem Gebre and Kiya Gezahegne (2014b) 'Early marriage and education: the complex role of social norms in shaping Ethiopian adolescent girls' lives', available at: https://www.odi.org/sites/odi.org.uk/files/odi-assets/publications-opinion-files/9183.pdf.

Jones, N., Presler-Marshall, Elizabeth, Bekele Tefera, Guday Emirie, Bethelihem Gebre and Kiya Gezahegne (2014c) 'Rethinking girls on the move: The intersection of poverty, exploitation and violence experienced by Ethiopian adolescents involved in the Middle East "maid trade"', available at: https://www.odi.org/sites/odi.org.uk/files/odi-assets/publications-opinion-files/9307.pdf (accessed 25 March 2020).

Juárez, F., LeGrand, T., Lloyd, C. B., Singh, S. and Hertrich, V. (2013) 'Youth migration and transitions to adulthood in developing countries', *Annals of the American Academy of Political and Social Science*, 648 (1), pp. 6–15.

Kandel, W. and Massey, D. (2002) 'The culture of Mexican migration: A theoretical and empirical analysis', *Social Forces*, 80 (3), pp. 981–1004.

Kaplan, S. (1993) 'The invention of Ethiopian Jews: Three models', *Cahiers d'Études Africaines*, 33 (132), pp. 645–58.

Kapur, D. (2003) 'Remittances: The new development mantra?', Paper prepared for the G-24 Technical Group Meeting (New York: United Nations).

Kaplan, S. and Rosen, Chaim (1994) 'Ethiopian Jews in Israel', *American Jewish Year Book*, 94, pp. 59–109.

Kelly, L. and Martinez, J. C. (2018) 'Can Ethiopia create 2 million jobs every year?', available at: https://ieg.worldbankgroup.org/blog/can-ethiopia-create-2-million-jobs-every-year.

Kiya Gezahegne (2013) 'The efficacy of benediction and prayer among the Amhara society: An anthropological study of the religious rituals of "Erfo Mereba" and "Shenecha" around Rayya Qobbo *wereda* of North Wollo Zone', Master's thesis, Department of Anthropology, Addis Ababa University.

————— (2019) 'Movements, relations, and land contestations along the Ethio-Sudan border of Metema Yohannes', in L. Manger, Fekadu Adugna, Munzoul Assal and Eria Onyango (eds.), *Borderland Dynamics in East Africa: Cases from Ethiopia, Sudan and Uganda* (Addis Ababa: Organization for Social Science Research in Eastern and Southern Africa), pp. 21–37.

Kosec, K., Hosaena Ghebru, Holtemeyer, Brian, Mueller, Valerie and Schmidt, Emily (2018) 'The effect of land access on youth employment and migration decisions: Evidence from rural Ethiopia', *American Journal of Agricultural Economics*, 100 (3), pp. 931–54.

Koser, K. and Kuschminder, K. (2016) 'Irregular migrants' decision making factors in transit', Occasional Paper Series no. 21, Department of Immigration and Border Protection.

Kurekova, L. (2009) 'Theories of migration: Critical review in the context of the EU East–West flows', Robert Schuman Centre for Advanced Studies, European University Institute.

Kuschminder, K. (2014) 'Shattered dreams and return of vulnerability: Challenges of Ethiopian female migration to the Middle East', IS Academy Policy Brief no. 18, Maastricht Graduate School of Governance.

Lancet Infectious Diseases (2017) 'Cholera in Yemen: War, hunger, disease … and heroics' (Editorial), 17, p. 781.

Landau, L. and Pampalone, T. (2018) *I Want to Go Home Forever: Stories of Becoming and Belonging in South Africa's Great Metropolis* (Johannesburg: Wits University Press).

Latour, B. (2005) *Reassembling the Social: An Introduction to Actor-Network Theory* (New York: Oxford University Press).

Leerkes, A. (2016) 'Managing migration through legitimacy? Alternatives to the criminalisation of unauthorised migration', in S. Carrera and E. B. Guild (eds.), *Trafficking and Smuggling of Human Beings: Policy Dilemmas in the EU* (Brussels: Centre for European Policy Studies), pp. 24–32.

Levine, D. (1965) *Wax and Gold: Tradition and Innovation in Ethiopian Culture* (Chicago: University of Chicago Press).

Li, T. M. (2007) 'Practices of assemblage and community forest management', *Economy and Society*, 36 (2), pp. 263–93.

——— (2017) 'After development: Surplus population and the politics of entitlement', *Development and Change*, 48 (3), pp. 1247–61.

Lindley, A. (2007) 'The early morning phone call: Remittances from a refugee diaspora perspective', Centre on Migration, Policy and Society Working Paper no. 47, University of Oxford.

Linz, J. J. and Stepan, Alfred (1998) *Problems of Democratic Transition and Consolidation: Southern Europe, South America, and Post-Communist Europe* (Baltimore: Johns Hopkins University Press).

Looney, R. (2004) 'Saudization and sound economic reforms: Are the two compatible?', *Strategic Insights*, 3 (2).

Madianou, M., and Miller, D. (2011) *Migration and New Media: Transnational Families and Polymedia* (London: Routledge).

Mains, D. (2007) 'Neoliberal times: Progress, boredom, and shame among young men in urban Ethiopia', *American Ethnologist*, 34 (4), pp. 659–73.

——— (2012) *Hope Is Cut: Youth, Unemployment and the Future in Urban Ethiopia* (Philadelphia, PA: Temple University Press).

REFERENCES

Mains, D., Hadley, C. and Fasil Tessema (2013) 'Chewing over the future: *Khat* consumption, anxiety, depression, and time among young men in Jimma, Ethiopia', *Culture, Medicine, and Psychiatry*, 37 (1), pp. 111–30.

Makoye, K. (2016) 'Tanzania threatens to deport migrants from drought-hit Ethiopia', available at: https://www.reuters.com/article/us-tanzania-ethiopia-migrants-idUSKCN0V4270 (accessed 13 April 2019).

Mallett, R., Hagen-Zanker, J., Majidi, N. and Cummings, C. (2017) 'Journeys on hold: How policy influences the migration decisions of Eritreans in Ethiopia,' available at: https://www.odi.org/publications/10728-journeys-hold-how-policy-influences-migration-decisions-eritreans-ethiopia (accessed 24 March 2020).

Manning, P. (2004) 'A millennium of meso-level analysis', *International Review of Social History*, 49 (3), pp. 500–4.

Marchand, K., Reinold, Julia and Silva, Raphael Dias e (2017) *Study on Migration Routes in the East and Horn of Africa* (Maastricht: Maastricht Graduate School of Governance).

Marchand, K., Roosen, I., Reinold, J. and Siegel, M. (2016) 'Irregular migration from and in the East and Horn of Africa', available at: www.merit.unu.edu (accessed 25 March 2020).

Markussen, B. (2018) 'The AU–EU summit, migration, mobility and youth,' *ECDPM Great Insights*, 7 (1), pp. 7–10.

Massey, Douglas S., Durand, Jorge and Pren, Karen A. (2016) 'Why border enforcement backfired', *American Journal of Sociology*, 121 (5), pp. 1557–600.

McCann, J. (1987) *From Poverty to Famine in Northeast Ethiopia: A Rural History 1900–1935* (Philadelphia, PA: University of Pennsylvania Press).

McDowell, C. and De Haan, A. (1997) *Migration and Sustainable Livelihoods: A Critical Review of the Literature* (Brighton: Institute of Development Studies).

Mehari Taddele (2016) *Migration Profile of Ethiopia* (Addis Ababa: IOM).

Mehari Zeru (2017) 'Anti-human trafficking responses in Ethiopia: Legal frameworks and local practices; The case of Saesi'e Tsada-Emba *woreda*, eastern Tigray', Master's thesis, Department of Political Science and International Relations, Addis Ababa University.

MGSoG (Maastricht Graduate School of Governance) (2017) *Ethiopia Migration Profile: Study on Migration Routes in the East and Horn of Africa*, available at: https://www.merit.uni.edu/publications/uploads/151747 5164.pdf (accessed 10 August 2018).

Mkandawire, T. (2015) 'Neopatrimonialism and the political economy of economic performance in Africa: Critical reflections', *World Politics*, 67 (3), pp. 1–50.

Monsutti, A. (2007) 'Migration as a rite of passage: Young Afghans building masculinity and adulthood in Iran', *Iranian Studies*, 40 (2), pp. 167–85.

REFERENCES

Morrissey, J. W. (2013) 'Understanding the relationship between environmental change and migration: The development of an effects framework based on the case of northern Ethiopia', *Global Environmental Change*, 23 (6), pp. 1501–10.

Müller-Mahn, D., Everts, J. and Stephan, C. (2018) 'Riskscapes revisited: Exploring the relationship between risk, space and practice', *Erdkunde*, 72 (3), pp. 197–213.

Mulugeta B., Kasahun D. and Zenebe Y. (2016) 'The aftermath of human trafficking in Ethiopia: Psycho-social impacts of human trafficking among North Wollo victim returnees from Arab nations', *Research on Humanities and Social Sciences*, 6 (13), pp. 71–9.

Mulugeta Gashaw and Bayissa Abdissa (2020) 'Globalization, smallholder agriculture, and rural livelihoods', *International Journal of Ethiopia Studies*, XXX (1).

NBE (National Bank of Ethiopia) (2013) *Annual Report, 2012/13* (Addis Ababa: NBE).

——— (2016) *Annual Report, 2015/16* (Addis Ababa: NBE).

——— (2017) *Annual Report, 2016/17* (Addis Ababa: NBE).

New Arab (2019) 'Ethiopia says 1,400 nationals freed from Saudi prisons pending deportation', 9 May.

Olivier, M. (2017) *Training of Trainers Manual: National Labor Migration Management Ethiopia* (Addis Ababa: IOM).

Olivier de Sardan, J. (2015) 'Practical norms: Informal regulations within public bureaucracies (in Africa and beyond)', in T. de Herdt and J. Olivier de Sardan (eds.), *Real Governance and Practical Norms in Sub-Saharan Africa: The Game of the Rules* (London: Routledge, 2015), pp. 19–62.

Osman, I. (2018) 'Why are migrants from the Horn flocking to war-torn Yemen?', *African Arguments*, 9 August.

Pankhurst, A. (ed.) (2017) *Change and Transformation in Twenty Rural Communities in Ethiopia* (Addis Ababa: WIDE).

——— (2019) 'Youth and globalisation in four WIDE Ethiopia sites: Communication media and cultural practices', *International Journal of Ethiopian Studies*, XIII (1), pp. 17–30.

Pankhurst, A. and Dom, C. (2019) 'Rural Ethiopia in transition: An overview', in A. Pankhurst and C. Dom (eds.), *Rural Ethiopia in Transition: Selected Discussion Briefs* (Addis Ababa: PDRC), pp. 1–23.

Pankhurst, A., Dom, Catherine and Bevan, Philippa (2018) 'Twenty rural communities in Ethiopia and how they changed: Introducing the WIDE research and the selected policy-relevant topics', in Alula Pankhurst, Philippa Bevan, Catherine Dom, Agazi Tiumelissan and Sarah Vaughan (eds.), *Changing Rural Ethiopia: Community Transformations* (Los Angeles, CA: Tsehai Publishers).

REFERENCES

Pankhurst, H. (1992) *Gender, Development and Identity: An Ethiopian Study* (London: Zed).

Pedersen, M. H. and Rytter, Mikkel (2018) 'Rituals of migration: An introduction', *Journal of Ethnic and Migration Studies*, 44 (16), pp. 2603–16.

Pessar, P. and Mahler, S. (2003) 'Transnational migration: Bringing gender in', *International Migration Review*, 37 (3), pp. 812–46.

Piper, N. (2005) *Gender and Migration* (Geneva: Global Commission on International Migration).

Poelma, R. T. (2019) 'The European securitisation of migration assemblage: A practices of assemblage analysis of joint operation Poseidon 2018 in Lesvos', Master's thesis, Faculty of Humanities, Utrecht University.

Porumbescu, A. (2015) 'Defining the new economics of labor migration theory boundaries: A sociological-level analysis of international migration', *RSP*, 45, pp. 55–64.

Ray, D. (2006) 'Aspirations, poverty, and economic change', in A. V. Banerjee, R. Benabou and D. Mookherjee (eds.), *Understanding Poverty* (Oxford: Oxford University Press), pp. 409–22.

Ray, L. (2007) *Globalization and Everyday Life* (London: Routledge).

REF (Research and Evidence Facility) (2016) *Cross Border Analysis and Mapping Field Report for Cluster 3: Western Ethiopia-East Sudan (Blue Nile and Sennar States)*, available at: https://www.soas.ac.uk/ref-hornresearch/research-papers/file115758.pdf (accessed 24 March 2020).

RMMS (Regional Mixed Migration Secretariat) (2014) *Blinded by Hope: Knowledge, Attitudes and Practices of Ethiopian Migrants* (Nairobi: RMMS).

RMMS (2016a) 'Djibouti: Country profile, updated July 2016', available at: http/www.regionalmms.org/images/CountryProfile/Djibouti/DjiboutiCountryProfile.pdf (accessed 24 March 2020).

———— (2016b) 'Ethiopia: Country profile', available at: https://reliefweb.int/sites/reliefweb.int/files/resources/EthiopiaCountryProfileMay2016.pdf (accessed 25 March 2020).

———— (2016c) *Young and on the Move: Children and Youth in Mixed Migration Flows within and from the Horn of Africa* (Nairobi: RMMS).

———— (2017) 'Weighing the risks. Protection risks and human rights violations faced by migrants in and from East Africa', RMMS Briefing Paper 5.

Robel Yohannes (2017) 'Ethiopia: Youth Revolving Fund; So far, so good,' *Ethiopian Herald*, 13 December.

Robertson, R. (2012) 'Globalisation or glocalisation?', *Journal of International Communication*, 18 (2), pp. 191–208.

Rogerson, M. (2015) 'Unpacking national policy towards the urban informal economy', in J. Crush, A. Chikanda and C. Skinner (eds.), *Mean Streets: Migration, Xenophobia and Informality in South Africa* (Cape Town: Southern African Migration Project, the African Centre for Cities and the International Development Research Centre), pp. 229–48.

REFERENCES

Rose, J. and Baird, J. A. (2013) 'Aspirations and an austerity state: Young people's hopes and goals for the future', *London Review of Education*, 11 (2), pp. 157–73.

RSA, Department of Home Affairs (2016) '2015 asylum statistics: Analysis and trends for the period January to December', available at: http://pmg-assets.s3-website-eu-west-1.amazonaws.com/160308Asylum.pdf (accessed 10 April 2017).

SAHAN (2016) 'Human trafficking and smuggling on the Horn of Africa–Central Mediterranean route', available at: https://igad.int/attachments/1284_ISSP%20Sahan%20HST%20Report%20%2018ii2016%20FINAL%20FINAL.pdf (accessed 24 March 2020).

Saleh S. A. (2019) 'Maternal absence and transnational labour migration: Implications for mothering, the left-behind child and gender labour dynamics', MA thesis, University of Leuven.

Salih, R. (2001) 'Moroccan migrant women: Transnationalism, nation-states and gender', *Journal of Ethnic and Migration Studies*, 27 (4), pp. 655–71.

Salt, J. and Stein, J. (1997) 'Migration as a business: The case of trafficking', *International Migration*, 35 (4), pp. 467–94.

Sanchez, G. (2015) *Border Crossings and Human Smuggling* (London: Routledge).

———— (2017) 'Critical perspectives on clandestine migration facilitation: An overview of migrant smuggling research', *Journal on Migration and Human Security*, 5 (1), pp. 9–27.

Sassen, S. (2006) *Territory, Authority, Rights: From Medieval to Global Assemblages* (Princeton: Princeton University Press).

Sayegh, N. (2019) 'Are Europe's failed migration policies finally getting a facelift?', TRT World, available at: https://www.trtworld.com/opinion/are-europe-s-failed-migration-policies-finally-getting-a-facelift-30808.

Schewel, Kerilyn (2018) 'Why Ethiopian women go to the Middle East: An aspiration-capability analysis of migration decision-making', International Migration Institute Working Paper no. 148, University of Oxford.

Schewel, Kerilyn and Asmamaw Legass Bahir (2019) 'Migration and social transformation in Ethiopia', International Migration Institute Working Paper Series, no. 152.

Schewel, Kerilyn and Fransen, Sonja (2018) 'Formal education and migration aspirations in Ethiopia', *Population and Development Review*, 44 (3), pp. 555–87.

Sen, A. (1999) *Development as Freedom* (New York: Anchor Books).

Serawit Debele (2020) 'Waiting as a site of subject formation: Examining collective prayers by Ethiopian asylum seekers in Germany', *Critical African Studies*, 12 (1), pp. 52–64.

SERI (Socio-economic Rights Institute of South Africa) (2017) 'Migration and the informal economy', presentation at the National Local Economic Development Conference.

REFERENCES

Serneels, Pieter (2007) 'The nature of unemployment among young men in urban Ethiopia', *Review of Development Economics*, 11 (1), pp. 170–86.

Shaban, A. R. A. (2017) 'Over 1,300 undocumented Ethiopian migrants expelled by Saudi Arabia', *Africa News*, 1 December.

Sharp, K., Devereux, S. and Yared Amare (2003) *Destitution in Ethiopia's Northeastern Highlands (Amhara National Regional State)* (Brighton: Institute of Development Studies).

Shewit Gebreegziabher (2013) 'The situations of trafficking women from Ethiopia to Sudan: The case of Metema Route', Master's thesis, Centre for Human Rights, Addis Ababa University.

Sisay D. (2019) 'The process and dynamics of irregular migration facilitation along the Wollo–Afar–Djibouti route', Master's thesis, Department of Social Anthropology, Addis Ababa University.

Skeldon, Ronald (2012) 'Migration transitions revisited: Their continued relevance for the development of migration theory', *Population, Space and Place*, 18, pp. 154–66.

———— (2018) 'A classic re-examined: Zelinsky's hypothesis of the mobility transition', *Migration Studies*, 7 (3), pp. 394–403.

Skjerdal, T.S. (2011) 'Development journalism revived: The case of Ethiopia', *African Journalism Studies*, 32 (2), pp. 58–74.

Solimano, A. (2010) *International Migration in the Age of Crisis and Globalization: Historical and Recent Experiences* (Cambridge: Cambridge University Press).

Solomon M. Gofie (2016) 'Emigrants and the state in Ethiopia: Transnationalism and the challenges of political antagonism', *African and Black Diaspora: An International Journal*, 9 (2), pp. 134–48.

Sommers, M. (2012) *Stuck: Rwandan Youth and the Struggle for Adulthood* (Athens, GA: University of Georgia Press).

Stones, R. (2005) *Structuration Theory* (New York: Palgrave).

Tariku G. Z. (2018) 'The social perception of technical and vocational education and training in Ethiopia', *International Journal of Research Publications*, 3 (1), pp. 1–14.

Teferi A. A. (1998) *Land, Labour and Capital in the Social Organization of Farmers: A Study of Local-Level Dynamics in Southwestern Wollo* (Addis Ababa: Addis Ababa University Press).

Tegegne G., Tassew W., Eshetu G. and Ezana A. (2015) *Poverty Level Assessment of Addis Ababa 2015* (Addis Ababa: Addis Ababa City Government Finance and Economic Development Bureau).

Teller, C. and Assefa Hailemariam (eds.) (2011) The *Demographic Transition and Development in Africa: The Unique Case of Ethiopia* (Dordrecht: Springer).

Tesfaye Tafesse (2007) *The Migration, Environment and Conflict Nexus in Ethiopia: A Case Study of Amhara Migrant-Settlers in East Wollega Zone* (Addis Ababa: OSSREA).

REFERENCES

Teshome Desta (2010) 'Irregular migration: Causes and consequences of young adult migration from southern Ethiopia to South Africa', Master's thesis, College of Development Studies, Addis Ababa University.

Teshome Desta Kanko, Bailey, A. and Teller, C. (2013) 'Irregular migration: Causes and consequences of young adult migration from southern Ethiopia to South Africa', Paper presented at the XXVII IUSSP International Population Conference, 26–31 August 2013, Busan, South Korea.

Thompson, W. S. (1929) 'Population', *American Sociological Review*, 34 (6), pp. 959–75.

Tibebe Eshete (1999) 'The Sudan Interior Mission (SIM) in Ethiopia (1928–70)', *Northeast African Studies* (NS), 6 (3), pp. 27–57.

Timmerman, C., Hemmerechts, K. and De Clerck, H. M. (2014) 'The relevance of a "culture of migration" in understanding migration aspirations in contemporary Turkey', *Turkish Studies*, 15 (3), pp. 496–518.

Todaro, M. (1969) 'A model of labor migration and urban unemployment in less developed countries', *American Economic Review*, 59 (1), pp. 138–48.

Trines, S. (2018) 'Education in Ethiopia', *World Education News and Reviews*, available at: https://wenr.wes.org/2018/11/education-in-ethiopia (accessed 22 March 2020).

Turton, D. (2006) 'Introduction', in D. Turton (ed.), *Ethnic Federalism: The Ethiopian Experience in Comparative Perspective* (Oxford: James Currey; Athens, OH: Ohio University Press; Addis Ababa: Addis Ababa University Press), pp. 1–31.

Turner, V. (1967) *The Forest of Symbols: Aspects of Ndembu Ritual* (Ithaca, NY: Cornell University Press).

Tyyskä, Vappu (2014) *Youth and Society: The Long and Winding Road* (Toronto: Canadian Scholars' Press).

UN (United Nations) (2015) *UN International Migration Report 2015*, available at: https://www.un.org/en/development/desa/population/migration/publications/migrationreport/docs/MigrationReport2015_ Highlights.pdf (accessed 1 April 2019).

UNCTAD (United Nations Conference on Trade and Development) (2013) *The Least Developed Countries Report: Growth with Employment for Inclusive and Sustainable Development* (Geneva: UNCTAD).

UNECA (United Nations Economic Commission for Africa) (2017) *African Migration: Drivers of Migration in Africa. Draft Report Prepared for Africa Regional Consultative Meeting on the Global Compact on Safe, Orderly and Regular Migration* (Addis Ababa: UNECA).

UNHCR (United Nations High Commissioner for Refugees) (2017) 'Yemen situation: Population movement between Yemen and the Horn of Africa', 31 March 2017, available at: https://reliefweb.int/sites/reliefweb.int/files/resources/YEM_SitnToFrom_31Mar2017.pdf.

REFERENCES

Van Gennep A. (1960) *The Rites of Passage* (Chicago: University of Chicago Press).

Van Hear, N. (2010) 'Theories of migration and social change', *Journal of Ethnic and Migration Studies*, 36 (10), pp. 1531–6.

Waite, L. and Lewis, H. (2017) 'Precarious irregular migrants and their sharing economies: A spectrum of transactional laboring experiences', *Annals of the American Association of Geographers*, 107 (4), pp. 964–78.

Wallerstein, I. (1974) *The Modern World-System* (New York: Academic Press).

Wehmhoerner, A. (2015) 'Lampedusa is everywhere: Migrants in South Africa', FEPS correspondent for southern Africa, Cape Town, February.

Weissleder, W. (1965) 'The political economy of Amhara domination', PhD dissertation, University of Chicago.

Wilson-Smith, H. (2019) 'On the move in a war zone: Mixed migration flows to and through Yemen', Migration Policy Institute, available at: https://www.migrationpolicy.org/article/mixed-migration-flows-yemen-war-zone

Wimmer, Andreas and Schiller, Nina Glick (2003) 'Methodological nationalism, the social sciences, and the study of migration: An essay in historical epistemology', *International Migration Review*, 37 (3), pp. 576–610.

Wood, Jason and Hine, Jean (2013) 'Policy, practice and research in work with young people', in Sheila Curran, Roger Harrison and Donald Mackinnon (eds.), *Working with Young People* (Los Angeles, CA: Sage).

World Bank (2011) *Migration and Remittances, Fact Book, 2011* (Washington, DC: World Bank).

——— (2016a) *5th Ethiopia Economic Update: Why So Idle? Wages and Employment in a Crowded Labor Market* (Washington, DC: World Bank Group).

——— (2016b) *Remittance and Migration Factbook*, 3rd edn (Washington, DC: World Bank).

Wyn, Johanna and White, Rob (2014) *Rethinking Youth* (Sydney: Allen and Unwin).

Wyss, A. (2019) 'Stuck in mobility? Interrupted journeys of migrants with precarious legal status in Europe', *Journal of Immigrant and Refugee Studies*, 17 (1), pp. 77–93.

Xiang, B. and Lindquist, Johan (2014) 'Migration infrastructure', *International Migration Review*, 48 (S1), pp. S122–48.

Yohannes Anberbir (2019) 'A new law which punishes human trafficking by the death penalty is about to be passed', *The Reporter*, 4 September 2019, available at: https://www.ethiopianreporter.com/article/16641 (in Amharic).

Yordanos Estifanos (2015) 'The political economy of transnational social

REFERENCES

networks and migration risks: The case of irregular migrants from southern Ethiopia to South Africa', Master's thesis, University of Oldenburg.

———— (2016) 'The Southern dream and migration risks: The case of young adult migrants from Southern Ethiopia to South Africa', in *Kabbo ka Muwala [The Girl's Basket]: Migration and Mobility in Contemporary Art in Southern and Eastern Africa* (Harare: National Gallery of Zimbabwe), pp. 44–57.

———— (2018) *Wayfarers: Travel Journal*, translated by Hiwot Tadesse (Addis Ababa: Central Printing Press).

Yordanos Estifanos and Zack, T. (2019) 'Follow the money: Tactics, dependencies and shifting relations in migration financing on the Ethiopia–South Africa migration corridor', MOOP Working Paper no. 63, December.

———— (2020) 'Migration barriers and migration momentum: Ethiopian irregular migrants in the Ethiopia–South Africa migration corridor', EU Trust Fund for Africa (Horn of Africa Window) Research and Evidence Facility, London and Nairobi.

Yordanos Estifanos, Zack, T. and Vanyoro, K. (2019) 'Challenges of the migration and integration of the Ethiopian entrepreneurs to South Africa', Policy Brief, African Centre for Migration and Society, University of the Witwatersrand, Johannesburg.

Zack, T. (2017) *Cross Border Shopping in Johannesburg's Inner City: Research Report Commissioned by the Johannesburg Inner City Partnership*, available at: http://www.jicp.org.za/news/cross-border-shopping-joburg-cbd/ (accessed 24 March 2020).

Zack, T. and Yordanos Estifanos (2016) 'Somewhere else: Social connection and dislocation of Ethiopian migrants in Johannesburg', *African and Black Diaspora: An International Journal*, 9 (2), pp. 149–65.

Zanker, J. H. (2008) 'Why do people migrate? A review of the theoretical literature', available at: https://mpra.ub.uni-muenchen.de/28197/1/2008WP002 (accessed 11 August 2019).

Zelinsky, W. (1971) 'The hypothesis of the mobility transition', *Geographical Review*, 61 (2), pp. 219–49.

Zeyneba Z. (2016) 'Cross border young female labor migration from Ethiopia to Sudan through Metema route', Master's thesis, Addis Ababa University.

Zhang, S. X., Sanchez, G. E. and Achilli, L. (2018) 'Crimes of solidarity in mobility: Alternative views on migrant smuggling', *Annals of the American Academy of Political and Social Science*, 676 (1), pp. 6–15.

INDEX

INDEX